WITHDRAWN

THOMAS WEELKES

THOMAS WEELKES

A Biographical
and
Critical Study
by
DAVID BROWN

FREDERICK A. PRAEGER, *Publishers*
New York · Washington

BOOKS THAT MATTER

Published in the United States of America in 1969
by Frederick A. Praeger, Inc., Publishers
111 Fourth Avenue, New York, N.Y. 10003

© 1969, in London, England, by David Brown

Library of Congress Catalog Card Number: 69–20021

Printed in Great Britain

TO
WALTER S. COLLINS
WHO SHOULD HAVE WRITTEN ONE HALF OF THIS BOOK
AND WHO HAS STILL CONTRIBUTED MUCH TO IT

CONTENTS

PREFACE

In recent years there have been signs that English Renaissance music is being subjected to a radical revaluation. A very important part in this has been played by Joseph Kerman's invaluable book, *The Elizabethan madrigal,* for anyone who has read this study is compelled to abandon any notion that the English madrigal was the climax of the whole development of Renaissance secular vocal music. Instead it must now be accepted that the splendid phase of late Elizabethan music was only a small and belated movement in the broader context of European musical culture. The stature of Byrd has remained undiminished; indeed, with these new and more balanced values, his pre-eminence has emerged more clearly, and his rightful position among the greatest masters of the sixteenth century is being more widely recognised. But the gap between him and his lesser English contemporaries is becoming a gulf, and there is perhaps a danger that our values may swing too far in the other direction, so that men like Morley, Wilbye, Gibbons and Weelkes will be accorded less credit than is their due. Such men were still major talents—even, on occasions, composers of genius.

This book is an attempt to assess one of these composers—perhaps the most interesting of them all. Weelkes is not the sort of composer likely to provoke many full-length critical studies, and the scholar must therefore feel all the more the responsibility to be comprehensive, and to cover Weelkes' work in as much breadth and detail as possible. At the same time, it is not possible to ignore what was going on around him either socially or musically, and some space must be devoted to sketching the background to his creative activities, and to comparing his compositions with those of certain of his contemporaries. Without such comparisons it is not possible either to be precise about those characteristics which are peculiarly his, or to make any sort of balanced assessment of his stature.

No book of this sort is ever written without the author becoming indebted to many people. My greatest debt is acknowledged in the dedication, but it requires more specific description here. It was originally intended that Dr. Collins should provide the biographical chapter and the study of the church music, the present author's share being an examination of the secular music, and of Weelkes' style. However, the increasing involvement of Dr. Collins in his duties as Dean of the Music Faculty of

Oakland University, Michigan, prevented him from pressing on with his portion. When it became apparent that he would be unable to complete this without a great deal of delay, he asked me to proceed with the whole book and, with the most liberal generosity, offered to pass on all the materials he had collected towards his abortive share. I was therefore able to make free use of his full edition of all the numerous incomplete anthems, and his preliminary transcriptions of five of the ten Services, and of some of the consort music. In addition, he gave me complete freedom to consult and use material from his study of the anthems. Because of the direction my study of the madrigals had already taken, the course followed in my own chapters on the anthems is quite distinct from that which Dr. Collins had originally pursued; his study of the anthems is therefore far from superseded by this book, and the reader will still find it profitable to consult Dr. Collins' original work.[1] Dr. Collins had also added his own biographical study of the composer, and although the first chapter of this present book is founded upon a direct examination of all the original source material, and supplies one or two omissions made by earlier biographers, I was greatly aided in several ways by Dr. Collins' previous researches. For instance, it was he who first made out the case for Parson John Weeke as the composer's father, a proposal which I have been able to support with a little more evidence. Other debts to Dr. Collins' work are acknowledged in footnotes throughout the book. His unselfish generosity is something for which I remain immensely grateful.

Many others have contributed their part to this book. It is not possible to name them all, but I must single out Dr. Peter le Huray of Cambridge University, who has readily made available to me his catalogue of the sources of English church music of the period; the list of sources for the Services I owe largely to him. In addition he has been most helpful in answering numerous questions that have raised themselves during the course of this study. Jeremy Noble kindly allowed me to use his masterly reconstruction of the seven-voice Service as the basis for my own examination of the work. I am indebted to my colleague, Rev. John Davies, Lecturer in Theology at Southampton University, and Mother Thomas More of Lady Margaret Hall, Cambridge, for guidance on the liturgical background to Weelkes' Services, and to Professor Thurston Dart of London University for making some helpful suggestions in the chapter on Weelkes' miscellaneous works. Numerous libraries and institutions have helped; Dr. Anthea Baird, my successor as Music Librarian of London University, has been most helpful in prompt replies to queries, and two members of Winchester College, Mr. Peter Gwyn and Mr. J. M. G. Blakiston, Archivist and Fellows' Librarian respectively, helped me in my

[1] W. S. Collins, *The Anthems of Thomas Weelkes* [unpublished dissertation].

investigations at the College. Canon C. E. Jarman, Librarian of Chester Cathedral, generously aided my enquiries into Chester records. The staff of the West Sussex County Record Office at Chichester have been unfailingly helpful in my biographical researches; Mr. J. M. L. Booker in particular rendered invaluable assistance in deciphering certain of the Latin records. For help in various other ways, my gratitude goes to Sotheby & Co., and Maggs Bros. of London, and to Miss B. N. Forder of Winchester Cathedral Library. My colleagues and students in the choir of the Southampton University Madrigal Society have cheerfully performed some of my reconstructions of Weelkes' fragmentary works, and in doing so have thrown considerable illumination upon these pieces. In the preparation of the typescript I received invaluable assistance from my mother, who typed the greater part of it. Finally there is my wife, who not only helped with checking, but who has borne my prolonged Weelkesian preoccupations with great patience.

University of Southampton   DAVID BROWN
January, 1967

NOTE ON QUOTATIONS, MUSIC
EXAMPLES AND REFERENCES

In quotations from documents of Weelkes' time, the spelling and punctuation have been modernised. In most instances there seemed no point in retaining the original spelling, while the original punctuation (when it exists at all) is often a hindrance rather than a help to understanding the sense of a passage. In the few cases where it did seem desirable that the original text should be printed exactly as it stood, the literal transcription has been placed in double quotation marks.

In a book of this sort, music-type examples should plainly be as numerous as the practical economics of book production allow, but the reader must treat them as illustrations of the points made in the main text of the book, not as substitutes for the full scores of the works themselves. In many instances, the point the music example is intended to make does not require a full presentation of the music, and in the interests of economy the score has been compressed. As a general principle, all examples printed in open score present the original text just as it stands; those in close score present the part-writing either explicitly or in a way that can in most cases be deduced with fair reliability, but do not attempt to indicate how the text fits the music in any part. Instead, the text (sometimes only the incipit) is printed once in square brackets. In a few cases it has only been necessary (and sometimes it has even been preferable) to reproduce a summary of the musical text; such instances are clearly marked.

The music-type examples of Weelkes' own works have been transcribed from the original sources (those from the incomplete verse anthems are drawn from Walter Collins' transcriptions). Note values have been halved in the examples of Weelkes' church music and in references to this music in the text. The organ scores of the verse anthems and verse Services have been retained in their original skeletal form, so that the reader may form a clear idea of how this music was presented to the early seventeenth-century performer. Examples of music by other composers are drawn from modern printed editions, and the author must thank the Royal Musical Association for permission to quote from *Musica Britannica*, vol. 15, and also Stainer & Bell and Schott & Co. for permission to reproduce examples from editions published by them.

The following abbreviations are used in referring to certain editions:

EMS   *The English Madrigal School* (edited by E. H. Fellowes, in process of revision by Thurston Dart as *The English Madrigalists*).

MB23   Thomas Weelkes, *Collected anthems* (edited by David Brown, Walter Collins and Peter le Huray. Published as *Musica Britannica*, vol. 23).

COL   W. S. Collins, *The Anthems of Thomas Weelkes* [unpublished dissertation; University of Michigan].

I. THE LIFE OF WEELKES

Early Years and Winchester

The visitor exploring the north aisle of Chichester Cathedral will come upon a series of stained glass portraits which commemorate notables from the history of the cathedral. Most are divines, but one is Thomas Weelkes who stands, recorder in hand, while before him a surpliced choirboy sings from a part-book of *Hosanna to the Son of David*. Since no known portrait of the composer survives, the window can offer only a conjectural likeness, but it is good to know that he has been accorded this recognition as one of the most distinguished individuals to have been connected with the cathedral. Yet the aptness of this memorial window must be in grave doubt to the scholar who has crossed the road to the County Hall and delved into the records of Weelkes' life and activities during the twenty or more years of his association with the cathedral. Could the choir of which he had charge in Chichester ever have adequately met the formidable challenge of *Hosanna to the Son of David*? Even more to the point—is it really possible that this mild and seemingly goodly man could really be the one who, three hundred and fifty years ago, had embarrassed and vexed the cathedral authorities with his drunkenness? How would Bishop Harsnett or Archbishop Bancroft have viewed this memorial window to the man whom they had to eject from his positions as Sherborne Clerk, organist and *informator choristarum* because 'he hath been and is noted and famed for a common drunkard and a notorious swearer and blasphemer'? One wonders with what sardonic amusement Weelkes himself might have gazed upon this idealised representation.

But what, indeed, are we able to discern of the man himself? No letter of his has survived and no certain music autograph; all we have is a signed will and two other signatures.[1] Trying to trace his biography is like proceeding from complete darkness into twilight. We know nothing definite of him until he is a grown, if still very young man. A few facts throw a thin shaft of light back into his earlier years, but nothing is ever illuminated with either precision or certainty. As his biography progresses, the

---

[1] One is Weelkes' subscription to the Act of Supremacy on graduation at Oxford (1602), the other is on his marriage bond (1603). What may be a third signature appears on a music manuscript of *Grace my lovely one*; a facsimile of this appears in the preliminary section of MB23. This manuscript was sold some years ago in London and its present whereabouts unfortunately cannot be traced. This third signature certainly closely resembles Weelkes' known signatures; if it is his, then the music may also be in his hand. Attention was first drawn to this source by Professor Thurston Dart.

evidence becomes less sparse, though many of the surviving facts are not the ones we would most wish to possess. Too many relate only to the circumstances or environment in which he lived and worked; there is nothing about his origins, his musical education, his musical attitudes, or the actual circumstances surrounding the birth of any of his compositions. Most of the documentary evidence tells only of his shortcomings, and can give but a very one-sided picture of the man. Sometimes we may deduce information, but all too often we can only speculate.

We have absolutely no concrete information about him before 1597, the year in which he published his first collection of music, *Madrigals to 3, 4, 5 and 6 voices*. In the dedication of this volume to 'the Right Worshipful Master George Phillpot Esquire', Weelkes writes of these madrigals as 'the first fruits of my barren ground, unripe in regard of time'; a year later in the dedicatory preface to his second volume, *Ballets and madrigals to five voices*, he again speaks of 'my years yet unripened'. It seems likely that he was at this time either in his late teens or early twenties, which would place his birth at some time between, say, 1575 and 1578.[1] An earlier rather than a later date is favoured by Weelkes' supplication for the degree of B.Mus., which he received in 1602 from Oxford University. This stated that he had been a student of music for sixteen years. Most English composers of this period seem to have reckoned the inception of their formal musical education from their mid-teens, and this would hint at a date rather earlier than 1575 for Weelkes' birth. Certainly it seems reasonable to assume that he was born during the middle or later 1570s.

In the absence of established parentage the biographer must resort, if he can, to marshalling the various potential fathers and testing the merits of each aspirant's claim. The number of persons or families with whom Weelkes may have had connections is greatly increased by the various ways in which the name might be spelt (Wilk(e)s, Week(e)s, Wick(e)s, Wyk(e)s, etc.), though it is perhaps noteworthy that the composer seems to have been particular about the way in which he spelled his own name (either Weelkes or Weelks). It is also worth remembering that he described himself as 'generosus' in his marriage bond and 'gentleman' in his will. This did not necessarily signify that he was of gentle birth, but it does suggest that he came from a family of at least some moderate social standing. But it seems that we possess an even more valuable clue to Weelkes' parentage in the record of his marriage preserved in the register of All Saints' Church, Chichester. For some unknown reason the clerk first wrote the whole entry incorrectly, inscribing '1602. John "Wilks"

---

[1] Myles Foster confidently stated that Weelkes was born in 1578; he also suggested, though with reservation, that Weelkes died in 1640. His authority, if any, for Weelkes' date of birth is unknown (see M. B. Foster, *Anthems and anthem composers*, p. 45).

and Katherine Sandham were married the fourth of February' (i.e. 4th February, 1603, according to our reckoning); he then struck through the names 'John Wilks' and 'Katherine' and interlined 'Thomas "Weelkes" ' and 'Elizabeth' (the date, which was over a fortnight too early, remained uncorrected).[1] Since Katherine Sandham was the name of the bride's mother, it seems not unlikely that John Wilks was the name of the groom's father, the respective parents having been entered first by mistake.

If this is so, it offers further support for the claims of a certain cleric, John Weeke (or Wyke), to be the composer's parent. Indeed, his paternity case is supported by enough circumstantial evidence for it to merit further exposition here.[2] John Weeke was Rector of Elsted in West Sussex when his son, Thomas, was baptised there on 25th October, 1576.[3] Elsted was in the diocese of Chichester; John had been inducted into the living two years before and remained there until his death in 1597. He had evidently been a scholar of Brazenose College, Oxford (though there is contradictory evidence about this) and was ordained by the Bishop of Chester in 1566.[4] Perhaps he was a member of the group of Wike families living in Cheshire and South Lancashire at this time. Parson Weeke's ordination

---

[1] Chichester Diocesan Record Office (hereafter referred to as CDRO), Par. 36/1/1/1, f. 77.

[2] It may be useful to record here some of the other suggestions which have been offered as possible clues to Weelkes' origins. Thomas Wilkes, who was one of the Clerks of the Queen's Council, has been suggested as the composer's sire. This Wilkes had connections with Winchester College, to which the composer was organist for several years; in 1582 the Queen petitioned the College to grant a lease of the parsonage of Downton, Wilts. to Wilkes the diplomat, a grant which the College accorded only reluctantly. A further connection with the Winchester area was the return of the same Wilkes to parliament for Southampton in 1593. But no sons are named in his will and, unless the composer was his illegitimate offspring, there is no reason to think he was the diplomat's child. There was also a large family of Weekes living in East Sussex at this time. A number of their wills are preserved in the East Sussex County Record Office at Lewes, but these provide no evidence to connect the composer with this family. Walter Collins has noted a certain John Wykes who appears frequently as a property holder in the Winchester City accounts in the mid-sixteenth century (see COL, vol. 1, p. 7). Fellowes has remarked a monument in Ripon Cathedral to a certain Stephen Weelkes (d. 1712) which traces his ancestry back four generations into the sixteenth century (see E. H. Fellowes, *English madrigal composers*, p. 191, and EMS9, p. ii. For further information about records of this family, who lived at Sawley, see COL, vol. 1, p. 9). It is also worth recording that there is a parish of Weeke on the outskirts of Winchester, where Weelkes held his first appointment. If he had been an illegitimate child born in this parish, he might have acquired the surname 'Weeke'. But in view of his claim to 'gentle' status, this seems an unlikely origin.

[3] CDRO, Par. 80/1/1/1, f. 2.

[4] There is no surviving record of his ordination at Chester, but there are many gaps in the records at this time; the information is afforded by the Bishop of Chichester's visitation of 1586. In this study the information concerning John Weeke has been extracted from the vast documentation of the Sussex clergy carried out by E. H. W. Dunkin; after Dunkin's death his papers were deposited in the British Museum. The relevant documents are Add. MS 39326, ff. 1016–18 and Add. MS 39333, f. 194v–95.

establishes the first feature in common with the composer, for it certainly seems that Thomas Weelkes had connections with the Chester area. The father of 'my trusty and well-beloved friend Henry Drinkwater', at whose house Weelkes died, came from Cheshire, and Fellowes has suggested[1] that 'Master George Brooke Esquire', to whom Weelkes dedicated his *Madrigals of 6 parts* (1600), may possibly be the second son of George Brooke of Norton, Cheshire. Weelkes makes it clear in his preface that he had never met George Brooke,[2] which suggests that they lived far from each other, and postulates the intervention of some other person. Perhaps one of Weelkes' suggested relatives in Cheshire interceded with Brooke for some subsidy to make possible the continuation of the 1600 volume of madrigals.[3]

In 1572 John Weeke became Vicar of Twyford and Owslebury in the Winchester diocese; thus he worked within the two dioceses in which the composer is known to have spent his working life. Twyford was a living licensed to be held in pluralism, and Weeke was authorised to hold two other livings within a twenty-six mile radius. Elsted became one of these two, and he continued as incumbent of Twyford until 1585. In Twyford a very close possible connection is established with the composer, for Twyford Church was barely one mile from Compton Place, a house belonging to the Phillpot family. One member of this family, George Phillpot, may very well be identical with the dedicatee of Weelkes' first madrigal volume. The Phillpots had a seat at Thruxton near Andover, but there are indications that George Phillpot lived at Compton, while his father, Thomas, who may have been a lunatic, was at Thruxton.[4] The incumbent of Twyford must surely have known the inhabitant of Compton Place, and the conditions would have been established for the later display of 'un-

---

[1] EMS10, Preface.

[2] Caution is needed in identifying any dedicatee who has no noble title, or who is not described more precisely than through his name alone. It is not impossible that Weelkes' dedicatee was the fourth son of Wm. Brooke, Lord Cobham. 'Master' and 'Esquire', as he is dubbed in Weelkes' dedication, would evidently have been quite proper titles by which to address him, though 'gentleman' is rather more questionable, even for a younger son of the nobility. Born in 1568, George Brooke was a prebend of York and was promised the Mastership of St. Cross, Winchester, though the appointment was not confirmed because of the death of the Queen. In 1603 he was executed at Winchester for conspiracy. Besides his Winchester connections (albeit these were seemingly later than Weelkes' own period at Winchester), this George Brooke was son-in-law to Lord Borough, upon whose death Weelkes wrote an elegy (published in 1598).

[3] But see below, pp. 96–97 for a further discussion of the curious presence of two dedicatees in Weelkes' single volume of five- and six-voice madrigals of 1600.

[4] Information drawn from J. S. Drew, *Compton near Winchester*. A further connection with Compton may be established in the lyric of one of Weelkes' madrigalian compositions (*Strike it up, tabor* from the *Ayres* (1608)) which refers to 'Martin of Compton'. The Martins were a notable, if not always law-abiding family, whose memory is perpetuated in the village in Martin's Close, a field abutting onto Compton Street.

deserved love and liberal goodwill' for which Weelkes acknowledged he was indebted to George Phillpot.

Beyond this it is not possible either to substantiate further or discredit John Weeke's kinship with the composer. If he was indeed Thomas Weelkes' father, then the composer's mother was named Johanne (John Weeke had married in Hampshire before taking the living at Elsted), and he had at least five brothers and sisters.[1] His brother John seems to have been older than he; William, Amy, Edward and Elizabeth were younger.

Passing from Weelkes' speculative origins to his childhood and musical training, we still find we can establish nothing with certainty. He may have been the chorister Thomas Wikes whose name appears in the Winchester Cathedral Chapter Acts during 1582–3/4.[2] Admittedly this child is not likely to have been also the son of Parson John Weeke, for he would have been very precocious vocally to gain a place in a cathedral choir at the tender age of six. One piece of information may be gleaned from the preface to Weelkes' second madrigalian publication, *Ballets and madrigals* (1598), where he reveals that he had passed some time in the service of 'his master Edward Darcy Esquire, Groom to her Majesty's Privy Chamber'. Weelkes dedicated this volume to Darcy, professing the need 'to remember one of your worship's least labours . . . the entertaining into your service the least proficient in music'. Darcy's court connections may have been of especial value to Weelkes in making certain people at court aware of his existence.

The appointment of Weelkes as organist of Winchester College brings the biographer onto firmer ground. Evidence of his position in the College is provided by the first title page to the volume of madrigals of 1600 on which he is described as 'of the College at Winchester, Organist', and his residence within the College is attested by the opening of the first dedicatory preface to the same volume: 'My Lord, in the College at Winchester, where I live . . .'. Even more concrete proof that he lived within the College itself is afforded by the College accounts for the first quarter of the financial year 1598–99 which record an entry for the glass in his bedroom: 'Item pro vitro pro cubiculo Mri Weelkes xxid'.[3] Unfortunately no record survives either of his appointment to the post of

[1] Information gathered from John Weeke's will, made 17th August, 1597, and preserved in Somerset House, PCC, 108 Cobham.

[2] Chapter Book, 1553–1600, ff. 100–4. He is first listed in November, 1582; on the last folio, which records the meeting of June, 1584, his name has been written down and then struck through.

[3] The accounts for each year ran from the middle of September. Information on the history of music at Winchester outside Weelkes' period at the College is drawn from A. K. Cook, *About Winchester College*, and H. C[hitty], *Winchester College: the organist and the Quiristers' Master*, a reprint (with some alterations) from an article in *The Wykehamist*, No. 523 (December, 1913), p. 84.

organist, or of his relinquishing it. Nevertheless, a broader examination of the musical situation within the College before Weelkes' appointment enables us to deduce a good deal about the first of these matters.

The history of the College organs in the years before Weelkes' arrival had not been a happy one. The College's founder, William of Wykeham, had made provision for music in the statutes which he had drawn up in 1387. There were to be sixteen choristers and three clerks, and by the beginning of the next century the College had an organ, although it still lacked a special organist. An organist proper first appears in the accounts for 1543–44, and his salary was 10s. a quarter. In 1558 this was doubled and remained thus until 1570.

In this latter year, when the Bishop made a visitation of the College, music suffered a severe blow. Robert Horne, who had been consecrated to the see in 1561, was a man of fanatically puritanical outlook, and was notorious for dismembering anything associated with popery, and for his assiduous destruction of catholic service books, as well as of any stained glass windows, statues and vestments which he judged to be superstitious. He silenced organs too, and during the 1570 visitation his ban fell upon the Winchester College instrument:

'Item, that the organs be no more used in service time, and the stipend for the organ player, and that which was allowed to a chaplain to say mass in the chapel in the cloister, shall be hereafter by the Warden and Fellows, with the consent of the bishop of Winchester, turned to some other godly and necessary purpose in the College.'[1]

Nevertheless, the organ at Winchester College was not destroyed. Its resurrection dates from the time of Thomas Bilson, a former Warden of Winchester College, who became Bishop of Winchester in May, 1597. Bilson was a very different man from Horne, and between 1598 and 1600 the College accounts reveal that repairs were made to the organ, and that an organist was once again appointed, for the accounts for the financial year 1598–99 include an entry under 'Stipendia famulorum in genere' for 'Item Organistae pro 3bus terminis xls'. Presumably this organist was Weelkes. Payment had evidently been made from just before Christmas 1598. The accounts for 1599–1600 record the organist's salary as 13s. 4d. a quarter. During this and the next year the organist's salary is listed with 'Stipendia capellanorum et clericorum capellae'.

Even allowing for bed and board within the College, this was a paltry stipend—much less, it will be noted, than that which had been paid to the organist before the post had been discontinued by Bishop Horne nearly thirty years before. Yet worse was to come, for the accounts for 1601–2

[1] Bishop Horne's Register (preserved in the Hampshire County Record Office, Winchester), f. 88.

show that the organist's stipend was reduced to only 10s. a quarter, while payment was now recorded at the end of 'Stipendia servientium in genere'. His removal in the accounts from the company of the chaplains to a position among the servants suggests a lowering of status.

This is the sum total of the biographical facts and pointers we possess about Weelkes' Winchester phase. There is no evidence to indicate just what his duties as organist entailed, or whether any of his surviving church music was composed for use in the College Chapel. The music we do definitely possess from this period of Weelkes' life are the sixty-eight madrigals issued in three volumes between 1597 and 1600, and the single madrigal he contributed to *The Triumphs of Oriana*, printed in 1601. The quantity is considerable, but the most remarkable feature of these works is the astonishing progress they record from the fumbling and unformed expression of some of the pieces in the first volume to the masterly maturity of the majority of the madrigals in the volume of 1600. Collectively these works are one of the most brilliant phenomena in English music of the time. But there must be grave doubts about whether the men of Winchester College would have received these pieces as enthusiastically as we greet them today.[1] It is not likely that many of the Fellows would have thrilled to the passions of *O care, thou wilt despatch me | Hence, care, thou art too cruel*, or have reeled admiringly before the fantastic imagery of *Thule, the period of cosmography | The Andalusian merchant*. Without doubt many viewed such compositions as wild eccentricities, and must have deplored that so much, if not all, of their organist's creative energies should have been spent on such outlandish creations. A strong hint of Weelkes' feeling of isolation within the College is to be detected in the preface of the five-voice madrigals of 1600. Evidently there were some men in the College who discounted the importance of music; certainly they had been at pains to deny that 'harmony' was an essential element in the soul of man:

'My Lord, in the College at Winchester where I live, I have heard learned men say that some philosophers have mistaken the soul of man for an harmony. Let the precedent of their error be a privilege for mine. I see not, if souls do not partly consist of music, how it should come to pass that so noble a spirit as yours, so perfectly tuned to so perpetual a Tenor

---

[1] In the Fellows' Library of Winchester College there is a set of four part-books of Italian and French madrigals and chansons. Some of these bear the compilation date of 1562 or 1564. Nevertheless, there is no evidence to suggest that they belonged to the College in the sixteenth century; the earliest mention of them in the College records dates from some two hundred years after Weelkes' time there. These books are usually cited as evidence that Italian madrigals were known in England early in Elizabeth's reign. They appear to be of Flemish origin, however, and, apart from the Tudor royal crest on the covers, there is nothing to suggest that they were in this country before the century was out.

of excellence as it is, should descend to the notice of a quality lying single in so low a personage as myself. . . . I confess my conscience is untouched with any other arts. . . .'.

The admission that he had no other special skills is reiterated later in the preface, when he pleads that

'this small faculty of mine, because it is alone in me and without the assistance of other more confident sciences, is the more to be favoured . . .', and the reader senses that Weelkes felt inferior (or had been made to feel inferior) to those who had other more highly rated abilities. Perhaps the evidence afforded by the accounts of 1601–2 of the down-grading of the organist, both in status and stipend, is a further sign that the authorities felt that their organist had been worth neither his position in the College hierarchy nor his remuneration, niggardly as that had been.

It seems unlikely that the Winchester College authorities would have taken such drastic action as to reduce the stipend of an organist actually in office (unless they were desperate to be rid of him). It seems more probable that they took advantage of a new appointment to do so, and there is strong circumstantial evidence to suggest that Weelkes joined the musical staff of Chichester Cathedral at about this time (September–October, 1601). A vacancy had just occurred at Chichester through the death in September of John Base (alias Martyn), one of the Sherborne Clerks.[1] Unfortunately the earliest actual evidence of Weelkes as a Sherborne Clerk dates from 1605,[2] but there is nothing to suggest that he had not held the position in the four years intervening since John Base's death. In addition, there is a slip made by the scribe of the Chichester Cathedral accounts in recording the payment to the organist for the financial year 1601–2. Unfortunately for us, the normal practice in the surviving Chichester accounts (as in those of Winchester College) was to record the office, not the holder, but for this year the accounts list a payment to 'Tho organist'.[3] 'Tho' has been struck through, but it seems possible that the scribe was about to write out Weelkes' name and then decided to let the record remain uncommitted.[4] Weelkes was certainly organist and *informator choristarum* by October, 1602, since the accounts for 1602–3

[1] His burial on 23rd September is recorded in the Subdeanery Parish Register (CDRO, Par. 44/1/1/1, f. 88).

[2] This is to be found in one of the papers associated with the Primate's visitation of 1605 (CDRO, Ep. 1/20/6). Weelkes is listed as the fourth of the first group of *Vicarii laici*. The first three are known to be the remaining Sherborne Clerks, all of whom were appointed before Weelkes' arrival in Chichester. In an account sheet, preserved in Cap. 1/10, he is specifically named as a Sherborne Clerk 'In vigilia Sancti Thomae: 1607'.

[3] CDRO, Cap. 1/23/4, f. 143.

[4] If it was Weelkes whom the scribe was about to specify, the reason for the deletion may have been that Weelkes was not appointed to this office at the beginning of the financial year, and had therefore to share the stipend with his predecessor, Jacob Hillary.

actually name him for both positions. It is therefore clear that he joined
the musical staff of Chichester Cathedral at some time between October,
1601 and October, 1602.

Before tracing further Weelkes' life at Chichester, two other matters
may be mentioned—his university degree and his marriage. The former, a
B.Mus. degree from New College, Oxford, was awarded on 13th July,
1602. He had supplicated for it on 12th February. As the Register reads:
'Supplicat . . . Thomas Weelks scholaris facultatis Musices e Collegio
Nova quatenus sedecem annos in studio et praxi Musicae posuerit ceter-
aque praestiterit omnia quae per statuta huius clarissimae Academiae
requiruntur ut ei sufficiant quo admittatur ad lectionem cuiuslibet liberi
musices Boëtii. Haec gratia concessa est modo hymnum coralem sex
partium componat proximis comitiis decantandum.'[1]

New College was the obvious one for Weelkes to choose for this
standard supplication, since it was William of Wykeham's twin foundation
with Winchester College. Choristers of the latter had often been granted
the favour of supplicating for a degree through New College, and presumably Weelkes was granted this privilege as organist of Winchester
College. Certainly the Oxford Registrar was determined to make it
clear that Weelkes was not a foundation member of New College, for to
the supplication is added:
'Intelligendum est quod nec dictus Thomas Weelks nec quisquam alius
est ex fundatione Sociorum in Collegio Novo si gratiam proponat aut in
Congregatione aut in Convocatione.'
It is tempting to speculate about what 'choral hymn of six parts' was
Weelkes' 'exercise'. Was it *Laboravi in gemitu meo*?[2]

Weelkes' marriage was solemnised on 20th February, 1603.[3] His
bride was Elizabeth Sandham, a member of a Chichester family of considerable means.[4] There were at least three children of the marriage, and

[1] *Oxford University Congregation Register, 1595–1606* (M.11), f. 128.
[2] See below, p. 154. Weelkes, like all graduates, was required to subscribe to the Act of
Supremacy, and his signature appears on f. 112 of the *Oxford University Subscription Register, 1581–1615*.
[3] The marriage is attested by four documents. One is the entry in the register of All Saints'
Church, Chichester, where the marriage took place (CDRO, Par. 36/1/1/1, f. 77); the
names were at first incorrectly written and the date, 4th February, is still wrong (see above,
pp. 18–19). There is also a marriage bond (CDRO, Sta. V), signed by Weelkes and William
Sandham. Such a bond was necessary when the marriage was taking place without time to
call the banns. The reason for the hasty marriage is clear; Elizabeth Sandham was pregnant.
There are also two copies of the marriage licence, one in the Act Book of the Exempt
Deaneries of Pagham and Terring (CDRO, Ep. IV/2/8, f. 24), the other in Diary B of the
Archbishop's Peculiars (CDRO, Sta. III/B, f. 22v).
[4] In the first of his two surviving wills, made in 1607 (Somerset House, PCC, 2 Wingfield),
William Sandham, Elizabeth's father, described himself as 'citizen and merchant' of Chiches-
ter, and left £200 to his wife, as well as bequests to five of his children (the three daughters

the eldest, Thomas, was baptised on 9th June, less than four months after the wedding;[1] he was to be admitted chorister of Chichester Cathedral on 1st August, 1614,[2] and was replaced on 2nd August, 1617.[3] Weelkes' daughter, Alice, was baptised on 17th September, 1606.[4] A second daughter, Katherine, is mentioned in Weelkes' will, but there is no trace of the record of her baptism, doubtless because many of the relevant registers between 1607 and 1618 are missing.

When Weelkes had established himself in the three positions he was to hold at Chichester Cathedral, his financial situation was much improved. Admittedly as organist he received only 13s. 4d. per annum, a rate of remuneration merely one quarter of that he had received at Winchester College, but the organist's post at Chichester was not a separate one; it was an additional duty discharged by one of the choir. As *informator choristarum* he received £3 12s. 4d. per annum,[5] but the most profitable of his posts was that of a Sherborne Clerk, a lay singer's position. There were four such clerkships at Chichester Cathedral, and the stipend of each was £10 16s. 8d. per annum. Thus, in all, Weelkes received £15 2s. 4d. Accommodation was evidently provided for him, and there were other gratuities attached to the offices.[6]

Life at Chichester Cathedral

For a while we will break off this account of Weelkes' career, and examine instead the context in which he lived. This is necessary because the remainder of this biographical study will be largely occupied with recording discreditable incidents from his life at Chichester; therefore, in order to keep his personal failings in perspective, it is necessary to know something of the whole environment in which he lived and worked. On his arrival in Chichester, the cathedral choir numbered twenty, of whom eight were boys and twelve were men. The men were grouped in three equal divisions, one made up from ordained priests (the four vicars choral), and the other two composed of laymen (four Sherborne Clerks and four singing-

were each to receive £80 on attaining eighteen years or marrying, and two sons were to receive property). Details of the Sandham family are to be found in COL, vol. 1, pp. 22–5.

[1] CDRO, Par. 44/1/1/1, f. 11v.   [2] CDRO, Cap. 1/3/1, f. 157v.
[3] *op. cit.*, f. 168.   [4] CDRO, Par. 44/1/1/1, f. 13.

[5] Of this, 22s. was realised from a lease on the 'choristers garden', 20s. was 'ex benevolentia', and 30s. 4d. was from an endowment of Bishop Sherborne's foundation. This last sum was paid 'pro eius obsequio quotidiano', or 'for his diligence to see the Choristers come to prayers', as Dr. Cox put it in his Rental of 1595 (CDRO, Cap. 1/26/4, f. 55v).

[6] For instance, in 1606 it was reported that each lay clerk received 'eight "caste" of bread every year' (CDRO, Ep. 1/20/7). The Chapter Acts indicate that in 1619 there was a twice weekly issue of bread to the choir members (CDRO, Cap. 1/10).

men). Formerly[1] all the adult members of the choir had been vicars choral, and in the fourteenth century there had been as many as thirty of them. During the next century they had established their own legal corporation, but their numbers had tended to decrease, and by the episcopacy of Robert Sherborne, Bishop of Chichester from 1508 to 1536, there were only twelve. By now the practice of employing laymen in the choir was well established, and in 1526 Bishop Sherborne had created four lucrative lay-clerkships as a means of strengthening the choir. The complement of vicars choral wavered further during the sixteenth century; by 1596 their number was down to four and was to remain thus for 300 years. The four Sherborne Clerks continued, and the adult section of the choir was completed with four lay singing-men.

From among the choirmen certain individuals were appointed to fulfil the functions of choirmaster, organist and subchanter (or succentor). The first two offices were sometimes combined in the same person; Weelkes occupied both positions for most of his time at Chichester. But the man who was evidently the real head of the musical establishment was the subchanter.[2] During Weelkes' period of service at Chichester this office was occupied by William Lawes, who had joined the Chichester establishment in 1596. His personal authority in the choir is attested by instructions given to him in 1597; besides being responsible for keeping a written check upon those absent from service, he was instructed to 'appoint what songs should be sung daily' and to see 'that all the singers should stand up the time that they did sing that they might be the better heard'.[3]

We are dependent upon three main sources for information about Weelkes and Chichester Cathedral. The first is the accounts of the cathedral, the second the Act Books of the Cathedral Chapter, and the third the papers of the various Bishops' or Archbishops' visitations. The surviving cathedral accounts are mainly a final record of the sums paid out during the financial year[4] to each member or department of the cathedral establishment, but there are a few account books in which expenditure is itemised in more detail. The Act Books[5] record the

---

[1] The history of the choir at Chichester Cathedral has been very fully traced in W. D. Peckham, 'The Vicars choral of Chichester Cathedral', *Sussex Archaeological Collection*, vol. 78 (1937), pp. 126–59. The above account of the choir before Weelkes' time relies upon this article.

[2] As the cathedral records put it: 'Cantor debet chorum regere quoad cantum, et potest cantum extollere vel deprimere, lectores et cantores nocturnos et diurnos in tabula notare, inferiores Clericos in choro introducere, in celebratione Ordinum Clericorum admissorum nomina litare' (CDRO, Cap. 1/1/2, col. 7).   [3] CDRO, Cap. 1/3/1, f. 116v.

[4] The accounts at Chichester ran from Michaelmas (29th September) of each year.

[5] A calendar of the Acts during Weelkes' time has been printed in W. D. Peckham (edr.), 'The Acts of the Dean and Chapter of the Cathedral Church of Chichester, 1545–1642', published as *Sussex Record Society*, vol. 58 (1959).

decisions of the Cathedral Chapter; they are mostly concerned with appointments, dismissals and vacancies, leases and other business matters, but they also record matters of discipline. They are not in fact very informative about Weelkes himself (infuriatingly they say nothing about his engagement, and he is not even mentioned by name until July, 1616), but they are full of pieces of incidental information about the musical life of the cathedral. The third source, the various visitation papers, record the business of the Bishop's or Primate's periodic general inspection of the cathedral and diocese. At Chichester this normally took place at two or three year intervals. Before each visitation a set of questions was drawn up which were put to the people concerned, and it is sometimes perfectly clear that these were pointedly framed with a foreknowledge that some aspect of the cathedral's life needed correction. Minutes were kept of the proceedings and of the answers given to the questions, and these are very valuable for direct evidence about Weelkes himself. Afterwards a set of statutes was drawn up to deal with shortcomings uncovered during the visitation. Evidence of these appears in the Act Books.

It is almost inevitable that the cathedral records should give an unfavourable impression of life in the cathedral, and of its personnel. Visitations were specifically campaigns of correction, not cavalcades of commendation, while the routine meetings of the Chapter were only concerned to note and combat indiscipline, not to extol virtue. Yet even allowing for their natural preoccupation with faults and deficiencies, the Act Books and visitation papers make it quite plain that Chichester was no Barchester. Between the routine succession of grants, leases, appointments and so on, as dead as the Latin in which they were written down, the Act Books offer choice snippets chronicling less formal events which stand out the more vividly for being perpetuated in blunt native English. A notable incident involved a certain William Payne, one of Weelkes' predecessors as *informator choristarum*, who threw down a colourful challenge to those who wished to take action against him for neglect of duty and defamation: besides an assault upon the verger, the Act Books record that he had pronounced

'that he that would go about to put him from his living in the church, he cared not "yf he did fill his skinne full of hayleshotte".'[1]

This was in 1571. Payne was not the only turbulent vicar, for on the very same occasion some dozen other people seem to have been in trouble, including two other lay singers who were charged with a nocturnal affray in which a knife had been drawn.

It is not always possible to say whether the administration of such reproofs and punishments to so many individuals indicates that the

[1] CDRO, Cap. 1/3/1, f. 64.

Chapter were faced with a 'crime wave', or whether they had simply decided to tighten discipline. The incident of the knife may still have been remembered two years later, for one of the orders and decrees promulgated in 1573 by the Dean and Chapter ordained that

'none of the vicars choral, lay vicars, singing-men or Sherborne Clerks shall be a fighter, common brawler, quarreller or drunkard either within the Close . . . or within the City or precincts of the City. . . . First and second times of so offending shall be had and taken for admonitions *ipso facto*, and after the third offence so committed [he] shall be expelled from such rooms and commodities as he hath within the said Church.'[1]

Such dissensions among the choirmen are in evidence nearer Weelkes' own time. In 1598 the Chapter had to admonish John Lilliatt, one of the vicars choral, to 'behave himself decently and quietly in the choir' and to 'be subject to the subchanter',[2] and seventeen days later they had to warn, on pain of deprivation,

'all the vicars choral, singing-men, Sherborne Clerks and all other officers of the Church, that none of them hereafter do either give out any slanderous report one of another, nor carry any tales one to another to make any contentions or brawls among them.'[3]

Evidently these disputes were serious enough to have precipitated legal action, for two days later an urgent admonition was added that they were not to 'go to law one with another', but were to bring before the Chapter any future disputes 'and all causes already begun between themselves'.[4]

At the same time there was evidently some incompetence among the choir, for in 1599 the Chapter decreed that

'hereafter no vicar, singing-man, chorister, or any other officer of the Church [shall] be admitted to the place absolutely but first he shall be a probationer the first year.'[5]

More was to be heard of this failing in Weelkes' own time.

But the biggest problem of all was absenteeism; indeed, it seems to have been rife among the whole cathedral establishment. Even on such occasions as the election of a new Bishop there seems to have been almost a tradition of non-attendance, with as many as half or more of the Canons being declared contumacious for failing to appear. It was widespread among the choirmen too, and there was a particularly bad rash of it in the mid-1590s. In 1595 eleven members of the choir were ordered

'that they, by their absence either in serving of Cures elsewhere or otherwise, [should] suffer not the Cathedral Church to be unfurnished of a sufficient number of them to discharge the service there on the Sabbath days.'[6]

---

[1] *op. cit.*, f. 71. [2] *op. cit.*, f. 118v. [3] *op. cit.*, f. 119.
[4] *ibid.* [5] *op. cit.*, f. 121. [6] *op. cit.*, f. 112.

This practice, even on the part of lay members of the choir, of holding livings as a means of augmenting their incomes may have been a major cause of absenteeism. The entry goes on to admonish the choirmaster, John Cowper, to apply himself more diligently to teaching the choristers; otherwise he will lose his office. Nine months later he was still at fault and was admonished for a second time because he continued 'his wonted disorder in haunting of alehouses, and also continued negligent in instructing the choristers'.[1] On the same occasion one of the singing-men, John Gregory, was admonished for the first time because he

'did often absent himself from divine service in the Cathedral Church, and did frequent bowling, and that in a public place, and sometimes in time of divine service. . . . [He] should refrain bowling publicly, and should do his duty in the Church better.'[2]

Gregory seems to have mended his ways, but Cowper had to be reproved yet again six months later, and only narrowly escaped expulsion; three bellringers were less lucky and were dismissed from the duties to which they had been appointed only a year or eighteen months before. Again the fault was apparently absenteeism. On 20th January, 1597, a newly appointed vicar choral, William Lawes (the subchanter mentioned earlier), was detailed by the Chapter to keep a book of 'perditions' for those absent without leave, the perditions to be greater for those absent on Sabbath or Holy Days.[3] For some years there may have been less absenteeism among the choirmen—at least, there are fewer references to it in the Act Books, though there was one bad lapse in 1601, when even Lawes himself was guilty; Godfrey Blaxton and John Lilliatt were charged 'that neither they nor any of the rest of their company were at Church one day in the week precedent to say service'. They were admonished not to absent themselves without leave, and were told that they 'should give warning and tell Mr. Leame and Mr. Lawes of this their [first] admonition'.[4]

An instance of absenteeism, which incidentally throws light upon the demands made upon the choir, occurred in 1619, when John Meade, one of the vicars choral, was charged that

'from Michaelmas last until Christmas thence next following he was absent from the choir one hundred [and] eighty three several services, and since Christmas last until this day [24th March] one hundred [and] forty and one several services.'[5]

His pre-Christmas absences show that the choir was required for certain other services besides the daily Matins and Evensong.

[1] *op. cit.*, f. 113.   [2] *ibid.*

[3] *op. cit.*, f. 116. A similar measure had been tried in 1585, and was to be applied again in 1608. In 1605 and 1610 special provision was made for fines to be imposed upon those who were absent without leave.

[4] *op. cit.*, f. 122.   [5] CDRO, Cap. 1/10.

Other lay officials of the cathedral were also repeatedly in trouble. The sextons were reprimanded for admitting people to the steeple; 'much detriment has been done to the Church thereby'[1] is the cryptic addition to this reproof in 1616. The 'detriment' suffered in 1587 had resulted in a sexton being dismissed 'for suffering strangers to ring ... whereby a bell is lately broken and lead stolen'.[2] The sextons were told more than once to keep order in the cathedral during service; as the Chapter put it in 1605:

'the two sextons ... with the assistance of the bell-ringers shall keep good and quiet order in the choir from disturbance of children, "Lewde parsons" [sic!] or any other during all the time of divine service and sermons.'[3]

Animals seem to have been a nuisance both inside and outside the cathedral. Some of the choir had evidently been bringing their dogs into service with them, for early in 1605 the Chapter had been constrained to decree that any of the choir or other lesser officials who

'shall hereafter bring or suffer to come with them into the choir in time of divine service any dog or bitch shall forfeit ... for every time so offending sixpence.'[4]

Among these lesser officials was the precular whose duty it evidently was to keep order outside the building. In 1616 the Chapter exhorted him that he should

'more diligently perform his office ... and purge the church yard of hogs and dogs and lewd persons that play or do worse therein.'[5]

In 1605, on the same occasion that had produced the decree concerning the exclusion of 'dogs and bitches' from divine service, the precular was reprimanded for neglect of duty, and admonished to abstain from drunkenness and all scandalous conduct, both within the church and outside it.[6]

Disorderly incursions into the cathedral and its precincts are laid bare in a further decree which resulted from the Bishop's visitation of 1616. It was ordered

'that the Principal see the outer doors of their cloister is locked up or fast barred every night by nine of the clock ... and that he repress all seditious brawls and other enormities there, or if they flame out so fast that he cannot, that then he relate them to the Dean.'[7]

This extended examination of the misdemeanours of the cathedral personnel before and during Weelkes' Chichester period effectively demolishes any lingering concept of that pleasant fiction, 'Merrie England'. Lawlessness, drunkenness, inefficiency and neglect of duty were repeated failings among the staff of Chichester Cathedral – and were no

[1] CDRO, Cap. 1/3/1, f. 164v.   [2] op. cit., f. 97v.   [3] op. cit., f. 130.   [4] ibid.
[5] op. cit., f. 165.   [6] op. cit., f. 129v.   [7] op. cit., f. 165.

doubt endemic in other comparable establishments throughout the country.[1]

Weelkes at Chichester Cathedral

Even though the evidence we do possess of Weelkes' life at Chichester is mostly discreditable to him, it is clear that he was not the only black sheep in the fold. In the context of life at Chichester Cathedral in the early seventeenth century, his career was not so very extraordinary. Nevertheless, when he first arrived there, he was probably determined to make the music within the cathedral the very best he could. Whatever the Fellows of Winchester College may have thought of them, those three volumes of madrigals must have made a deep impression in certain musical circles. Weelkes was still very young, and his transference to Chichester could well prove to be a further step towards that most coveted of all musical positions, a Gentleman's place in the sovereign's Chapel Royal. His B.Mus. degree added to his professional prestige, and within the year he had married the daughter of a wealthy Chichester merchant. He had good reason to feel that life was treating him well, and all seemed set for a brilliant career.

It is a pity that there is so little direct evidence about him during his first years at Chichester, though perhaps his influence may be detected behind the thorough overhaul of the organ made in 1602–3; Dr. Henry Blaxton's account book for this financial year lists a large variety of expenses connected with repairs to the instrument.[2] The very silence of the cathedral records suggests that the authorities had no cause for complaint. The papers recording the events of the Primate's visitation of 1605[3] contain nothing suggesting that the musical affairs of the cathedral were unsatisfactory. The questions asked seem routine enough, and the answers given, though mostly evasive, are not incriminating–unless evasion is incriminating. The following year there was another visitation made by the newly installed Bishop, Lancelot Andrewes. Jacob Hillary, Weelkes' predecessor as organist, and a fellow Sherborne Clerk, made the replies on behalf of the Sherborne foundation. Perhaps we may sense a certain edginess behind Hillary's statements for, though he gives all the Sherborne Clerks a good moral report, he hastens to provide what sounds suspiciously like diversionary fire by drawing attention to neglect in the precular's

[1] We may note, for instance, the scathing portrait of 'common singing-men' drawn by John Earle, a Bishop of both Worcester and Salisbury, in his *Micro-cosmography or, A Piece of the world discovered; in essays and characters*, (1628) (quoted in M. C. Boyd, *Elizabethan music and musical criticism*, pp. 26–7). Though grossly exaggerated, the portrait must have had some foundation in fact.

[2] CDRO, Cap. 1/26/5, ff. 78–9.   [3] CDRO, Ep. 1/20/6.

sector: 'But the churchyard lieth in most uncleanly sort, and not like a place appointed for Christians to bury in'.[1]

In view of Weelkes' early brilliance, it seems amazing that the coveted royal appointment should have eluded him. It was once within his grasp, for on the title page of his one remaining volume of madrigalian compositions, the *Ayres or fantastic spirits for three voices* (1608), he styles himself 'Gentleman of His Majesty's Chapel', but this is the only record of such an appointment. It seems that he was at most a Gentleman Extraordinary, for his name is never mentioned in the records of the Chapel itself. We shall probably never know why he failed to secure a permanent appointment. It is not until 1613 that he is known to have been in trouble for drunkenness, though we may suspect that this disorder had started before then, and may have made the Chapel Royal authorities reluctant to take into their establishment a man whose reputation was, in one respect, questionable, and whose behaviour was unreliable.

Yet up to this time there is no sign in the Chichester records that Weelkes had proved in any way unsatisfactory. Indeed, on 8th July, 1608, when the Chapter found it necessary to reprove six of the choirmen for negligence in their duties, Weelkes was not among the delinquents.[2] It is in the next year, 1609, that there is the first positive instance of Weelkes incurring the displeasure of the cathedral authorities, when he was declared contumacious for absence throughout the whole visitation of Bishop Andrewes.[3] The record states that he was to be disciplined, but there is no further information about what happened. Since a large number of the cathedral officials, including the Dean himself, were also guilty of contumacy by absence from at least part of the proceedings, the enormity of Weelkes' truancy seems less. His complete absence suggests that he was right away from Chichester at the time.

The beginning of 1610 saw a sharp change in the temper of authority within the cathedral, for on 30th January, Samuel Harsnett was installed as the new bishop. Harsnett had become Master of Pembroke Hall, Cambridge in 1605 when the former master, Lancelot Andrewes, became Bishop of Chichester, and he became Andrewes' successor yet again when Andrewes was translated to Ely in 1609. The two men were quite different characters. Andrewes was a man of immense learning—a middle-of-the-road cleric, straightforward, unaffected in manner, and humorous. Harsnett, on the other hand, is reputed to have been overbearing in manner; in ecclesiastical affairs he was a high churchman, and a great advocate of ceremonial in worship.

[1] CDRO, Ep. 1/20/7. The precular was an officer of Bishop Sherborne's foundation; this explains why Hillary should report on him.
[2] CDRO, Cap. 1/3/1, f. 139v.   [3] CDRO, Ep. 1/18/29.

The diocese of Chichester now found that it had at its head a man with a reputation for strict discipline, and the cathedral was quickly to hear the crack of his whip. It is echoed in a decree of the Chapter issued on 3rd May, 1610:

'for so much as the vicars choral and other singing-men of this Cathedral Church are very negligent in their service and duties, . . . especially on Sundays and Holy days, . . . any vicar choral . . . absenting himself . . . on the Sabbath days or Holy Day shall forfeit and lose out of his wages . . . ii*s* vi*d* . . . and any other singing-man . . . ii*s* [for each absence].'[1]

Discipline was tightened further when Harsnett made his inaugural visitation of the cathedral. This turned out to be a prolonged affair which resulted in a series of decrees agreed in the Chapter on 30th October, 1611. A number of these refer specifically to members of the choir. Absenteeism was forcefully attacked:

'the ancient and laudable orders and customs of perditions by the Dean . . . [should] be weekly and duly executed every Friday upon the absent without leave.'[2]

A fine of 2s. 6d. for each absence was to be imposed upon all offenders, and the total was to be deducted at the next quarterly payment of the delinquent's wages. Repeated absence would entail dismissal.

The ceremony-loving Harsnett was also clearly dissatisfied with the conduct of the choir during divine service, and two injunctions sought to correct this. The first ordained

'that no unreverend gesture nor unseemly talking be used by any of the vicars, lay vicars, or Bishop Sherborne Clerks in time of divine service upon pain of an admonition, and after three admonitions precedent, upon pain of deprivation.'[3]

—while the second ordained

'that no vicar or Clerk do presume to go out of the choir in time of divine service without leave first asked and obtained of the Dean.'[4]

A further decree, entitled 'Church officers not to frequent tippling houses', was designed to combat drunkenness and disorderly behaviour in general. But as far as Weelkes was concerned, two decrees are even more pertinent:

'that no Clerk, vicar or chorister be actually admitted into his place until he first make public trial of his voice and skill in presence of the Dean and Chapter, together with the Master of the choristers or the Subchanter . . .

'that the Master of the choristers bestow three hours at the least in every day in teaching the choristers, and if he become negligent herein, then after three admonitions to be, *ipso facto*, deprived of his place or places.'[5]

---

[1] CDRO, Cap. 1/3/1, f. 147. [2] CDRO, Cap. 1/1/2, col. 23.
[3] *op. cit.*, col. 24. [4] *ibid.* [5] *op. cit.*, col. 25.

These are the first real signs that Weelkes was giving cause for dissatisfaction. To what extent the first of these reflects direct blame upon him is uncertain; after all, the subchanter was the real head of the cathedral music, and doubtless inside influence played their part in some choir appointments. But there is an undeniable implication in the second decree that Weelkes had not been properly discharging his duties as *informator choristarum*.

From this time forward the surviving evidence about Weelkes is primarily a catalogue of complaints and proceedings against him for inefficiency, neglect of duty, and drunkenness. The first reference to the last failing occurs in the records of the next visitation when, in December, 1613, Weelkes (together with another lay singing-man, Thomas Leame) was charged 'quod fuit et est detectus et presentatus . . . quadam fama publica ebrietatis'.[1] Weelkes denied the charge, and was instructed (as also was Leame) to 'purge' himself by producing witnesses to his good character.

Nothing drastic happened as a result of this enquiry, and Weelkes may have been heartened a little the next year when two of his pieces appeared in Sir William Leighton's *The Tears or lamentations of a sorrowful soul* (1614). These were the only settings by Weelkes of religious texts ever to be published in his lifetime, and they proved to be the last of his works which he was to see in print. In the next year, 1615, the clouds gathered again as the Primate himself descended upon the cathedral for a full-scale visitation, loudly decreeing a dire doom upon all who were found to be beyond correction:
'within a short time [he] would send such refractories home again either well reformed, or at least weed them out from among them as cockle from among good wheat.'[2]
His wrath hung over the heads of Weelkes and ten other members of the choir who were presented for 'intolerable negligence in not coming to Church since their monition given to them by . . . Mr. Booth, President of the Chapter'.[3] The Chapter, it seems, were uncertain of themselves when it came to discipline, for instead of proceeding vigorously against this insubordination, they had simply issued another admonition. The minutes record this in one virtuoso sentence:
'Yet notwithstanding the premises [promises?] . . . Doctor Barker [a Commissary in the Dean's jurisdiction] thought it good to give them another peremptory monition, and therefore did warn and admonish all and singular the vicars choral and singing-men before named, and also enjoined . . . Mr. Meade to admonish . . . Mr. Blaxton, so as aforesaid being absent, that they should every one of them repair diligently to the Church every day to say Morning and Evening Prayer as they ought to

[1] CDRO, Ep. 1/18/31, f. 7v.　　[2] CDRO, Ep. 1/18/32, f. 18v.　　[3] *ibid.*

and are enjoined by the statutes and orders of the said Church, upon pain of perditions and such other penalties as His Grace shall think fit to inflict upon such as shall offend herein between this Tuesday next, and to certify in this place the same day that they have so done.'[1]

Even then there seem to have been no disastrous consequences for the offenders, and the Archbishop, who had started his visitation with such noisy threats to the guilty, contented himself with an enjoinder that they should be more diligent.

But for Weelkes the crisis was approaching. The next year, 1616, started inauspiciously with a lawsuit in which his wife and mother-in-law were involved; next came an order to him from the Chapter for greater efficiency, which was followed in turn by another visitation from Bishop Harsnett. Scarcely had he suffered these tribulations than matters came to a head, and at the beginning of 1617 the ultimate catastrophe befell him— dismissal.

The first of these troubles, the lawsuit, did not affect Weelkes directly,[2] and there is no need to go into great detail about the case. The cause of the trouble is clearly set out in the evidence of one of the witnesses, a servant called Gertrude Lynch. The incident complained of had occurred at the house of Weelkes' mother-in-law, Katherine Sandham, when a certain John Egle,

'sitting by the fire in the kitchen of the dwelling house of Katherine Sandham . . . on an evening about supper time, and being somewhat overcome and sick with drinking, and hearing Anne Blaxton, Marie Ward, Elizabeth Weelkes litigant, and the wife of the said John Egle talking to- gether in the same room near unto him, and supposing (as the deponent thinketh) that they had talked of him, rose suddenly in a very furious manner and said they were all whores, having no manner of occasion offered him so to do, and so continued in that outrageous manner a long time, insomuch that those who were sat down to supper were compelled to rise again and pacify him, which they could hardly do.'[3]

The slander which had stung Katherine Sandham especially was that she had

'heard the said Egle, many and sundry times since the publishing of the aforesaid words of defamation, call the said Elizabeth Weelkes whore, and that she was Weelkes his whore, and was with child before she was married.'[4]

While her maternal discomposure is understandable, it was a charge so

[1] *ibid.*

[2] Perhaps we may be forgiven for feeling a secret regret that this was not in fact one of Weelkes' personal troubles. If he had been called to give evidence, he would have had to provide a brief autobiography which would have answered many questions about him.

[3] CDRO, Ep. IV/3/1, f. 12.　　　　　　　　　　[4] *op. cit.*, f. 10.

patently true (as she herself was forced to admit under cross-examination) that it was amazing that it should ever have become a court issue. As it was, the whole case seems to have fizzled out on 28th July[1] without ever coming to judgement.

The measure to combat Weelkes' inefficiency occasioned the first reference to him by name in the Act Books of the cathedral. The order, approved by the Chapter on 4th May, was designed to improve the standard of the choristers' singing. It was decreed

'that John Juxon, John Little, Thomas Trigges and Richard Mose shall from henceforth every day go to the Song School to Mr. Weelkes, organist and instructor of the choristers, at nine of the clock in the forenoon, by him there to be instructed and made more perfect in singing until ten, and then to go with the rest of the choristers to Church, and so likewise in the afternoon to be there present to the intent aforesaid from three to four, and then to go to Church as aforesaid . . . Nicholas Windres, Thomas Weekes [Weelkes' son], Robert Randoll and Thomas Butcher (junior choristers) shall from henceforth every day repair and go to the said Song School at eight of the clock in the forenoon, to be there instructed and to practise there [their?] singing until ten, and then to go to Church as abovesaid, and so likewise in the afternoon at two of the clock, there to remain to the same intent until four, and then also to go to Church according to the order above set down.'[2]

Defaulters' wages were to be stopped at the quarter day by the communar, and each chorister was to provide himself with either a 'double psalter or a Communion book', and was to bring it to the choir. After the four vicars choral had been admonished for absenteeism, the subchanter opined that two of the choristers mentioned earlier were 'insufficient to perform such duty to the Church in singing . . . and unlikely ever to prove sufficient'.[3]

The Bishop's visitation took Weelkes even deeper into trouble. The list of 'Articles to be ministered to the Dean and Chapter', drawn up before the visitation, reflect some canny appraisals of disorders within the establishment. Five of the articles sought to probe deficiencies (musical and personal) within the choir:

'Item, whether do the vicars or singing-men duly and diligently attend the performing of divine service in the Cathedral Church; whether to your knowledge within these three years last past have not all or the most of them been absent at once at beginning of divine service; whether have not some of them within the time above named been absent by the space of one, two, three or six or ten months in a year; who are the parties so

[1] CDRO, Ep. IV/2/11, f. 7.   [2] CDRO, Cap. 1/3/1, f. 162.
[3] *ibid.*

notoriously offending, and how hath the Dean and Residentiaries proceeded against the offenders for the same.

'Whether is the choir furnished with voices fitting the several parts of song; whether are the singing-men sufficient and skilful in church music; who is in principal fault that the choir is not so furnished.

'Whether are the choristers duly and diligently taught and instructed in their music; how are they furnished with skill and voice to perform their parts; in whom resteth the cause of their insufficiency and defect; and how have the Dean or Residentiaries proceeded against him in whom the fault resteth.

'Whether are there not amongst the choir some disorderly, scandalous or defamed persons in their lives; who are they, and for what vices are they scandalous, defamed or grievously suspected, as you have credibly heard or do believe; how long they have been so noted or defamed, and how far hath the Dean proceeded against any of them. . . .

'Item, In whom the true cause is (as in your conscience you are persuaded) that the choir and choristers are so deficient, the vicars and other church officers so audaciously contemn the performance of their duties, and that so many enormities and disorders do walk in the Church and Church officers not controlled and suppressed.'[1]

The visitation was duly made, and the subsequent list of decrees was approved by the Dean and Chapter on 30th September. The whole staff of the cathedral seem to have come in for reproof, and these orders provide some interesting information about musical matters in the cathedral generally, and about Weelkes himself in particular. The system of fines for absence, instituted in 1610 and confirmed by the Archbishop on his recent visitation,

'hath not taken so good effect as it were to be wished; we therefore decree, that if this prevail not, that every vicar choral or lay vicar . . . delinquent herein after three several admonitions . . . shall be expelled finally, *ipso facto*.'[2]

Evidently some of the Sherborne Clerks were once again holding livings, and this practice was roundly condemned: it was ordered

'that Bishop Sherborne's Clerks peruse their founder's statutes; there are they reputed mere *laici*, and consequently may serve no Cures.'[3]

The subchanter, besides being instructed to keep the perditions, was enjoined

'that he order the choir, and in case there happen any disorder that he reform it: if in the choristers by correcting them, if in any other by complaining to the Dean.'[4]

[1] CDRO, Cap. 1/1/2, cols. 109–10. [2] CDRO, Cap. 1/3/1, f. 165v.
[3] *op. cit.*, f. 165. [4] *op. cit.*, f. 165v.

He was also told to look into the condition of the cathedral's music books, to

'immediately survey all the church song books, what they are, how conditioned, preserved and pricked; that he bring in a catalogue thereof within one week next, and for that we are informed our best Services are conveyed away, that he enquire them out if he can, and that henceforth he permit no book or Service to be had out of the choir without special leave of the Dean *in scriptis*.'[1]

In the early seventeenth century, cathedral and collegiate choirs still had to rely almost exclusively upon manuscript part-books for their musical repertoire. It was sometimes a condition attached to the appointment of a singer to the Chichester Cathedral choir that he should 'prick his own part', and there are records of occasional payments to members of the musical staff for music copying. Unfortunately, the inventory of 1616 has not survived, but a list extant from five years later shows that Weelkes himself had copied music for the cathedral. The list is of special interest, since it gives some idea of the repertoire in use at Chichester during Weelkes' last years:

'A catalogue of all the song-books for the performance of divine service appertaining to the Cathedral Church of the Holy Trinity in Chichester: taken January 18, A.D. 1621.

    Ten new books in folio for Men and M[eans?]
    Eight new books in folio for men only
    Eight books in long quarto of Mr. Weelkes his pricking
    Eight books of Mr. Wm. Cox his Service
    Eight books without covers of anthems
    Eight scrolls in royal paper of Mr. Wm. Cox his anthem
    Eight scrolls of the anthem: *Thou art my king, O God*
    Eight scrolls of Mr. Jurden's anthem
    Eight books in a long quarto of *Christus resurgens*
    Eight scrolls of the anthem, *The Lord hath granted*
    Six books in a long quarto: *A poor desire I have to amend mine ill*
    Ten books of the Gunpowder Treason
    Eight books of Mr. Strogers' Service, called As
    Ten long anthem books, called Bs
    Eight books of Mr. Tallis his Service, called Cs
    Mr. Farrant's Service in books, called Hs
    Eight books in quarto of Mr. Shepherd's Service
    Eight books in quarto of Mr. Byrd's Service
                  per me John Lilliatt'.[2]

It is very irritating that this list is so summary, and that the contents of

---

[1] *ibid.*   [2] CDRO, Cap. 1/10.

the various anthem anthologies are not listed. The cathedral music books suffered sorely during the Commonwealth, and it is very doubtful whether we shall ever know just what they contained. Nevertheless, one of the separate anthems listed, *A poor desire I have to amend mine ill*, must surely be Weelkes' verse anthem, *If King Manasses*, the first chorus of which opens with these words, and 'Mr. Wm. Cox his anthem' must be *Deliver us, O Lord our God* for five voices.

Others of the statutes of 1616 are even more pertinent to the efficiency of the choir. The choristers were ordered to give good notice of their intention to leave the choir:

'every chorister that shall depart the Church without six months' notice given beforehand to the Dean . . . shall at his departure be deprived of his "dismission" money.'[1]

Choristers had sometimes tried simultaneously to serve a trade apprenticeship, but this was not to be tolerated: 'every chorister that becomes an apprentice whilst he is chorister shall be expelled his choristership'.[2] Incompetence had evidently reared its head again, and it was laid down that

'the Master of the choristers or subchanter henceforth "oppose" each chorister before his admission, and faithfully relate his aptness or ability of voice . . . to the Dean.'[3]

Two other orders referred even more specifically to Weelkes. The first of these reflected his continued neglect of the training of the choristers, for he was ordered to

'teach them each morning from eight to ten, and so conduct them to church to and fro; likewise from three to four each afternoon, and so again bring them to church, ranking them orderly by two and by two; thus shall he guide them more especially on Sundays and Holy Days.'[4]

This was largely a reiteration of the Chapter's orders made nearly five months earlier, but the second of these injunctions, referring specifically to Weelkes, was new, and reflected the inadequacies of the cathedral choir:

'that the organist remain in the choir until the last psalm be sung, and then he go up to the organ and, there having done his duty, return into the choir again to bear his part all along, under the "amerciament" of iiid *toties quoties*. This is thought a meet manner in all double choirs, much more is it necessary in all half choirs as ours is.'[5]

This last decree is especially interesting for the information it provides about performance practice at Chichester Cathedral in the early seventeenth century. The description 'half choir' suggests that the *cantoris* and

[1] CDRO, Cap. 1/3/1, f. 165.   [2] *ibid.*   [3] *ibid.*   [4] *ibid.*   [5] *ibid.*

decani division of the choir was not practiced at Chichester. But more important still is the light this passage throws upon the role of the organ within the church service. One of the most uncertain points about the performance of church music at this period is the function of the organ in anthems and services in which the instrument had not been given a specifically independent part. There is considerable doubt about whether such church music was always sung unaccompanied, or whether it was in fact supported by the organ throughout. There are in existence several collections of organ scores compiled at about this time containing organ versions of 'unaccompanied' anthems; these scores give the outer voice parts of the texture at all times, and indications of important inner parts. It is difficult to believe that so much time and expense would have been spent on compiling these collections if they had been intended solely for rehearsal purposes. On the other hand, this injunction to Weelkes makes it plain that at Chichester the service was to be sung unaccompanied until after the psalms, and that the later stages of the service were likewise sung without the support of the organ. It is infuriating that the order should be so vague about just when the organist was to return to the choir; what in fact seems most likely is that he was ordered up to the organ after the psalm in order to play a voluntary. Support for this is to be found in Clifford's *The Divine Services and anthems* which, though printed as late as 1663, describes practices deriving from pre-Commonwealth times. Clifford notes in his 'Brief directions for the understanding of that part of the Divine Service performed with the organ' that for both Matins and Evensong there should be 'after the psalms a Voluntary upon the organ alone'.[1] It appears likely therefore that the service was sung unaccompanied throughout at Chichester (unless, of course, a verse anthem or verse Service was being used).

Events now moved rapidly to the ultimate catastrophe for Weelkes. Only three weeks after these decrees had been passed by the Chapter, he was once again presented to be disciplined. The charge was
'that he hath been, and is noted and famed for a common drunkard and a notorious swearer and blasphemer; his usual oaths are that which is most fearful to name, by the wounds, heart and blood of the Lord.'[2]
Weelkes denied the charge and was ordered to purge himself four weeks later. On the appointed day (18th November) he was unable to produce

---

[1] J. Clifford, *The Divine Services and anthems usually sung in the cathedrals and collegiate choirs in the Church of England.*

[2] CDRO, Ep. 1/18/33, f. 16v. Once again Thomas Leame was also presented for the same offence. It was stated that he 'hath been, and is taken and famed for a notorious drunkard, to the great scandal of the Church, and the causing the people to abhor the service of God: and that he often times curseth his mother, being a woman of good respect: *quem defectionem idem Leame negat*' (f. 16).

the witnesses ('nullos produxit in compurgatores'[1]). The proceedings were adjourned, but at the beginning of the following year (16th January, 1617) the final blow fell, and sentence of dismissal was pronounced: ' "D[i]c[t]us Weelkes . . .(?) defecisse in purgan[acio]ne et h[ab]eri pro Convicto Q[u]o die Comp[arui]t personal[ite]r d[i]c[t]us Weelks in Cuius p[rese]ntia d[omi]n[u]s Ep[iscop]us legit tulit et promulgavit quandam s[ente]n[t]iam in script[is] conceptam p[ro]mulcando declar-and[o] amovendo deprivand[o] ac cetera faciend[o] p[ro]ut in eadem continent[ur] tunc et ib[ide]m Geo Elgger p[re]bend[o] de Hyghley Johnes Lilliett et Wmo Lawes Cl[er]ic[is] testibus etc Super quibus d[o]m[inu]s R[ichar]dus pr[elatus] requisivit me no[st]r[u]m aud[i]c[ori]-um unum vel plura instrum[en]tu[m] vel instrum[en]ta conficere ac testes etc in p[u]n[i]ti[on]e D[omi]n[i] Weelkes tacent[is]." '[2]

The scribe first noted that Weelkes protested (' "Weelks dissen[tis]" '), but then struck through ' "dissen[tis]" ' and declared that he accepted his fate silently (' "tacent[is]" ').

The authorities had evident difficulty in finding a replacement as *informator choristarum*, for they had to go outside the choir to fill this post; on 3rd May John Fidge was appointed[3] on the understanding that he would be given the first vacancy to occur in the choir's establishment. He had in fact to wait a whole year before he was appointed a singing-man. Although there is no actual record of his appointment as organist, it is clear from the cathedral accounts that Fidge also held this post, for, al-though these accounts do not attach a name to either post, payment for both is clearly made to the same person.[4] Nevertheless, Weelkes was ultimately to be reinstated as organist, for the accounts of the financial year ending Michaelmas, 1622 once again name him as organist,[5] while the

[1] *op. cit.*, f. 17.

[2] *op. cit.*, f. 20. Neither the scribe's hand nor the Latin itself is as clear as it might be, and it is not always possible to decipher the passage with complete certainty. The gist of the passage appears to be: 'The said Weelkes [was reported?] to have failed to purge himself and to be considered guilty. On which day the said Weelkes appeared in person, in whose presence the Lord Bishop read and made public a certain sentence set out in writing for publishing, declaring, for removing and depriving, and for doing such other things as are contained in it. [This was done] there and then with George Elgar, prebend of Higheleigh, John Lilliatt and William Lawes, clerks, present as witnesses. In whose presence the Lord Archbishop Richard [Bancroft] required me, [as part of] our ecclesiastical court, to prepare one or more instrument or instruments as witnesses to the punishment of Master Weelkes, who remained silent.'

[3] CDRO, Cap. 1/3/1, f. 167v.

[4] From 1617 to 1621, after the payment to the organist has been listed, the following entry for the *informator choristarum* starts 'eidem' (CDRO, Cap. 1/23/4, ff. 206v, 211, 215v, 220, 224v).

[5] CDRO, Cap. 1/23/4, f. 229. This is confirmed by the entry recording the burial of Weelkes' wife on 7th September, 1622: ' "Eliza: Welkes: the wyfe of Mr Tho: Welkes:" organist of the Cathedral Church' (CDRO, Par. 44/1/1/1, f. 99).

payment for this post is now detached from that to the *informator choristarum.*

Nevertheless, all was not lost for Weelkes, for in one respect the Chapter evidently did not carry out the Bishop's sentence, and Weelkes continued to hold his position as a Sherborne Clerk. We know from the evidence of the next visitation that he remained in the choir establishment. In 1619, Bishop Harsnett was translated to Norwich, and the new bishop, George Carleton, made his primary visitation of the cathedral. During this, William Lawes reported:

'most of the choir and other the officers of the same (as many as come to Divine Service) demean themselves religiously all the time of prayers, save only Thomas Weelkes, who divers times and very often comes so disguised either from the tavern or alehouse into the choir as is much to be lamented, for in these humours he will both curse and swear most dreadfully, and so profane the service of God (and especially on the Sabbath Days) as is most fearful to hear, and to the great amazement of the people present. And though he hath been often times admonished by the late Lord Bishop, the Dean and Chapter to refrain these humours and reform himself, yet he daily continues the same, and is rather worse than better therein. . . . I know not any of the choir or other the officers of the Church to be a common drunkard but Mr. Weelkes'.'[1]

Even now no action seems to have been taken against him, for when Carleton again inspected the cathedral in 1622, the replies given by Jacob Hillary and Valentine Austen make it clear that Weelkes was not only still definitely considered a Sherborne Clerk, but also that he was still quite unreformed:

'We do answer that there are four of the foundation of the said Bishop Sherborne's Clerks, whose names are Jacob Hillary, Valentine Austen, Thomas Weelkes and John Clifford. . . . Three of our foundation are sworn to observe the statutes of our foundation, but Thomas Weelkes, being the fourth, is not sworn thereunto, nor never was to our knowledge. . . . Three of us do observe the said statutes accordingly, but Thomas Weelkes, being the fourth, does not. . . . Three of us do perform our duties in the choir according to the foundation of our said statutes, but Mr. Thomas Weelkes, being the fourth, does not so.'[2]

It seems clear that Hillary and Austen assumed that when Weelkes had been dismissed from his position as a Sherborne Clerk in 1617, the oaths which he had previously taken on being admitted to the post had lapsed, and that Weelkes' readmission into the position was unofficial. Whether or not this was the real situation, they used it as a means to sidestep deftly any obligation to present him for discipline themselves:

[1] CDRO, Ep. 1/20/9. By this time Thomas Leame was dead. [2] CDRO, Ep. 1/20/10.

'and further for Mr. Thomas Weelkes, who was one of our foundation of Bishop Sherborne's Clerks, but being expelled by your Lordship's predecessor, Bishop Harsnett, in his last visitation, since which time we never knew him admitted or sworn into his place again, and therefore, being at this present time none of our foundation to our knowledge, we think it not fit to present him for any misdemeanour or disordered life, but refer it to your good Lordship, and the right worshipful the Dean and the Chapter's discretions.'[1]

Just before the last visitation Weelkes' wife died;[2] his own end came only a year later. From his will and the record of his burial, it is discovered that he died in London, and was buried on 1st December, 1623 in St. Bride's, Fleet Street. The site of his grave remains unknown. The fact that his will acknowledges a debt of 50s. to his 'well-beloved friend Henry Drinkwater . . . for meat, drink and lodging' suggests that he had been spending considerable periods in London.[3] The will, which was proved at Chichester on 5th December and which is preserved there, reads:

'In the name of God, Amen. That I, Thomas Weelkes of Chichester in the County of Sussex, gentleman, sick of body, but of good and perfect mind and memory, God be thanked, do make this my last will and testament in these words following. That is to say, I bequeath my soul to God who gave it, and my body to the earth from whence it came: and as for all other my lands, tenements, goods, chattels, bills, bonds, debts or demands due to me by any person or persons whatsoever, unto my trusty and well-beloved friend, Henry Drinkwater, of the parish of Saint Bride's, London, cutler, whom I make my full and absolute executor of this my said last will and testament. And the reason why I should make the aforesaid Henry Drinkwater my executor is for that I, the said Thomas Weelkes, at the making and day and date hereof, am indebted unto him, the said Henry Drinkwater, in the sum of fifty shillings of good and lawful English money for meat, drink and lodging, and suchlike necessaries which is already due unto him. And do farther likewise desire the said Henry Drinkwater, if it please God to take me out of this world into his heavenly mercy, to see me buried like a man of my profession, and to pay himself as well such monies as shall hereafter be laid out and disbursed about my burial, as also all such monies as formerly he hath laid out and disbursed and [are] due unto him before the day and date hereof. And the rest of my goods and chattels to be divided amongst my children, that is to say, to my son Thomas Weelkes five shillings, to my daughter Katherine Weelkes five

---

[1] *ibid.*   [2] CDRO, Par. 44/1/1/1, f. 99 records her burial on 7th September, 1622.
[3] His absence from the entire visitation of 1609 has already been noted; perhaps he was in London on that occasion.

shillings, and all the rest of my goods, lands, chattels, and hereditaments whatsoever to my daughter Alice Weelkes; and do, as is before mentioned and expressed, make him, the said Henry Drinkwater, my full and absolute executor of this my last will and testament. In witness whereof I have hereunto put my hand and seal, the thirtieth day of November in the one and twentieth year of the reign of our Sovereign Lord, King James, and in the year of our Lord God, 1623

[Signed] "Tho: Weelkes".[1]

Despite the 'lands, tenements, goods, chattels, bills, bonds, debts or demands due to me', this does not sound like the will of a wealthy man; otherwise why should he leave so very little to his son and one of his daughters? Weelkes must have died later the same day, for he was buried in St. Bride's the day following; as the parish register records it: 'Thomas Weelkes from Henry Drinkwater's the 1 [st December]'.[2]

Weelkes' biography is a sorry tale. His first three books of madrigals had promised the most brilliant of careers, and the decline of the later years appears all the more tragic after such an auspicious beginning. These early madrigal volumes had shown that he could work quite fast, and the quantity of his remaining compositions is much less than might have been expected after those four brilliant years—even allowing for all the pieces that are likely to have vanished without trace in the intervening three and a half centuries. Couple this to the portrait of a demoralised and doubtless very disillusioned man which emerges from the Chichester records, and the biographer cannot help wondering whether these last years were not in fact creatively barren. Does the best—and the bulk—of his church music belong to the earlier part of his Chichester period? Nevertheless, any assumption of a complete degeneration during these last years must be tempered by the hard fact that Weelkes was retained on the cathedral staff, even after he had been expelled by the bishop. In general, his masters must have had a high regard for him; perhaps their action is also an indication that he was well liked as a person.

But it is not profitable to speculate further. The one thing that is really definite about him is his surviving music—at its best thoroughly positive, clear-headed, imposing and imaginative. The extant corpus consists almost exclusively of vocal music—madrigals and church music; his surviving instrumental compositions are very few, which is all the more surprising in view of the strongly instrumental manner which appears in some of his vocal music.[3] Except for the two pieces printed in 1614, none of his

[1] CDRO, STD II/Box 3/130.
[2] Corporation of London, Guildhall Library, MS 6538.
[3] It is worth noting that both halves of the madrigal volume of 1600 describe their contents as 'apt for the viols and voices'.

music to religious texts was published during his lifetime, and the manuscript sources in which it survives are mainly too late to give any indication either of when it was composed, or for what purpose. These are all matters which will be considered in due course. First it is necessary to examine the sources that contributed to the formation of his style, and the nature of the synthesis he evolved from these sources in his madrigals.

The roots of Weelkes' madrigal style

Weelkes grew up during a time of rapid change in English musical life. In 1588, a mere nine years before his first works appeared in print, the madrigal had broken to the surface of Elizabethan musical life, speedily transforming the whole appearance of English music, and giving 'art music' a wider popularity than it had ever enjoyed before. In fact, the madrigal became an economic venture, propagated not in isolated manuscripts, but in printed copies for an extensive upper and middle class public. The times were exciting for a composer, for here was not only a new musical style and a larger musical audience, but also an atmosphere in which novelty stood a fairer chance of acceptance than it would have done a few years before. The extraordinary phenomenon of Weelkes' most advanced madrigals would certainly have been unthinkable in the England of a mere fifteen years earlier.

Yet, for all its charms, the Italian madrigal did not stifle the indigenous line of composition. The musical circles which it first captivated were mainly groups of amateurs—middle class merchants and professional men who had contacts with the Continent, were aware of what was happening there, and who were more likely to be receptive to a new style and technique than many musical professionals. Nor was the resistance of others simply the instinctive opposition of older men to change. English composers were still largely church musicians, living in a world which had a natural distrust of new ideas, and which would have judged the novelties of the Italian madrigal not only unnecessary but repellent (though it must be remembered that Nicholas Yonge, the man behind *Musica Transalpina* (1588), was a lay clerk at St. Paul's Cathedral). As for the average English Christian, he would have found the dramatic and volatile manner of the madrigal unacceptable in music for worship. The newly imported style was to influence English church music, but it could never seduce it.

Nor was the native tradition perpetuated simply because it was still needed for church music. Inborn English conservatism (and, at this time in particular, a strong streak of puritanism) ensured that in secular music too, the older, more serious English tradition should persist doggedly alongside the frivolities and passions of the madrigal. As a result the English composer of the 1590s found himself in a situation which was exciting for its possibilities, but problematic in that he had to decide what was to be his own creative standpoint within it. William Byrd, the greatest English composer of the time, chose to continue in the native manner in which he had composed for a quarter of a century; Orlando Gibbons, his pupil, and forty years his junior, was to be the main champion of this line in the early seventeenth century. On the other hand, another of Byrd's pupils, Thomas Morley, performed a stylistic *volte face*, capitulated completely to the new Italian idiom, and became its foremost exponent in England. John Wilbye, who seems to have been Weelkes' exact contemporary, and who was the one English composer who could challenge him as a madrigalist, chose to follow Morley, though with a greater seriousness of purpose and occasional excursions towards the manner of Byrd.

Weelkes' solution was quite different. He was gifted with the most restless musical imagination of all English composers of the time, and in his madrigals he applied this gift to a musical style which was basically Italian, but which incorporated substantial elements of the native English manner. This may sound a simple enough process, but in fact any attempt to mix the Italian and English manners was hazardous. Byrd seems to have tried it once—if he did, he failed.[1] This stylistic dilemma was as acute for Weelkes as for any composer, and certainly more problematic than it was for either Morley or Wilbye. It is not therefore just for completeness of the record that any study of Weelkes must go back to his very earliest years to isolate the various stylistic currents in English music during his student period. These first experiences proved to be of vital importance to him.

We have Weelkes' own authority for deducing that his musical education began in 1586,[2] and presumably his primary musical instruction was received in some church establishment. It is certainly improbable that Italian madrigals were part (or any large part) of his early musical diet. At this time the normal manner of English composition was restrained and, compared to what was soon to come, unspectacular—but the range of music to be heard was not small. Most of the Services and anthems which existed for the rites of the Reformed Church were comparatively modest in their expressive aims, but some were by no means unworthy in their achievement. Far more highly evolved music was still being composed to Latin texts, although in much reduced quantity. Thomas Tallis and Byrd had published a joint set of *Cantiones sacrae* in 1575, and Byrd was to offer two more volumes of his own maturer Latin works in 1589 and 1591. The only other English music which could compare with such works in quality and complexity was certain of the viol-accompanied songs which seem to have been bred in the court circles and especially in the choirboy plays of the earlier years of Elizabeth's reign. The lyrics were often laments, and elicited a remarkable expressive

[1] See below, p. 52.
[2] From his supplication for the B.Mus. degree of Oxford University in 1602 (see above, p. 25).

response from some composers. Nevertheless, these consort songs were highly professional music whose performance must have been restricted to fairly limited circles.

Beside these, the part-songs of the time are far humbler. Their counterpoint is gentle and their expression restrained; compared to the later madrigal, they seem unambitious. Even simpler are the musical offerings in the numerous psalters published during Elizabeth's reign. These were products of that puritanism which was strong in England in the latter half of the sixteenth century, and were intended to serve primarily a domestic, non-liturgical function. They presented mostly simple, four-part settings of the standard tunes associated with the psalms. Yet their importance is greater than the average quality of their contents would suggest, for they were evidently the musical primers by which many Elizabethans gained their first skill in reading music.

Through this truly indigenous English vocal music Weelkes would have become familiar in his earliest student years with an undemonstrative polyphonic technique, simple in the psalters, part-songs and some of the English church music, but more complex in much of the music to Latin texts and in certain of the consort songs—a technique not given to sudden dramatic eruptions or abrupt expressive changes. By continental standards it was antiquated, a fact of which some English musical circles were being made increasingly conscious by the growing currency of imported Italian madrigals. Because of developing musical literacy and the growing awareness of an expanding class of amateurs, change was inevitable.

As a living and still creative force, this native tradition was embodied during the last years of the century in the mighty genius of Byrd. The death of Tallis in 1585 had left him the unchallenged head of English music, and he consolidated this position by the publication of four further volumes of his music between 1588 and 1591. Byrd's greatest work is to be found in his compositions for the liturgy and devotions of the Roman Catholic Church, of which he remained a faithful member all his life. In his works to Latin texts he composed freely in a fully evolved manner deriving originally from Flemish polyphony—a manner which the Reformation had restricted in England, but never stifled. Thus Byrd escaped the technical and expressive dilemmas which faced his contemporaries who were trying to provide music in accord with the demands of the Reformed Church. This broad polyphony was at the root of all Byrd's vocal music, no matter how much he might modify it to suit a particular purpose. Yet his conservatism was of manner only; in some ways he was the most progressive English composer of his time.[1] Although English

[1] This is apparent, for instance, in the modulatory practices of certain of the three-voice psalms in his *Songs of sundry natures* (1589). Some of the 'modulations' in these works are

music of the 1590s was falling firmly beneath the spell of newfangled Italian ways, the fact that Byrd's all-powerful genius remained committed to the native tradition was a guarantee that this tradition should not die. Indeed, some younger composers, notably Gibbons, chose to follow Byrd's path rather than submit to the lure of Italian enchantments.

Morley, however, surrendered to them completely. He was certainly not the first composer to introduce Italian elements into composition in England, for in 1571 Thomas Whythorne, a gentleman and musical amateur, had published a large collection of his own vocal compositions in which there is an avowed and some apparent Italian influence, though the moral tone of some of the texts betrays the force of that English puritanism which was producing the metrical psalters. A few of the things in Whythorne's volume must have sounded quite startlingly new to English ears, but the prosaic quality of much of the music doubtless reduced its influence. Much more important musically were the madrigals of Alfonso Ferrabosco the elder, Byrd's exact contemporary, who lived in England between 1562 and 1578 and who adopted in his madrigals a solemn mien to accord with the prevailing English musical taste. Ferrabosco helped to acclimatise English musical circles to the madrigal, and he remained a powerful influence in English music for the remainder of the century.

Weelkes must certainly have made Ferrabosco's musical acquaintance after 1588, the year in which Nicholas Yonge included fourteen of his madrigals in *Musica transalpina*. Though this large collection of Italian madrigals (furnished with English texts) marked the 'coming out' of the madrigal in England, it still remained for an English composer to set a precedent for a viable English madrigal. This was Morley's achievement. His Latin-text compositions which have survived in manuscript sources show that he had thoroughly mastered the older polyphonic technique of his teacher Byrd, but the musical and financial attractions of the madrigal induced him to embrace its style wholeheartedly. Morley's first madrigal print, *Canzonets . . . to three voices*, appeared in 1593, and contained twenty works. The magnitude of the change in musical style becomes apparent if these first madrigals of Morley are placed alongside some of the most

not simply inflections of the prevailing mode through the use of *musica ficta*, but are unequivocal and extended changes of tonic which impart a feeling of progress within the expressive uniformity of each work. The later English madrigalists, Weelkes included, showed nothing like so developed an attitude to tonal organisation, since their sectionalised, volatile works would neither have favoured nor required modulation as a way of transforming a static into a dynamic form. For instance, it was characteristic of Wilbye, being a true madrigalist, that his most important application of modulation was to move between tonic-major and tonic-minor, a modulation whose effect is highly expressive (see *Draw on, sweet night* (madrigals of 1609), or the extended major-mode endings of *Adieu, sweet Amaryllis* (madrigals of 1598) and *Sweet honey-sucking bees/Yet, sweet, take heed* (madrigals of 1609)).

recent compositions by Byrd—for instance, the three-voice secular works of his *Songs of sundry natures* (1589), of which more will be written a little later. Straightway a fundamental change in the relationship between the melodic lines and the harmonic structure is revealed. For Byrd the linear aspect of the music is paramount, with the harmony a controlled subordinate factor; for Morley the harmonic element has quite as much importance as the melodic. In Morley's volume the harmonic progressions have become clearer, and the harmonic rhythm, now moving in semibreves and minims, is more regular, and founded largely upon fundamental bass movement in fourths or fifths, or by step. In other words, it is manifesting strong characteristics of diatonic harmony. Crotchet chords often sound like mere inflections of this broad harmonic scheme; where the harmonic rhythm is in crotchets, the music is often homophonic or sequential. The points of imitation are designed to accommodate this firm harmonic idiom, often forming themselves round the notes of a triad, or else suggesting a straightforward harmonic progression. Thus it is easier to retain these melodic points intact upon their repetitions. Byrd's melodic points, despite their modifications in successive entries, play a large part in determining the harmonic progress of the work; Morley's often appear to be simply contrapuntal decorations of a chord or progression, and have a pithiness or catchiness which makes them easily remembered. His madrigals split into more definite sections marked out by clearer intermediate cadences, and these sections may be sharply contrasted in mood. Asymmetrical rhythm is used to provide fascinating texture rather than to produce virile rhythmic counterpoint. The rhythmic life of the music is nearer the surface, is more obvious, and more deliberately attractive; the texture itself is both more decorated with quavers and, at the same time, more lucid. The approach to dissonance is less virile and more exquisite; suspensions are confined more to the cadences, and are almost always both approached and quitted by step. Certain formulae, especially cadential ones, are used so widely as to become clichés; in fact, the whole conception is more artificial. Last, but by no means least, the declamation of the text is altogether lighter, and the union of text and music far more essential. The hallmarks of the new style are directness, effectiveness and refinement.

By 1597 Morley had published four more volumes of his own madrigals —the English madrigal had arrived. When Weelkes was composing his first madrigals, the English musical scene was dominated by the two figures of Byrd and Morley. Byrd had the greater authority, the greater genius and prestige (and also, one gathers, the greater personal attractiveness, although it must be remembered that Weelkes numbered Morley among his friends). Morley offered a new glittering manner, facile and shallower than Byrd's, but full of new possibilities, and alluring to a young composer ambitious for success.

Before examining the synthesis which Weelkes made from these two streams, it is worth returning to Byrd to take a closer look at the brief but rather disastrous attempt he seems to have made to unite the Italian and English styles, for it demonstrates the problem of reconciliation. This crisis can be seen in the three-voice secular pieces of his *Songs of sundry natures* (1589) which have already been contrasted with Morley's madrigals. Byrd's volume contains compositions for from three to six voices, a precedent followed by Weelkes in his first volume. The first fourteen works are for three voices, and fall into two equal groups, the first consisting of penitential psalms in eight-line metrical versions, treated to a thoroughly polyphonic (and characteristically Byrdian) technique. Although Byrd occasionally breaks each line of text into two, he usually allots a single broad melodic point to each line, modifying pitch and rhythm to suit the harmony or the proportions of the piece. The breadth he achieves within the limitations of three voices is often most impressive. The other seven works for three voices set, with one exception, secular texts, and are strikingly different. The thematic material is much briefer and more prolific; in most instances Byrd divides each line of text into two, giving a short melodic point to each half. The movement is mainly in crotchets, as in the later madrigal prints. Clearly Byrd was aiming at a more succinct expression, but the technical approach is still thoroughly polyphonic. The results are unfortunate. Gone are the sweeping melodic lines; the employment of up to a score of brief and unremarkable melodic fragments makes for shortwindedness in detail and diffuseness in the whole, while the rhythmic vitality which Byrd tries to inject into the music sounds contrived. Their gaiety is joyless.[1] Byrd, it seems, has tried to enter the madrigal on his own terms, only to prove how incompatible were his own spacious polyphony and the epigrammatic, volatile character of the madrigal.

The trouble was that the two styles could not simply be compounded. The composer had to choose one or the other, although, having once taken his stand, there was no reason why he should not fertilise or expand his chosen style with elements from the other. Byrd in fact did this very profitably in some of his later music. To cite but one example—his justly renowned *Ave verum corpus*[2] is composed in a plastic, economical yet genuine polyphony, but is suffused with a fervent mysticism which must surely derive from years of conditioning by the passionate warmth of

---

[1] The arresting modulatory practices of the preceding psalms are replaced by incidental inclinations to other tonal centres, typical of the coming English madrigal.

[2] *Gradualia* (1607).

Mediterranean music and its English offspring. Against this, the early *Emendemus in melius*,[1] while essaying essentially the same expressive manner, exhibits more clearly cut phrases, a more severe harmonic language and a less sensuous treatment of dissonance. By comparison, it sounds almost austere.

Weelkes approached this dichotomy from the opposite side, as a madrigalist following naturally in the Morley line, but treating the form with truly polyphonic intentions deriving from the hardy English manner which he had known from his earliest years. His attitude will be seen more clearly if we compare some passages from his earliest madrigals with similar incidents in works of Byrd or Morley. Of course, many similarities between sections in works by different sixteenth-century composers are quite coincidental, arising from the repeated use of melodic points drawn from the common stock of melodic formulae, and also from the circumscribed technique available for working these points. Whether the resemblances between the passages in Examples 1 and 2 are accidental or not, the differences are more significant than the similarities. In Example 1 the melodic point and the sequence of entries in both extracts are vir-

Ex. 1

a

MORLEY: Why sit I here complaining? (1594)

b

WEELKES: Ay me, my wonted joys (1597)

¹ *Cantiones sacrae* (1575).

53

tually identical, but whereas Morley closes immediately with a conventional madrigal cadence, Weelkes proceeds to elaborate further upon the point (to different words), modifying it rhythmically and melodically to

Ex. 2

suit the harmony, just as Byrd had done in his secular three-voice works of 1589. Morley is smooth in rhythm and the verbal stresses fall consistently upon the strong pulses; Weelkes is altogether less pat, rhythmically more virile, with stresses on all pulses. The melodic material of Example 2 is likewise identical, and both extracts employ a $\frac{5}{4}$ structure for segments of their melodic lines. Morley makes six entries with the point in three bars, the second pair sequentially following the first; all three pairs of entries are regularly spaced, the harmonic scheme is steady and crystal clear, and the final entries are followed without more elaboration by a conventional madrigal cadence. Polyphonic gestures remain, but the unpredictable progress created by the thrust of independent melodic lines has gone. Weelkes achieves nine completely unsequential entries in four bars, the entries occurring on all crotchet pulses; the underlying harmonic scheme is neither clear nor steady, the rhythmic life is again more virile, and the approach to the cadence is more extended and less completely conventional.

The undigested mixture of the Byrd and Morley styles in Weelkes' work is nicely demonstrated in Example 3. Weelkes' contrapuntal approach is immediately apparent in the genuine linear independence of the opening imitative duet which might well have come from a work of Byrd. The melodic point is a full nine crotchets long and is maintained intact, the false entry of the alto prolonging Weelkes' self-imposed *canti fermi* until

Ex. 3

WEELKES: Now every tree renews (1597)

bar seven, and compelling the tenor and bass voices in bars four to six to find their way along lines which will accord with the harmonic limitations imposed by the combination of the upper two voices. So far, so Byrd-like. But, the last entry completed, Weelkes proceeds to a smooth, thoroughly Morleyish madrigal cadence.[1]

As well as an inclination to genuine polyphony in his madrigals, Weelkes gained from Byrd an understanding of the expressive power of organic growth. This is evident in the opening of the very first madrigal of his first volume (Example 4), in which, by progressively more intense

Ex. 4

rhythmic activity and quickening harmonic rhythm, Weelkes contrives a broad and deliberate growth quite lacking in the neat entries with which Morley so often launches his madrigals. Example 4 has a closer affinity with the opening of a work like Byrd's *O Lord, who in thy sacred tent*,[2] even though in this instance Byrd achieves a sense of organic growth

[1] The opening of the next madrigal, *Young Cupid hath proclaimed*, shows similar features, though here the fourth voice is not allowed to complete its entry before the conventional madrigal cadence intrudes.

[2] *Psalms, sonnets, and songs* (1588).

through the use of a very restrained chromaticism distantly related to his modulatory practices. On the other hand, the melodic point to 'Amyntas joys' and Weelkes' handling of it are closer to Morley in manner.

All the examples of Weelkes' work quoted in this chapter are from his first madrigal collection, in which the young composer's technique and style are imperfectly integrated. But it would be quite wrong to assume that all the music of this 1597 volume grew out of precedents set by Byrd and Morley. One madrigal at least, *Cease sorrows now*, introduced a new expressive experience into English music; even Morley had never tried anything as radical as the pathos and chromaticism of this piece. From the beginning Weelkes was striving not merely to work out a new synthesis from the compositional practices current in English music, but to seek out new expressive possibilities. Without this adventurous attitude the incredibly rapid progress to the achievement of the great madrigals of 1600 would have been impossible. The newness of *Cease sorrows now* may be gauged by placing one of its most striking passages beside an extract from one of Byrd's three-voice psalms which momentarily pursues a very similar course; indeed, for three bars they are virtually identical (Example 5). Byrd employs a well defined melodic point (*a*) firmly set within clear,

Ex. 5

a

BYRD: Lord, in Thy rage (1589)

WEELKES: Cease sorrows now (1597)

measured harmonic progressions. The final approach to the cadence is deliberately delayed both by the longer note values and by the expressive reversion from B natural to B flat, suggested perhaps by the word 'troubled'; the cadence itself, though interrupted, is clearly defined. This passage, which starts at the apex of a calculated climax which Byrd has been building for a dozen bars, is typical of his spacious and proportioned manner, and of his profoundly *musical* approach. Weelkes, on the other hand, uses little recognisable basic thematic material, nor have his progressions anything like the measured quality of those of Byrd. Instead he relies for his effect upon dissonance, the pathetic descent of the voice parts, and the greater emphasis upon the reversion to B flat by placing it in the most extreme dissonance of the whole passage. Byrd demands that each moment should be heard in relation to the whole passage; the proportions are vital. Weelkes does not demand such an architectural ear, but strikes the senses with each move to a new sound, only requiring spatial attention to sense the chromatic alterations he effects to G and B. The whole section is less vertebrate, more deliberately effective, and less truly musical than is Byrd's. Byrd, the polyphonist, commands our waking mind; Weelkes, the madrigalist, charms our twilight senses.

Besides the new integration of old sounds and the quest for new ones, the first twelve works of Weelkes' first madrigal volume show him searching for new ways of unifying a work by all sorts of repetitive procedures—by literal repetition in places where there is no conventional precedent for such repetition, by varied repetitions of sections, by relationships between the main thematic points of a work, and by progressive evolutions of imitative points or whole sections. He also applies recompositional processes, allowing an earlier section to shape a subsequent passage without cramping the freedom of the later passage to be new. Such recomposition is neither exact enough nor deliberate enough to warrant the term 'variation', and it often very clearly results from instinct rather than design. This search for ways to a truly musical unity was by no means a new thing in English music. There is some evidence of it in the three-voice secular works of Byrd's *Songs of sundry natures* (1589),[1] and certain madrigals of Morley show very definite signs of a calculated, purely musical organisation. Long before this, the use of headmotifs in masses, or the employment of a repeated *cantus firmus* (especially when used as obviously as in a work like John Taverner's Mass, *Western wind*) reveal an urge to establish such unity. But before the madrigal this had not been an urgent problem to the composer, since the expressive uniformity, typical of the earlier Renaissance motet or mass movement, ensured a feeling of oneness within a movement. So, also, the repeated use of universally known texts, such as the Ordinary of the Mass, the Magni-

[1] Since this was written, H. K. Andrewes' *The Technique of Byrd's vocal polyphony* has appeared. Andrewes presents much evidence to show that Byrd employed numerous thematic cross references in his work (see Andrewes, *op. cit.*, pp. 266 ff.).

ficat, or the Marian antiphons, enabled the listener to orientate himsel throughout a piece by reference to the words. However, the madrigal's characteristic juxtaposition of the most diverse moods within a single work (and the increasing importance at this time of purely instrumental music) created an acute need to find purely musical ways of countering diffuseness and imprecision, and of creating an exclusively musical logic. No English composer made use of greater extremes of expression within one work than did Weelkes, and the following chapters on the madrigals will be much concerned with these integrating techniques.

But before embarking on this detailed study, a word of caution is needed. In the following examination, it may seem that the resourcefulness and novelty of his work must make Weelkes a major historical figure. In fact, it is unlikely that, as an influence upon subsequent musical events, he had much importance—certainly not to the degree that Byrd or Morley had. There is no doubt that Weelkes was a composer of immense talent, at times of genius, but it is equally certain that he was a composer who failed lamentably to fulfil the promise of his early works. The unhappy personal decline already recorded in the biographical chapter was clearly connected with this, but it is also true that Weelkes was a creative artist out of place in the England of his time. As a madrigalist he almost certainly became too 'hot' for the prevailing taste of his English contemporaries, and it is doubtful whether the madrigal volume of 1600 enjoyed the appreciation which we can see it deserved, for only his *Ballets and madrigals* of 1598 ran to a second edition (in 1608). Interest was shifting to the lute-accompanied solo song, a form which could afford to be more esoteric since it was the province of the solo singer-cum-instrumentalist, in general a more highly skilled and sophisticated performer than the homely amateur who rejoiced in the madrigals of Morley or of Weelkes' first two volumes. But even in this field it must be noted that the most extreme compositions of the greatest of the lutenist song-writers, John Dowland, were reserved for his last book issued in 1612.

Whatever the causes (and these will be considered more fully later on), the fact is that after four years of most vigorous activity, Weelkes' madrigal output ceased abruptly. Works like the madrigal pairs, *O care | Hence, care* or *Thule | The Andalusian merchant*, were, for all their originality and attainment, early works. It is only to be expected that some structural procedures in these and their companion madrigals would not yet have crystallized into the more evolved forms that might have resulted if Weelkes had continued to compose madrigals instead of turning his attention to the more traditionally-minded field of church music (though even here he was to prove much more advanced in his structural practices than any of his major English contemporaries).

This raises a particular problem in the study of his development. When a trend that has been growing in a composer's work reaches its fulfilment in compositions written much later in his creative lifetime, it is easy to point wisely to the embryonic manifestations of that trend, and to demonstrate that these were very real and valid. But when fulfilment has not been reached, it is much more difficult to assess the importance of these imperfectly formed phenomena. Was the trend a major feature of his style, or an incidental (or even accidental) trait? The problem is greatly exacerbated in Weelkes' case because he was a composer working within a period of radical musical change, when empiricism was widespread, and when experiments which were to evolve into fully formed musical phenomena existed side by side with others which proved abortive, or which could have only a limited importance. For instance, the embryonic ritornello procedures in certain of Weelkes' madrigals can be seen to reach a far more advanced stage in the inter-chorus relationships of certain of his verse anthems; on the other hand, his device of recomposition was essentially a technique for a polyphonic context, and could therefore only evolve to a limited extent, since the life of polyphony was nearly ended (in any case, it was a far less satisfactory device than other more literal forms of repetition).

These factors must be borne in mind if some of the observations in the following chapters are to be seen in perspective. The surest guide to the significance of these new probes is the consistency and breadth with which Weelkes applied them. This requires close scrutiny of all his works, and the following chapters will not only comment critically and analytically upon Weelkes' individual compositions, but also attempt to establish the common characteristics which link them together as the work of the same composer. Later we shall have to stand back from these pieces to restore some sense of perspective. But even if certain of Weelkes' searches did only remain probes, and if their significance is not proved by fulfilment, it is still reasonable to expect signs of a searching and experimental attitude in the work of a composer as imaginative and restless as Weelkes.

III. THE MADRIGALS OF 1597

1597 was rich in English music publications. In the preceding year the music printing monopoly, granted in 1575 to Tallis and Byrd, had expired, and though Morley made a fierce bid for the licence, it was not until 1598 that he secured it. Weelkes' *Madrigals to 3, 4, 5 and 6 voices* was one of the splendid crop of volumes to appear in the intervening year while the monopoly was vacant. The twenty-four compositions in the volume (six for each of the vocal forces specified) are unequal in quality; they were, as Weelkes pleaded in his preface, 'the first fruits of my barren ground, unripe in regard of time, unsavoury in respect of others'. Sometimes they offer passages worthy of his most mature compositions, at other times they betray all too clearly the imperfect condition of his technique. They show him leaning upon the example of other composers, experimenting, discovering, restless to strike out on his own but often scoring only a partial success, yet evolving and refining stage by stage his own personal musical manners and techniques. His wakeful imagination enlivens these works, but at times threatens to flaw the musical unity of the complete work through the very strength of its response at individual moments. To balance this there is Weelkes' concern with techniques for knitting a work more closely through purely musical means.

This concern emerges in the symmetrical planning of the first madrigal in the volume, *Sit down and sing*.[1] An introductory section, already proffered as evidence of the architectural proclivities in Weelkes' musical personality (see Example 4), passes into a 'mirror' structure centring upon a triple-time section (Example 6). The dissonant cadential formation in Example 6a, in which the sharpened leading note follows hard upon the flattened form, echoes a practice common in earlier sixteenth century English music and freely employed by Weelkes in his church music, although castigated by Morley in his *A Plain and easy introduction to practical music* (1597).

The triple-time sections interjected into a number of these madrigals often play an important part in the structural scheme. It was customary at this time to associate dancing or merriment with triple time,[2] and Weelkes' application of it here could have been instigated by the text.

---

[1] Surely it is not an accident that this summons to musical activity should be complemented in the very last line of the final madrigal of the volume: 'I need not sing another song'?

[2] A thorough, though very dry analysis of Weelkes' madrigalian symbolism is made in D. Morse, *Word-painting and symbolism in the secular choral works of Thomas Weelkes* [unpublished Ph.D. dissertation].

Elsewhere, however, he ignores many instances where the text might have been expected to provoke triple time, and on other occasions uses this device in seemingly inappropriate contexts. In fact, the function of these triple-time passages is often not descriptive but structural; they act either as central episodes contrasting with flanking duple-time sections (thus producing rhythmically a ternary effect), or else as structural landmarks (as in the next three madrigals). Hence Weelkes uses them

Ex. 6

primarily in the most extended and most contrapuntal works whose evenness of expression and whose length make clear structural pointers the more desirable. Triple-time passages occur in five of the three-voice madrigals, but in only two of the four-voice works, which are generally shorter. The works for five and six voices in this volume employ or grow from the balanced periodic structure of the canzonet, and are on average even briefer. These never employ triple-time passages.

The links between the next three madrigals, *My flocks feed not, In black mourn I* and *Clear wells spring not* (Nos. 2–4), are quite positive. Each madrigal repeats the music of lines one to four for lines five to eight, each uses triple time at the head of the central portion of the stanza, and each includes a passage of a more affective character in its central area, and one of greater pictorialism towards its end. There is an affinity between the openings of the first and third of these works, while in the second and third of them a marked use is made of the accidentals D sharp, G sharp and B flat as the music enters the final section of the stanza.[1] By allotting a

[1] This list of relationships is by no means exhaustive, since clear echoes of one madrigal are sometimes to be heard in another of this triptych. Compare, for instance, the setting of

different line of text to each of the three voices at the beginning of each madrigal, Weelkes simultaneously despatches three lines—a salutary reminder that the Elizabethan approach to setting words was not always as meticulous as is popularly supposed. It is sometimes all too clear that Weelkes made the words fit the music.

Weelkes' touch becomes surer as he progresses through this triptych. In the centre of *My flocks feed not* his contrapuntal instincts become increasingly assertive, culminating in a passage of true linear independence such as Morley never put into a madrigal (Example 7). Indeed, for a while

Ex. 7

it looks as though Weelkes may fall into the sort of trap which had ensnared Byrd in the three-voice secular works of his *Songs of sundry natures* (1589). The characterisation is more precise in *In black mourn I*, which offers the first example of Weelkes' use of chromaticism—a sudden twisting of the tail of a G major phrase onto a B major chord at the suggestion of the word 'afraid' (Example 8). As it stands, it sounds contrived, for Weelkes overemphasises the incident. It appears less eccentric when heard

'My curtall dog, that wont to have played, plays not at all' in *In black mourn I* with that of 'Poor Corydon must live alone; other help for him there's none' in *Clear wells spring not*; or the momentary anticipation of the opening of this latter madrigal at the end of *My flocks feed not* (EMS9, p. 12, bars 4–5).

in relation to the subsequent direction taken by the music; the fault lies not so much in the idea as in its inflation.

Ex. 8

[but seems afraid.]   [My sighs so deep]

Weelkes' imagination seems freer still in *Clear wells spring not*. The attraction which the *alla breve* manner had for him is more apparent, even though the opening paragraph shows that he had not yet learned how to maintain an organic musical life beyond the initial imitative entries. The paucity of thematic interest is somewhat balanced by the neat chromatic slide onto an E major chord which deflects the music towards the supertonic for a couple of bars. The *alla breve* setting of 'to us is fled' is better, since the sequential use of a three-note descending figure gives the passage some melodic substance. By now Weelkes' imagination is on the move, and the rest of the madrigal is mostly first-rate. 'All our loves are lost, for love is dead' is affectingly treated, and the protracted B major-E major progression of 'Farewell, sweet lass' is the more striking for following so closely upon G minor. Poor Corydon's loneliness, conveyed by the conventional device of contrasting one voice with the full vocal forces, is nevertheless touchingly realised. Altogether this is the best madrigal so far in the volume.

The musical integration of *A country pair* (No. 5) is as positive as it is unselfconscious, for not only is the setting of the third line of the lyric a variation of the first (Example 9*b* and *d*), but the two melodic points used successively for the final section are derived from the double counterpoint of the opening (Example 9*a* and *c*). In character this is a rustic piece in the line of Morley's madrigal pictures, *Arise, get up, my dear* and *Ho! Who comes here?*,[1] and presents a hearty front. The middle of the work sags somewhat when Weelkes follows the text's precept to 'take time' by moving into minims and semibreves, but the request 'kiss me, Kate' restores the interest all round.

The last of these three-voice madrigals, *Cease sorrows now* (No. 6), is the best known, and employs a deeply pathetic expression unprecedented in English music. The progressive expansion and the increasing assertive-

[1] *Canzonets to three voices* (1593) and *Madrigals to four voices* (1594) respectively.

Ex. 9

ness of the musical phrase to 'lo, care hath now consumed my carcase quite' shows a typically Weelksian growth, although the frequency of the cadences and their tonal uniformity constricts progress. Chromaticism such as Weelkes uses towards the end of this madrigal is usually cited as a progressive tendency. Expressively it is advanced, but technically such chromaticism is more frequently associated with dying modality than rising tonality. This is certainly the case here, for *Cease sorrows now* is

Ex. 10

thoroughly modal, offering only one mild suggestion of a change of tonal centre.

The opening bars are dimly reflected in the entry to the central area (Example 10)—a further symptom of Weelkes' habit of haunting a new inspiration with something already passed. The over-faithful reflection of textual details deprives the central area ('no hope is left . . . doth cut off pleasure quite') of breadth, but the last section recovers. The famous chromatic passage is nicely placed, especially in the way it follows the dying and inconclusive cadence of the preceding section (see Example 5*b*). Italian composers may have become sated with chromaticism, but this did not mean that an English composer to whom it was fresh could not find stimulus in it.[1] The *coup de grâce*, the prolonged simultaneous false relation in the final phrase (Example 12), sets a seal upon the profoundly pathetic expression of this remarkable work.

Ex. 12

[my faint farewell]

No doubt it was because he still lacked skill in handling the more complex vocal textures that Weelkes chose to place his most elaborate texts in these three-voice settings; excluding any conventional repetitions,

[1] Recognition of the patent Italianism of this madrigal is tempered by observing the resemblance of a passage in it to the opening of a pre-1570, and very English, viol-accompanied song, *Pandolpho*, by Robert Parsons (Example 11). This provides another small

Ex. 11

a PARSONS: Pandolpho *[transposed]*

Pour down, pour down,

b WEELKES: Cease sorrows now

[Yet whilst I hear the knolling of the bell]

suggestion of Weelkes' inbred association with the indigenous English tradition, as well as emphasising the change which had been wrought to that tradition by the Italian madrigal.

they are on average twice as long as the later ones for five voices. In all but one of these latter works Weelkes employed the simplest type of canzonet structure. The musical manner of canzonets is light: certainly Morley sounded rather contemptuous when he defined them as 'little short songs (wherein little art can be showed, being made in strains, the beginning of which is some point lightly touched and every strain repeated except the middle) which is, in composition of the music, a counterfeit of the madrigal'.[1] Put schematically, its form is AABCC, but in practice it was not uncommon for the middle 'strain' to be omitted altogether, so that it became a binary movement. The shadow of canzonet structure has already appeared in the three-voice *A country pair* (No. 5), but the four-voice works move much closer to the form; the approach is seen in the more frequent observance of sectional repetitions, the greater brevity of these pieces, and the more consistently light character of the music.

The first two of the four-voice works, *Now every tree renews* (No. 7), and *Young Cupid hath proclaimed* (No. 8) seem to have grown from the same stock. The stylistic division in the opening of the first of these, already noted in the preceding chapter (see Example 3), confirms that Weelkes had no intention of capitulating completely to Morleyism. A considerable thematic concentration is achieved by using in the final section a melodic point very like that which is worked at the beginning of the madrigal. In the thematic material of *Young Cupid hath proclaimed* an evolutionary process seems to be at work (Example 13).

If the musical imagination has been restrained in these first two four-voice madrigals, it reappears more fully in the third, *Ay me, my wonted joys forsake me* (No. 9).[2] *A note nere* passages, founded primarily upon dominant-tonic progressions and using dissonance sparingly, are sharply contrasted with affective *alla breve* sections employing much suspended dissonance, a wider range of chords, and melodic movement by step. It was an original and felicitous idea to repeat the *alla breve* music already used for the second and fourth lines as the dressing for the final line. Weelkes' attitude to dissonance is quite emancipated in this *alla breve* section (Example 14); particularly notable are the unprepared dissonance which becomes a suspension at*[3] (written under a growing awareness of the dominant seventh as an autonomous chord) and the tense chord

---

[1] Morley, *A Plain and easy introduction to practical music*, edited by R. A. Harman, p. 295.

[2] Yet the tangible debt to Morley is as great in this madrigal as in any: see Morley's *Why sit I here complaining* (Example 1 above), and also his settings of 'O strange tormenting' and 'And you that do disdain me' in *Lady, why grieve you still me?*; both works are from his *Madrigals to four voices* (1594).

[3] This type of dissonance is to be found in earlier English music, notably in the work of Tallis.

Ex. 13

progression starting at ★. This madrigal concludes 'on the dominant' as was Weelkes' usual practice in the first madrigal of a pair, but this is one of the only two instances in his work of a single madrigal finishing out of key.[1] Is the inconclusiveness intended to express a collapse ('and yet I die'), or 'misery' without end?

Ex. 14

[deep despair doth overtake me]

Three virgin nymphs (No. 10) deploys its upper three voices (all equal range sopranos) as the three ladies of the lyric, while the bass assumes the role of 'rude Sylvanus'. The robustness and scale of Weelkes' treatment of the line 'till rude Sylvanus chanced to meet them' are greater than Morley would have accorded it, nor can Morley anywhere match the rhythmic virility of Sylvanus' attempted assault on the nymphs. This

[1] The other is *O Jonathan*, one of Weelkes' two 'sacred' madrigals, which also seems to finish on the dominant.

piece is really a canzonet, but Weelkes' handling of the first section is noteworthy, for the repetition of the opening four bars is both expanded and ornamented (Example 15), the initial two-bar C major chord being inflected by the $\frac{F}{D}$ minor third on the strong crotchet pulses, and the final bars augmenting the earlier cadence.

Ex. 15

[summary] '[Three virgin nymphs were walking all alone]

Our country swains (No. 11) is a rustic picture which again recalls Morley, though the extra virility marks it down as Weelkes' work, as does the placing of a triple-time section in the middle of the piece, and the change to an *alla breve* manner at the end. A distant recomposition of the

Ex. 16

a

[morris dance they woo and win their brides]

[I die in grief and live in fear]

b [note values halved]

second half of the first section is used to form the conclusion of the work (Example 16). In Example 16*b* the earlier passage is both stretched and compressed, and has in any case been converted into an *alla breve* section (in order to prevent it from becoming disproportionately long, Weelkes excises three and a half bars from the original). The similarities are not close enough for the second to be considered a straightforward variation of the first, but there seems little doubt that Example 16*b* was composed in the mental presence of 16*a*.

The last of these four-voice madrigals, *Lo, country sports* (No. 12), introduces the first real example in Weelkes' work of a device which he was to use in a variety of ways, and which was to constitute one of his most individual practices. Basically it involves the invention of melodic material which permits close exact imitation at the unison, and which may be deployed repetitively throughout the whole texture so that there is little or no need of other material. The result is a kind of ostinato. It was not a new technique in itself, and may have been suggested to Weelkes by incidents in madrigals of Luca Marenzio printed in *Musica Transalpina* (1588), or in compositions by Morley.[1] But where Marenzio and Morley only hinted at ostinato devices, Weelkes elaborated them into major effects. The technique, as used in *Lo, country sports*, involves two 'associated subjects' producing the effect of 'pseudo-antiphony'.[2] Two examples of it from this madrigal should make the process clearer (Example 17). In each a two-bar pair of associated subjects is used, with the canonic

Ex. 17

a

[pipe on, for we will have the prize]

b

[with merry, merry pipes we bring]

---

[1] Notably such an incident as occurs in both *Why sit I here complaining?* ('with sobs and groanings') and *Lady, why grieve you still me?* ('O no, you love me') from Morley's 1594 volume. Incidentally, both these madrigals were particularly fruitful sources for Weelkes.

[2] The term 'associated subjects' is used rather than 'double subjects', since in these instances there is none of that character contrast which is usual between the two parts of a true double subject. 'Pseudo-antiphony' seems a fair description of the product of this technique, since its effect resembles the statement and repetition common in antiphonal writing, but is produced by the same voices with the musical parts redistributed; there is therefore no possibility of a spatial separation of the musical forces which perform the statement and answer(s).

parts following one bar later. There is no technical reason why the interlocking repetitions should not be carried on indefinitely, producing the
reiteration of a very brief, melodic-harmonic cell.

Pseudo-antiphony is effective when used sparingly, but in *Lo, country
sports* Weelkes applies it very extensively. At the same time his individual
applications are tentative; the possibilities of some of the associated subjects are unfulfilled, and after one canonic entry Weelkes proceeds immediately to new material. Nor, when faced with the extra technical
demands of the device, does he always seem to have his material under
control. The work has some rough moments, and there is even a blatant
pair of consecutive fifths between bars six and seven. But the widespread
use of this device creates a notable consistency of manner which is reinforced by the numerous thematic kinships between different sections.

It is vital not to lose a sense of proportion in evaluating the relationships
within or between these twelve madrigals. Thematic material used in one
may turn up in another, and it is sometimes even possible to find a few
bars in one work similar to a passage in another quite unconnected madrigal. Examples have been cited from Weelkes' work which might be related
to passages in compositions of Morley, Byrd and even Parsons. In
Weelkes' own madrigals, ideas which have shaped one work spill over
into another. This is not surprising for, with the one exception of Morley,
Weelkes' rate of production was the highest of all the English madrigalists.
However, what is striking about the internal musical relationships within
single madrigals is not the force with which they are presented, but the
persistence with which they appear, and the variety of ways in which they
are established.

These three- and four-voice works contain much to admire and enjoy.
They restored something of the former vigour of polyphony, and moved
away from the temptation to refined triviality which lurked in Morley's
manner. But the Italian madrigal had not brought into England merely a
remodelled technique, associated with a new approach to verbal declamation; it had also changed the quality of the sound. 'Effective' is a word
which constantly springs to mind in talking of madrigal style, for the
clarification of the polyphonic texture, and the deliberate attractiveness
of the declamation were designed to give the music a new appeal. Associated with these was a movement of the sound medium into a higher,
brighter register. Symptoms of the change are the use of divided sopranos
in works for five or more voices, and the use of two sopranos and an alto
for three-voice works, rather than the soprano, alto and tenor disposition
favoured by Byrd in his *Songs of sundry natures* (1589). The last four of
the madrigals that have just been discussed have an uncommonly high
tessitura.

Nor was the search just for brilliance of sound. The greater awareness of the appeal of certain sound qualities, and of the expressive power of harmony and texture in themselves, encouraged a more intensive exploration of colour, contrast and sonority for themselves alone. No English composer of the time understood these possibilities better than Weelkes, and we may see him revelling in these effects in some of his grandest madrigals and anthems. Nevertheless, he still sought out these delights as far as possible through contrapuntal means, even though the technique might have to be radically modified to achieve them. The evolution of these new technical resources is to be traced pre-eminently in the six-voice madrigals of this volume, although signs of them appear earlier in the book.

Yet the five- and six-voice works did not serve merely as exercises for expanding Weelkes' vocabulary and the scope of his musical language. There were more basic things to be accomplished, for he had still to learn to handle the more complex syntax of these larger textures grammatically and stylishly. Some of these compositions are all too clearly student exercises, unworthy of publication for their own merits, but affording interesting evidence of his growth as a composer. A survey of these twelve works suggests that they were printed closely, perhaps even exactly, in chronological order, for there is a progressive improvement observable in them when they are taken in turn.

Weelkes chose to make his first attempts at handling these more challenging forces through the most undemanding of forms, the simple canzonet. In this he was wise, to judge from the trouble they caused him. The first of these five-voice works, *Your beauty it allureth* (No. 13), is as dispiriting a piece as he ever wrote, starting unremarkably, and creaking into its second half with a weak set of entries and bungling continuations. This would be a strong candidate as the worst passage in all Weelkes' surviving music. In a forlorn attempt to save the work, he changes to an *alla breve* manner for the close, but the passage is thematically amorphous and technically feeble. All too clearly the bass and upper two voices were composed first, the former functioning mostly as a pedal, and the latter descending stepwise. The upper pair of voices contrive a good many dissonant moments between themselves and in collision with the bass, but these incidents are tame musical opportunism. The remaining two voices complete the texture, or merely fill in.

There is no point in dilating further upon such mediocrity, and the canzonets immediately following may be passed over quickly. *If thy deceitful looks* (No. 14) opens with a square set of entries upon a conventional melodic point, moves stiffly to the expected cadence, and forthwith suffers repetition. The remainder is equally dull. The next two canzonets have more interest because they set English texts which Weelkes was to use again in their (presumably) original Italian versions in his last madrigal volume, the *Ayres . . . for three voices,* issued in 1608. *Those sweet delightful lilies* (No. 15) employs much the same basic material as *I bei ligustri e rose* for all except its central section, but the Italian version has greater breadth, despite being written for only three voices. This is especially conspicuous in the final *alla breve* section which is broader, tidier, more precise in outline, and more calculated in dissonance. *Lady, your spotless feature* (No. 16) uses the same thematic material for its first half as its Italian counterpart, *Donna, il vostro bel viso.* Neither of the imitative sections which make up the English version is particularly noteworthy, but each produces a less meagre impression than any passage in the preceding five-voice works. These signs of a more expansive life in Weelkes' counterpoint are encouraging; he is chafing under the restrictions of the small-scale canzonet. The improvement is maintained in *Make haste, ye lovers* (No. 17), where a greater skill is apparent in the manipulation of the voices in the opening paragraph, not so much during the imitative entries themselves as in their continuations. Weelkes is also learning to handle his transitions better, for the two sections of the second half are neatly welded together.

The eruption from the confines of the simple canzonet occurs in the last of the five-voice works, *What haste, fair lady* (No. 18). After a fairly orthodox initial paragraph, duly repeated, the second half of the work turns into an extended unrepeated section, carefully planned both in the varied vocal groupings of its first part, and in the ordering of the twenty-two imitative entries which make up its second.

Schematically these groupings and entries appear thus:

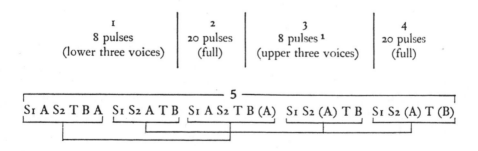

1	2	3	4
8 pulses	20 pulses	8 pulses [1]	20 pulses
(lower three voices)	(full)	(upper three voices)	(full)

5

S_1 A S_2 T B A S_1 S_2 A T B S_1 A S_2 T B (A) S_1 S_2 (A) T B S_1 S_2 (A) T (B)

[1] The first two of these pulses are musically inactive; nevertheless, the scheme is exactly symmetrical. The bracketed entries in the sequence of voice entries in the fifth section do not occur because the alto settles onto a sustained A which it maintains for the final nine bars. The final bass entry is forestalled by the concluding cadence.

Within the scheme Weelkes manoeuvres freely, and although the music of this section does not have the clarity and distinctiveness of outline which are features of his work at its best, there is control behind the expansion. With the larger scale there re-appears some evidence of a significant thematic unity between different sections.

Pseudo-antiphony returns in the first of the six-voice works, *Retire, my thoughts* (No. 19). Its use here is still free; in any case, the associated subjects are twelve crotchets long and, with entries every four crotchets, it proves impossible to use the upper subject for the third entry (Example 18). Weelkes scatters this material among the upper five voices, saturating

Ex. 18

[Retire, my thoughts, into your rest again]

the texture with it. To prolong its life while avoiding monotony, he moves onto another pitch level at bar seven, and dilutes his material with a freer contrapuntal manner. Compared with the first section of the preceding work, from which it seems to have borrowed some material, these first eleven bars are altogether tighter. The final imitative paragraph of the work balances the textural solidity of the opening, and gives the impression of having been heard as a sonorous block of sound rather than as a contrapuntal network. The deliberate, clear harmonic progress and the widely spaced texture (rarely spanning less than two octaves) achieve the maximum possible sonority. The method is still ostensibly contrapuntal, but the entries of the melodic point decorate rather than create the texture; hence the modifications to the point and the more arbitrary way in which it is used are less damaging to the musical character. This emerges clearly from a comparison with the final paragraph of the preceding work, which had employed the same melodic point as a generating force in which the implications of each entry had determined the next stage in the musical progress.

This move away from the purely contrapuntal to a more sonorous, cohesive texture is seen more clearly in *Say, dear, when will your frowning* (No. 20). The opening is admirably clean, the thematic concentration is

sustained, and the contrasting *alla breve* section (which borrows its opening bars from the *alla breve* incident in *Ay me, my wonted joys forsake me*
(No. 9))[1] is nicely fashioned and proportioned. The opening to the second
half is excellent—a completely committed application of pseudo-antiphony,
using two-bar associated subjects (Example 19a). Weelkes moves easily
to new pitch levels in applying this device, and soon substitutes a fresh
upper subject (Example 19b); thus concentration is not accompanied by
stagnation. Unfortunately, however, only four voices are required for

Ex. 19

this pseudo-antiphony, and the remaining two voices can only fill in—
which they do very obviously. The concluding *alla breve* passage is brief,
and contains some arresting harmonic moments. It is notable that in his
multi-voice *alla breve* passages Weelkes relies for his dissonance as much,
if not more, upon minim passing notes as upon suspensions. Morley, on
the other hand, had favoured suspensions, although he did not neglect
passing dissonance. While the effect of the suspension is exquisitely
excruciating, that of passing dissonance is more massive, and an excellent
aid to textural sonority, as this *alla breve* conclusion demonstrates. Despite
the redundancy of some voice parts in the pseudo-antiphony, and the
textural density of the second half, this is the best work so far in the
second half of the volume, and the first worthy example of Weelkes'
'massive' manner.

Those spots upon my lady's face (No. 21) is on a less ambitious scale
than the preceding two. More rests are introduced into the final *alla breve*
section than had appeared before in the course of similar passages; while

[1] Weelkes seems to have especially liked this opening. He reworks it in *What have the
gods?* (*Madrigals of 6 parts* (1600)), bars 10–12.

exploring the powers of sonority, Weelkes is also perceiving the virtues of clarity.

If beauty be a treasure (No. 22) is as thoroughly integrated a work as any in the volume. *A note nere* passages flank an *alla breve* centre, and there are clear rhythmic, thematic and textural affinities between the final repeated passage and the treatment of 'Sweetheart, enjoy your pleasure' in the work's first section. So, too, the opening section and the central *alla breve* passage are related through the virtual identity of a major portion of the uppermost voice part of each (Example 20). For each of the four

Ex. 20

lines treated in these two sections Weelkes uses a different manner, each merging smoothly into the following one, thus:

Line 1	Line 2	Line 3	Line 4
homophonic *a note nere*	homophonic into polyphonic *a note nere*	*a note nere* rhythmic pulse, but steadier lines and *alla breve* harmonic rhythm	*alla breve* manner, but with consistent sprinkling of *note neri*

The segregation of *a note nere* and *alla breve* manners in the three- and four-voice works has now become less clear, and the increasing engagement between the two styles has resulted in all sorts of subtle gradations, greatly increasing the precision of Weelkes' expressive vocabulary, and making possible the smoothly wrought transformation of manner effected in this work. The clumsy apprentice of *Your beauty it allureth* (No. 13) has become the accomplished master. But not quite; the extraordinary maladroit moment in the *quintus* shows that all is not yet under control (Example 21).

My tears do not avail me (No. 23) contains hints of two of Weelkes' madrigals of 1600, for the opening closely resembles the first three bars of *Hence care, thou art too cruel*,[1] and the concluding melodic point is similar to that used at the end of *Like two proud armies*,[2] although its use

[1] *Madrigals of 5 and 6 parts* (1600). [2] *Madrigals of 6 parts* (1600).

Ex. 21

here is tentative compared to its masterly application in the later work. Premonitions of the final fa-la of *O care, thou wilt despatch me*[1] occur in the first part of the concluding section of *My Phyllis bids me pack away* (No. 24). Weelkes' control of the broad contrapuntal paragraph is revealed in the thematic concentration of this passage, its easy admission to the texture of all note values from semibreve to quaver, the purposeful, firm shape of the lines, even when not actually engaged in imitation, and the sure sense of direction which nevertheless avoids a trite harmonic progress. The prolonged delay of the initial entry of the two lower voices anticipates a practice not uncommon in the madrigals of 1600. As used here it enables Weelkes to achieve a striking increase of power when they finally join in, and in the meantime to restrict himself to the four voices which are all that are required for the pseudo-antiphony near the beginning. The internal thematic relationships are simple and clear (Example 22). In scale and accomplishment this is quite a splendid piece; it is no great step from here to the madrigals of 1600.

Ex. 22

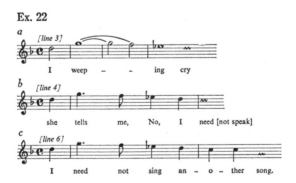

This study has already referred several times to Weelkes' ear for textural effects. However, in these works such effects do not always serve simply an expressive purpose. In the five-voice works no problem of structural coherence had arisen as long as Weelkes restricted himself to the simple periodic structure of the canzonet. As soon as he moved out of the form,

[1] *Madrigals of 5 and 6 parts* (1600).

however, the conscious shaping of the structure becomes clearer, and this has been achieved in these works as much through relationships of texture as of material. A balanced plan with clear divisions into types of texture is clearly perceptible in these larger works. There are, for instance, the precise proportions of *What haste, fair lady* (No. 18):

1	2	3
polyphony for five voices (61 pulses) *repeated*	strictly proportioned antiphony (see p. 73)	polyphony for five voices (68 pulses)

—or of *Say, dear, when will your frowning* (No. 20):

1	2	3
(a) *a note nere* polyphony (37 pulses) (b) *alla breve* polyphony (47 pulses)	pseudo-antiphony (42 pulses)	(a) *a note nere* polyphony (40 pulses) (b) *alla breve* polyphony (39 pulses)

Not all are as balanced as this, but all are clear.

These five- and six-voice works are a remarkable record of progress. They reveal a rapidly growing command of the more complex vocal textures, and a notable expansion of Weelkes' compositional techniques. The compounding of a new madrigalian polyphony 'by Byrd out of Morley' has been achieved, and more plastic gradations of this manner have evolved from the interaction of *a note nere* and *alla breve* styles. The *alla breve* sections have become more shapely, the thematic material more focussed, and the massive power of these sections has been enhanced by the liberal use of passing dissonances, often multiple, on the weaker minim pulses. The evolution of pseudo-antiphony has added a new and valuable item to Weelkes' expressive equipment, and his vocabulary has been expanded by the exploitation of sonorous texture, which may also, however, be used as a means of articulating structure. The whole volume impresses less by its absolute musical achievement (though there are some first-rate pieces in it) than by the signs it contains of a wide-ranging, restless musical talent, flexing itself to command elaborate structures, and to strike out into new expressive adventures.

IV. THE BALLETS AND MADRIGALS OF 1598

The canzonet had done Weelkes good service, but it could not detain him long. Being no more than a mould for pleasant and facile music, it neither challenged him nor offered him ready opportunities for original, imaginative adventures. He had quickly expanded into more ambitious and characteristic works, still well controlled, but tending towards a more massive musical manner. It was natural enough for the young composer to turn now to the ballet, the other closed madrigalian form which Morley had established in England. Again the structure was clear and simple, but the musical character was quite different, and much more congenial to a composer of Weelkes' temperament. It had epigrammatic compartments, immense rhythmic vitality, and natural contrast between verse sections and fa-las. It offered scope for his musical imagination, yet the small scale of the composition did not impose extended demands upon his technique. Although there are signs of an expansive tendency in some of the ballets, it is nothing like the consistent or drastic trend it had been in the canzonets. Weelkes had no need to expand; indeed, the shorter ballets are generally the more successful.

There was also the inducement of the excellent models proffered by Morley's *The First book of ballets* which had appeared three years earlier. The form had been established in Italy by Gian Giacomo Gastoldi's *Balletti* (1591), and Morley had taken not only the scheme, but had even modelled a number of his own works upon the lyrics and music of specific compositions by Gastoldi. In doing this he had transformed these simple ballets into the brilliant and witty form that attracted Weelkes. Weelkes knew Morley's madrigalian compositions thoroughly, and in his ballets there are passages clearly founded upon actual incidents in Morley's works. Indeed, it looks as though Weelkes started his own volume with the intention of parallelling Morley's scheme, but as the volume proceeds, the tidy sequence of Morley's book is abandoned. Morley had segregated the six madrigals of his publication from the fifteen ballets, and had then grouped each of the categories tidily according first to key signature, then to mode. Weelkes' volume gives far less impression of orderliness; the madrigals are scattered among the ballets, and there is less regularity of modal grouping. This may imply some chronological significance in their printed order, a hypothesis which gains some support from the echoes which certain works contain of some other composition printed close by in the volume.

Fundamentally the ballet is a lively, dance-like composition in binary form, each half ending with a refrain to the syllables 'fa-la' (or some other meaningless sounds), and each half being repeated. Usually a ballet had two verses, and since the same music had to serve two sets of words, word painting or highly characterised expression had normally to be restrained or avoided.[1] The absence of meaning or any predetermined verbal stress in the fa-la sections left the composer completely free to devise his own musical dressing for them, and these sections show a notable variety. Three basic types of fa-la may be distinguished. First, there is the very simple type—perhaps some four bars of conclusion balancing the preceding verse, or simply rounding off a section in a manner more homophonic than polyphonic. Secondly, there is the freely contrapuntal type in which there is little thematic focus, although there may be a certain limited amount of decorative exchange of material between the voice parts. Morley and Weelkes employed both these types, but it was the third, the imitative fa-la, that occupied them most, and which shows the most revealing divergencies between their respective practices. Weelkes tended to work his imitation more intensively than Morley, and he made less use than Morley of two points (either simultaneously or successively) within a single fa-la. Filling-in by the alto and tenor voices is often patent in the ballets of both composers, especially during homophonic passages, and implies some definite polarity between the upper two voices and the bass. This is more obvious in Weelkes' ballets, in which there is also more frequent and systematic movement in chained thirds between the two sopranos. The fuller or brighter texture produced by pairing imitative entries obviously had its own attractions for Weelkes; thus it may not have been merely an attempt to give an appearance of organic respectability to what is often an unshapely and even redundant tenor that led him to his practice of linking this part in parallel thirds or sixths with an imitative incident in another voice.

Weelkes' use of ostinato in these fa-las is particularly striking, the effect often being achieved by the repetition between a pair of voices of a short, two-bar fragment (Example 23). This device is closely allied to the pseudo-antiphony which had already appeared prominently in the madrigals of 1597. Finally, we may note that his fa-las make greater use of

[1] The fact that seven of Weelkes' ballets do not have a second verse does not necessarily mean that there was not one, or that it was incompatible with the music, for there are many instances in Weelkes' work to show that he was not particularly scrupulous in treating his text. The partbooks themselves suggest that the deficiency of a second verse in any of these seven ballets may have been simply a matter of insufficient space; the music of each of them fills the page (or even overflows it) in every partbook. Second verses are also omitted in any individual voice part of the other ballets if the printed notes have already claimed the whole page.

Ex. 23

sequential and repetitive devices. Morley's fa-las are lighter and more airy, more essentially wedded to the sound of the insubstantial syllables upon which they grew. Their charm and sheer facility is often irresistible, and in such passages as the final section of *Fire! Fire!*, profound admiration must surely be added to the listener's delight. Weelkes' touch was less delicate, and his brilliance more studied. The counterpoint of his fa-las is less fleet, their average length is greater, and they gain additional weight from their higher thematic concentration and more intensive use of sequence and repetition—features which are also signs of Weelkes' inclination to focus inward upon his material, an inclination which is consistent with the instinct towards thematic unity already noted in some of the madrigals of his earlier volume.

Weelkes' ballets, like Morley's, divide into two categories—the simple ballet and the canzonet-type ballet. The difference lies in the verse sections, those of the simple ballet being homophonic and dance-like, while those of the canzonet-type ballet employ the contrapuntal manner or the more supple homophony of the canzonet. The most rudimentary is *Welcome, sweet pleasure* (No. 15) which joins verse and refrain in a clearly balanced phrase structure. The other simple ballets are a good deal more elaborate than this. Of these, the first three in the volume make up a group with certain details common to two or all of them. A concrete debt to Morley is immediately uncovered when a fa-la from each is placed beneath their obvious prototype from Morley's ballet, *Dainty fine sweet nymph* (Example 24). *All at once well met, fair ladies* (No. 1) is a masterly example of the simple ballet, well proportioned, technically polished, with a lightly contrapuntal texture employed for the second line of text which shows Weelkes gravitating towards the more expansive canzonet-type ballet. A certain kinship of the prime thematic ingredients binds the work together unobtrusively. *To shorten winter's sadness* (No. 2) founds the opening of its second half upon the corresponding moment in Morley's *No, no, Nigella*, but the ostinato effect of the two sopranos in the first fa-la is thoroughly Weelksian. The two fa-las are related, especially through the constant use of the figure in Example 25. The third of the initial group, *Whilst*

Ex. 24

a MORLEY: Dainty fine sweet nymph (fa - la 1)

b WEELKES: All at once well met (fa - la 1)

c WEELKES: Whilst youthful sports (fa - la 1)

d WEELKES: To shorten winter's sadness (fa - la 2 *(opening)*)

youthful sports (No. 4), is technically clean, and perhaps most readily memorable for its very sprightly second fa-la.

There are two other simple ballets, *We shepherds sing* (No. 17) and *Now is my Cloris* (No. 22). The former is one of those patchwork compositions which, it seems, Weelkes was from time to time guilty of fabricating from existing material. The opening verse section recalls that of *To shorten winter's sadness*,[1] and the first fa-la is founded upon the corres-

[1] The setting of the second line of both these ballets is the same as that of Morley's ballet *Those dainty daffadillies*.

ponding passage of Morley's *My bonny lass she smileth*. Weelkes' version is less polished and more selfconsciously worked. The change which Morley makes from an *a note nere* to a broader *alla breve* style is rather what we would have expected of Weelkes, but Morley makes the change smoothly and without emphasis; the easy transition is the delight of the

Ex. 25

device. Weelkes would have used it for dramatic effect.[1] The second half begins with a triple-time derivative of the Morleyish second line; 'dance' and 'prance' were doubtless the cue for this rhythmic switch. The final fa-la must surely have been conceived for some other context, and is, in fact, like the organ openings of certain of Weelkes' verse anthems. In this context it sounds incongruous and prosaic, and seems to have no relevance at all to the preceding music.

The fa-las of *Now is my Cloris* are even busier than any so far encountered, though the technical accomplishment of the whole work is high. It is very well integrated, with one momentary but very audible similarity between the fa-las (Example 26). During the second of these, Weelkes

Ex. 26

introduces music which he also uses in his anthem *O mortal man*;[2] even more thought-provoking is the virtual identity of the openings of the second verse section and Morley's funeral anthem, *I am the resurrection and the life*. Weelkes was to use this phrase again to open *Te Deum* of his

---

[1] But this generalisation must be qualified; Morley makes a more abrupt transition to an *alla breve* manner in another ballet, *Thus saith my Galatea*. So, too, the change to triple time for the second fa-la of *My bonny lass she smileth* is something which would have been expected rather from Weelkes than Morley.

[2] See MB23, p. 61.

Short Service (No. 7). So much for any indestructible unity of words and music!

The remaining ballets are of the canzonet type, employing contrapuntal passages in their verse sections, and adopting a more variable, plastic rhythm during homophonic incidents. On average the verse sections are about twice as long as those of the simple ballets, although the fa-las tend, if anything, to be shorter than those of their simple counterparts. For all but one of his simple ballets just discussed, Weelkes chose lyrics with four-line stanzas of simple or regular metrical pattern. Three such poems are also treated in his canzonet-type ballets, but these usually employ more involved texts—lyrics with unconventional metrical schemes, six-line stanzas, or with four-line stanzas containing longer lines (nine or more syllables) which would suit less well the snappy phrases of the simple ballet style.

Two of the most striking canzonet-type ballets, *On the plains* (No. 5) and *Hark, all ye lovely saints above* (No. 8), have much of the simplicity and regularity of the simple ballet. Echoes of Morley may be detected in the first of these, but the whole work has a 'fantastic' flavour far removed from that composer's ingenuous sophistication. There is enchantment in the capricious rhythmic life, and fascination in the alternation between homophonic triple-time sections and duple-time counterpoint. *Hark, all ye lovely saints above* is perhaps even more individual.[1] The concluding fa-la adopts a lively manner, and uses modal characteristics strikingly. The expressive extremes of this second half make it as entrancing as it is brief.[2] This is altogether one of the most captivating of all Weelkes' works.

These last two pieces enjoy the best of both worlds, retaining a good deal of the terse, homophonic utterance of the simple ballet, while employing epigrammatic contrapuntal contrasts. This juxtaposition heightens their brilliance, yet they remain completely committed to the ballet concept. The only other canzonet-type ballet to keep something of the simple ballet's laconic expression is *Unto our flocks* (No. 23). The beginning of the first fa-la, used also in *Farewell, my joy* (No. 21), is clearly related to the ballet's opening bars, and the second fa-la abandons tripping Morleyish facility in favour of a less pat counterpoint, placing jabbing semiquaver pairs within an altogether more virile sound. This is a concise distinctive miniature with a fresh and varied rhythmic life.

Critical enthusiasm wanes in the face of most of the remaining eight

---

[1] The text of this ballet seems to be freely derived from *Ode 14* in Barnabe Barnes' *Parthenophil and Parthenophe* (1593), which also furnished the lyric of *On the plains* (see E. Arber (edr.), *An English garner*, vol. 5, p. 462).

[2] Five bars of the *alla breve* passage in this second half presage the four *alla breve* bars of *Lady, the birds right fairly* (*Madrigals of 5 and 6 parts* (1600)), where its use is more concise and taut.

canzonet-type ballets. Weelkes was not really to blame if his imagination took little fire from the plainer mixture of ballet and canzonet used in these works. The two forms, one witty and pithy, the other innocuous and amiable, were as incompatible as the madrigalian ideal and abstract polyphony. The canzonet tended to expand the ballet, quenching its pungency, emasculating its rhythmic vitality without compensating with extra breadth, and weakening or destroying the engagement between verse and fa-la refrain. In *Give me my heart* (No. 7) Weelkes tries to counter this last failing by employing for the second 'no-no' the same bass (but with changed rhythm) that had rounded off the preceding verse.[1] Nevertheless, it remains a pedestrian and technically raw piece—no better than the work from which it drew some ideas, Morley's *Singing alone* (also the first canzonet-type ballet of his volume).

Nor does *Say, dainty dames* (No. 9) arouse much more enthusiasm. It does its pictorial duty by 'run', 'valleys' and 'high hills', but balances off the ascending and descending scale passages too mechanically. The second half is better, shorter, and more Weelksian in its simple antiphonal effects and its sprightly ostinato in the bass (Example 27). This is a pleasant

Ex. 27

[fa - la]

enough composition, but it centres too firmly on G, and has little sense of progress. On the other hand, *In pride of May* (No. 11) is more characteristic and accomplished—and just because of this it emphasises the canzonet-ballet dilemma all the more. The saturated opening is easily recognisable as Weelkes' work, and a process of thematic evolution seems to be at work throughout the piece (Example 28). The second half threatens to be prosaic, but the lift onto a cadence on D is the more effective because so much of the preceding music has been firmly centred upon G. But as a ballet it is not really a success; the opening verse especially raises expectations of a more solid continuation than the first fa-la provides.

Sing, shepherds, after me (No. 14) seems to be another patchwork composition. The framework for the setting of the second line is extracted from Weelkes' own *Lo, country sports*;[2] Morley's *Besides a fountain*[3] may have suggested Weelkes' opening, and certainly provided four bars in

---

[1] The first part of this bass had already initiated the first 'no-no'.

[2] *Madrigals to 3, 4, 5 and 6 voices* (1597). This passage may also draw upon the first madrigal of this earlier volume (*Sit down and sing*).

[3] *Madrigals to four voices* (1594).

the second half.[1] However, the expansion of this quotation to become the second fa-la is typically Weelksian.[2] A tangible integration of verse and

Ex. 28

fa-la is also to be found in the second half of *I love, and have my love regarded* (No. 18), this time effected by the repetition of the broad harmonic progression which had concluded the former as the foundation for

Ex. 29

the fresh, quaver-animated music which enters with the latter (Example 29). This ballet has three verses in its first half, but the second half uses the same text on all three occasions, and is thus able to characterise freely

[1] Morley had also used this incident again in his own *Clorinda false* (1594).

[2] Weelkes' use of black notes for 'black are our looks' is evidently a piece of 'eye music'.

'laugh', 'weep', 'play' and 'sleep' with *a note nere* and *alla breve* alternations. The similar outlines of the *a note nere* sections further tightens the
structure (Example 30).

Ex. 30

[which makes me always laugh]

[and play with love]

Stylistically *Sing we at pleasure* (No. 12) steps aside from the main
trends in the volume. Really it is a work for two sopranos and bass; only
in passages where four voices are required for pseudo-antiphony does the
tenor really become organic, and the alto fills in throughout—towards
the end all too obviously. Nevertheless, this is a solidly attractive work,
expressively consistent, very English in flavour, and far more instrumental
than vocal in idiom. An ostinato effect emerges from the combined
soprano parts during the final fa-la (see Example 23). Verse and fa-la are
indivisible throughout, and there is a strong impression that the last
twenty bars are an expanded recomposition of the opening eight.

The canzonet-type ballet had lost the punch of the simple ballet; it
could only compensate for this by extra weight. The remaining two ballets
are on a decidedly more ambitious scale, and show Weelkes expanding
out of the restricted dimensions of the ballet as decisively as he had burst
out of the simple canzonet in his 1597 volume. Having (apparently) only
one verse each, both works are free to characterise textual details. *Lady,
your eye my love enforced* (No. 16) shows no evidence of thematic unity,
but knits the structure by a design common to both halves of the work:

First half			
a note nere section, founded first upon F, then upon C	*alla breve* section	related conclusion	D–C ostinato in soprano
Second half			
a note nere section, founded first upon F, then upon C	*alla breve* section		D–C ostinato emerges in bass

The ostinato this time is a true one, not a product of two voices. *Lady, your eye my love enforced* has a breadth and even massiveness absent from any of the ballets so far discussed. Admittedly the *alla breve* section of the second half[1] is unventilated and lacks the expressive precision of some similar passages in the madrigals of 1600; nevertheless, it is undeniably effective, and the chromatic change on 'cry' is striking.

Morley crops up again as a definite source in *Farewell, my joy* (No. 21). This time it is the second fa-la of *My lovely wanton jewel* upon which Weelkes founds his second fa-la, characteristically working the idea at greater length than Morley, and building a denser texture.[2] There are numerous thematic relationships within Weelkes' ballet, and it is especially notable how the melismatic writing at the beginning of the second verse section (the only writing of its kind to appear in the ballets) anticipates the sequential treatment which dominates the working-out of the concluding fa-la. Yet, despite its obvious ambitions, this ballet is something of a disappointment, for the clear treatment allotted to each line results in an excessively episodic impression, which is aggravated by the unusual division halfway through the first fa-la. It is not exactly a poor piece, but the intensity of Weelkes' imagination hardly seems commensurate with the scale of the composition.

Some of Weelkes' ballets are splendid and contain imaginative and captivating music, but it must be admitted that the composition of some of them was obviously 'not a little hastened', as Weelkes confessed in his preface. Indeed, it is not unlikely that the small scale of the ballet (and the ease with which such works could be turned out) may have been an additional reason why he turned to the form. The ballets have tended to overshadow the madrigals which are scattered among them—which is a pity, since the latter are far more consistent, both in craftsmanship and expression, and are of great interest because they stand between the enlarged canzonets of the 1597 volume and the madrigals of 1600.[3] In these madrigals of 1598 Weelkes had neither the obligations, restrictions—nor the aid—of the clear periodic structure of the canzonet or ballet: yet one of their most striking features is the clear and deliberate structural articulation, despite the less frequent employment of thematic relationships. The texts chosen are all brief (four or six lines only), and thus do not produce

[1] This passage is closely related to the first *alla breve* section of one of the madrigals in this volume, *Phyllis, go take thy pleasure* (No. 10).

[2] This second half offers the one instance in Weelkes' canzonet-type ballets of a clear break between verse and fa-la. This had occurred frequently in Morley's canzonet-type ballets, and had loosened even more the already slack structure.

[3] In addition to the madrigals, Weelkes added an extra piece at the end of the 1598 volume. *Cease now delight:* 'An elegy in remembrance of the Hon. the Lord Borough' is a *pièce d'occasion* for six voices. Consideration of it will be reserved until the next chapter.

the sprawling outlines of the first four madrigals of the 1597 volume. A clear overall shape is often established by the orderly balancing of sections, each clearly defined in manner, whether *alla breve* or *a note nere*, homophonic, polyphonic, or employing pseudo-antiphony. The sure handling of the pseudo-antiphony is notable, but it is in the fashioning of the contrapuntal paragraph that Weelkes' achievement is the most striking. Though the expression is completely madrigalian, the combination of breadth with linear autonomy brings some of the contrapuntal incidents as close as any passages in Weelkes' madrigals to the ideals of traditional polyphony. Weelkes' command of organic concentration within the broad contrapuntal paragraph seems all the more remarkable for following so closely upon the undigested contrapuntal style of the majority of the 1597 madrigals. The handling of the melodic lines is economical yet characterful, and the texture, though sometimes showing a typically Weelksian thickness, is never turgid or muddy.

The simple double subject which opens *Sweet love, I will no more abuse thee* (No. 3) is the first genuine one so far encountered in Weelkes' work. This is a poised composition, and if the sectional and cadential scheme is set down, the symmetry of the piece is exposed:

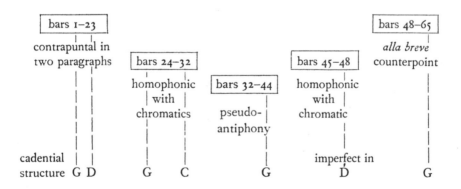

There are also identities of material between the corresponding sections. The chromatic relationship between the homophonic sections is easily perceived, but at first only contrapuntalism and the free employment of the accidental B flat may seem to relate the outermost sections. This is not the whole truth; it is as though the sound of a fragment of the opening section (Example 31*a*) had haunted the composition of the first bars of the conclusion (Example 31*b*). The central section of pseudo-antiphony contrives to employ purposefully all five voices. The conclusion is both delicately and penetratingly chromatic, though with one very revealing

Ex. 31 *[summaries]*

[Sweet love, I will no more abuse thee]

[what wanteth concord soon doth perish]

'fault' in the resolution of a suspension (Example 32). The explanation is obviously that the expected F sharp resolution occurs in the appropriate place in another voice, and Weelkes calculated that it would be *heard* as a normal resolution. There could be no stronger evidence that Weelkes heard some passages as a homogeneous texture, and not as purely linear writing.[1]

Ex. 32

[what wanteth concord soon doth perish]

Sweetheart, arise, why do you sleep? (No. 6) is composed upon material derived from the four main melodic points of Byrd's *Laudate pueri*[2] (Example 33). Compared to the characteristically dense sound of this work by Byrd from a quarter of a century earlier, Weelkes' texture seems finer; yet, when set beside an Italian madrigal like Marenzio's *Cantai gia* (*I sung sometime,* as it was translated for *Musica transalpina* (1588)), its

[1] Weelkes used this transferred resolution at the opening of Gloria in *Magnificat* of his First Service, and near the beginning of his setting of *The Cries of London* (see Example 70), though in both cases the resolution is made even bolder by being transposed an octave.

[2] *Cantiones sacrae* (1575).

Ex. 33

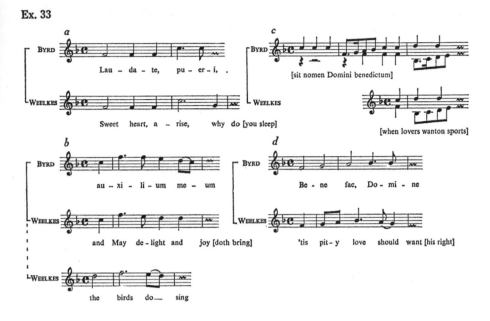

facture seems rather stiff, and the melodic lines less flexible and lyrical. This madrigal of Marenzio may have been in Weelkes' mind when he composed a section of this work (Example 34); yet there is a decidedly

Ex. 34

English flavour to *Sweetheart, arise, why do you sleep,* especially during its square and unsophisticated opening.

As a structural principle for *Phyllis, go take thy pleasure* (No. 10) a distinct musical section is allotted to each of the first four lines, the odd-numbered sections employing triple-time homophony and an *a note nere* manner, and ending on the dominant, while the even-numbered use duple-time polyphony and an *alla breve* manner, and close in the tonic. In the final couplet these expressive extremes are relaxed. There is an unusual dissonant moment in an intermediate cadence in the central *alla breve* section (Example 35); this is to recur in *What have the gods?*[1] *Phyllis, go take thy*

Ex. 35

[those wounds thy looks laid open]

pleasure is very characteristic of Weelkes, despite the echoes of Morley's *Fire! Fire!* (second fa-la) to be heard in the concluding section. Yet, oddly enough, this is the only madrigal in this volume not to employ pseudo-antiphony.

On the other hand, it is only the pseudo-antiphony in *Now is the bridals of fair Choralis* (No. 13) which immediately proposes Weelkes as its composer, although his authorship is quietly established in its free, accomplished counterpoint, especially well demonstrated in the extended setting of the final line. One incident is built upon a direct quotation from Morley's *Lady, why grieve you still me?*[2] (Example 36). As in the pre-

Ex. 36

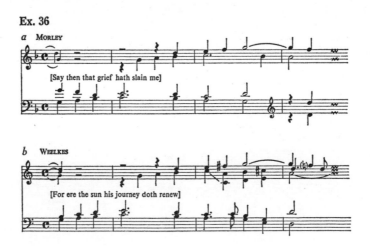

a MORLEY

[Say then that grief hath slain me]

b WEELKES

[For ere the sun his journey doth renew]

---

[1] *Madrigals of 6 parts* (1600).

[2] *Madrigals to four voices* (1594). Further suggestive comparisons may be made with this madrigal, starting from the *pointilliste* setting of 'Ah, break!' (that is, from just after the

ceding madrigal, the alternation of dominant and tonic cadences is clear. This is an attractive, bright piece, generally open in texture.

The last two madrigals, *Come clap your hands* and *Phyllis hath sworn* (Nos. 19 and 20), make up a pair. Much the same comments made upon the last work apply here—the light, Morleyish approach, the Weelksian pseudo-antiphony, and far greater contrapuntalism. In this pair thematic unity is also prominent; as Kerman has observed, Weelkes seems to have devised a kind of Leitmotif for the name 'Phyllis',[1] and this lady's textual ubiquity ensures a considerable thematic concentration, further increased by the clear relationships of the opening idea of *Come clap your hands* to the 'Phyllis' motif (Example 38). The unity of the two works is finally

Ex. 38

incident which had already provided Weelkes with the beginning of the *alla breve* passage in *Ay me, my wonted joys forsake me* (1597)). The incidents in Example 37*a* and *b*, which precede the parallels quoted in Example 36, may not be coincidental in their resemblances.

Ex. 37

Deliberate parody hardly seems likely; it is more probable that the earlier work was at the back of Weelkes' mind so that, during gestation, it conditioned the embryo of his own work.

[1] J. Kerman, *The Elizabethan madrigal*, p. 229.

sealed by their identical conclusions, for the last eighteen bars of both are the same, except for adjustment of the final cadence.

No doubt for most of the first enthusiasts who bought this set of part-books, it was the ballets which proved the main attraction; yet it was the six madrigals which were the most portentous works. The ballet, like the canzonet, had served Weelkes well, but by now it was as exhausted for him as the canzonet had been a year before. This volume of 1598 was evidently hastily compiled, with manufactured music and imperfectly realised conceptions scattered among some really excellent pieces. 1599 passed without issue, for the next volume was to be of real madrigals in which the skills and lessons learned in the first two volumes were to be applied. There was to be no haste about these, no stereotyped formula for mass production. These works were to be personal in their vision and power, and masterly in their structure and composition. When the volume of five- and six-voice madrigals appeared in 1600, the lapse of a year proved to have been well worth while. Not all of these twenty works are beyond reproach, but the very best of them are among the finest of all the English madrigals.

V. THE MADRIGALS OF 1600

Although he was a thoroughly committed madrigalist, it was inevitable that Weelkes should move farther away from the intimacies and refinements of Morley's madrigalian manner, and more into line with the indigenous musical stream. His natural virility ensured this; so, too, did his inclination to genuine contrapuntalism which had been exercised and strengthened in the madrigals of 1598. When, two years later, he published his five- and six-voice madrigals, the trend was confirmed. The purging of some of the more facile Morleyisms of the earlier volume is especially noticeable in the cadences, which take on a more unsophisticated, blunt strength, rarely using (except in *alla breve* passages) the 'suspended dominant seventh' formula (Example 39) which

Ex. 39

is such a feature of Morley's madrigals, and common in Weelkes' own first two volumes. But there was, of course, no question of him adopting the broad sweep of the older English manner. Concentration, both in the composition of the individual sections and in the panorama of the whole work, is one of the most notable features of these madrigals of 1600. The pruning of superfluous notes is more strict, and some of the freely contrapuntal passages are enriched by the use of two thematic ingredients (on occasions a single idea which falls into two parts). The acme of concentration is reached in a completely new technique which founds an extended section upon a melodic point which not only saturates the texture but, in a gigantic augmentation in the bass, determines the harmonic structure of the section.

Thematic relationships had receded in most of the madrigals of 1598, but here they reassert themselves as strongly as ever, and recompositional processes even produce embryonic ritornello structures. The sectional clarity, typical of the madrigals of 1598, is apparent in some of these pieces. The textural shades between homophonic and polyphonic manners are more numerous, subtle, yet precise. This finer variety is also reflected in the varying vocal groupings which may be used within or between sections. Weelkes' response to textual details is, admittedly, quite often tempered in the interests of musical coherence, and there are occasions when he ignores a possible expressive or symbolic point altogether, but at other times his imagination blazes out into some of the most vivid moments in English music of the time. A few passages hark back to the more abstract manner of earlier English music, but some of the most advanced sounds and concepts to be fashioned by an English composer are to be heard in the chromaticism of *O care, thou wilt despatch me / Hence, care, thou art too cruel*, or in the radical aesthetic of *Thule, the period of cosmography / The Andalusian merchant*. Yet, simultaneously, the debt to modal polyphony is constantly evident in the melodic lines and rhythmic counterpoint of some sections, which introduce chromatic inflections not for expressive purposes, but simply to make the linear progress more smooth —even sometimes at the cost of a twinge of harmonic awkwardness. Indeed, even such a purple patch of chromaticism as that at the beginning of *Hence, care, thou art too cruel* is, like that of *Cease sorrows now* (1597), set in a work which elsewhere shows thoroughly modal behaviour. In the *O care / Hence, care* madrigal pair Weelkes shows himself able to modulate convincingly to distant tonal regions, yet without creating any feeling that modulation is being used as a structural device. Rather he sees it as a means of tension and colour—an immensely elaborated and heightened form of expressive *musica ficta*. This subtle interplay of modal and tonal possibilities is typical of the enormous scope of these works. It is amazing that Weelkes should have compassed so quickly and thoroughly such diverse manners and techniques, and commanded such a broad expressive range.

The single volume in which the five- and six-voice madrigals of 1600 were issued[1] is exceptional in that it contains two dedicatees. The title page at the beginning reads *Madrigals of 5 and 6 parts, apt for the viols and voices*, and is followed by a dedication to 'Henry Lord Winsor, Baron of Bradenham'. But after the ten five-voice madrigals, there appears a new, full title page, *Madrigals of 6 parts, apt for the viols and voices*, and a new dedication to 'Master George Brooke Esquire'. Thurston Dart has pointed out that the printer's signatures run continuously through the part-books, clearly showing that he set them as a single entity. It has already been suggested in this book that Brooke may have financed the publication of the six-voice madrigals, and thus earned their dedication. Yet it still seems possible that Weelkes may have conceived the five- and six-voice madrigals

[1] It was Professor Thurston Dart who first noted that these madrigals were issued as a single set of part-books.

as two separate collections, and may have arranged his two dedicatees, intending to issue them separately. The point is that the five-voice works, taken by themselves, do show a textual coherence lacking in Weelkes' other volumes. A simple love story may be traced through the ten lyrics: the awakening of love with the coming of summer (Nos. 1–3), disappointment and despair (Nos. 4–6), spirits revived by the merriment and festivities of May (Nos. 7 and 8), and salute to a new love with chorus of birds on the morning of a new day (Nos. 9 and 10). The individual poems are not completely consistent to the story, but Weelkes' arrangement is certainly neat, and the three compositions which involve a flat key signature are placed as centrally as possible in the scheme. There is also some orderliness in their modal succession: three major, three minor, two major, two minor. The six-voice madrigals, on the other hand, are a disjointed sequence. It seems most likely therefore that it was at a late stage that it was decided, probably by the printer, Thomas East, to issue them as a single volume. Published separately, they would have been far shorter than any of the preceding English madrigalian publications; East may have calculated upon a better profit by making the buyer purchase both sets.

Turning to examine the five-voice madrigals individually, we find that *Cold winter's ice* (No. 1), like the first work of Weelkes' volume of 1597, shows a rhythmic growth which is apt in the piece which is to inaugurate the volume. Pronounced features of this work are conciseness, and strong contrapuntalism within subtle variations of texture. Expressively both this and the following madrigal, *Now let us make a merry greeting* (No. 2), are temperate, and the English tradition is strongly evident in the latter's homophonic opening. This second madrigal displays a taut periodic structure, reinforced by clear thematic relationships. The pattern of alternating homophonic and polyphonic sections is like that already employed in *Phyllis, go take thy pleasure* (1598). The scheme is intersected by a second division into duple- and triple-time sections, thus:

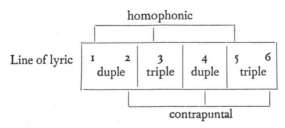

Thematic affinities bind the first two contrapuntal sections (Example 40*a* and *b*), and there is common material to open the second and third homophonic sections (Example 40*c* and *d*). The long delay of the initial entry in the bass voice is a typically Weelksian touch.

Ex. 40

a

and thank god Cu - pid for our meet — ing

b

since thou art here, mine on - ly trea - sure

c

My heart is full of joy and plea - sure

d

Now will we dance

Concentration and purpose are just what the opening and closing sections of *Take here my heart* (No. 3) lack. The trouble starts insidiously in the broad opening paragraph, when the second segment of the melodic point beguiles Weelkes into a quasi-ostinato texture of descending scales which chime on happily in thirds – very pleasant in itself, but showing no real growth.[1] Evidently this failure to establish any thrust left Weelkes at a loss, and the unsubtle set of entries which follows is the weakest incident in the whole volume. He recovers as he turns to an *alla breve* manner for the reassuring 'fear not, my dear' which, like the opening paragraph, is founded upon two thematic ideas. This passage is admirable for its open texture, complete absence of melodic padding, and consequent clarity of dissonance. But the rest of the madrigal falls off, with contrapuntal trundlings upon 'desire will make it range', and mundane counterpoint in the closing bars. Perhaps there is some feeling that the

---

[1] The failure is the more apparent when this passage is compared to Byrd's success within similar restrictions at the opening of his keyboard piece, *The Bells* (see W. Byrd, *Collected works* (edited by E. H. Fellowes), vol. 20, p. 96). Weelkes himself managed this sort of thing much better in the (presumably) earlier *Noel, adieu, thou court's delight* (*Madrigals of 6 parts* (1600)).

treatment of 'love but my heart' near the end echoes the quasi-ostinato texture of the opening, but otherwise there is no evidence of any significant thematic or recompositional relationships. Despite the quality of its middle area, this is the dullest piece in the book.

The next pair of madrigals more than compensate for this relapse. Between them, *O care, thou wilt despatch me* (No. 4) and *Hence, care, thou art too cruel* (No. 5), make up one of the finest and most imaginative of all Weelkes' compositions. Each employs a four-line verse made up of two

Ex. 41

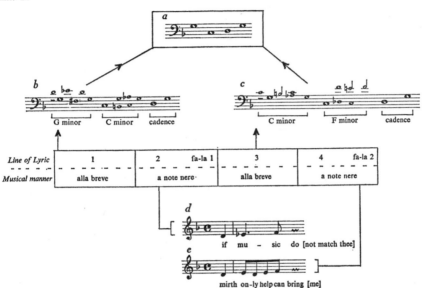

couplets of deplorable quality, to whose despairing sentiments are annexed fa-la refrains. This incongruous conjunction promises a tragic ballet—if such a thing is conceivable. The astonishing thing is that Weelkes not only conceives it, but carries it off magnificently. The conception is as daring as anything in English music of the period, and its complete musical success depends upon a combination of careful planning with a strong instinct to establish musical relationships between separate sections. To ensure engagement between the couplets and fa-las, Weelkes binds the latter and the second line of the former into one musical paragraph; consequently the fa-las do not contradict the couplets with unseemly gaiety, but instead intensify the sorrow by nostalgically reflecting the joy of which the lyric despairs. Then within each madrigal he relates the two *alla breve* sections through the fundamental outline of the bass line, using the same outline (Example 41a) for both sections of *O care*, but in *Hence, care* balancing the sequential drop of a tone in the first *alla breve* section (Example 42*a*) with a rise of a tone in the second (Example 42*b*). So, too, the *a note nere* sections are connected, thematically in *O care* (Example 41*d* and *e*), by close variation in *Hence, care* (Example 42*d* and *e*).

Ex. 42

So much for general principles. The melodic point and the actual openings of the two *alla breve* sections of *O care* are the same (except for octave transposition) and, after diverging for a couple of bars, the second rejoins the first in a recomposition (Example 43). In each of the *alla breve* sections of this madrigal, Weelkes uses the three notes of the melodic point upon each of the initial two notes of the outline bass (Example 41*a*), using the point's inverted form in the second of these sections; he then allows the implications or possibilities of these applications to determine the tonal direction (Example 41*b* and *c*). At the same time he exploits the possibilities of *musica ficta*, capping the second section with a quite devastating simultaneous false relation.

Ex. 43

But even more amazing things are to come. Unlike its counterparts in the other four madrigal pairs published in Weelkes' volumes, *O care* ends not on the dominant but on the tonic, thus confirming the tonal centre which is to be opposed in the sensational passage at the beginning of *Hence, care* (Example 44). As the foundation of the extraordinary harmonic procedures of this section, Weelkes brings in the chromatic fifth between the two falling fifths of the outline bass of this section (see the bracketted notes in Example 42*a*); the course of the music, though highly unusual, is still very clearly directed, and tonal liberty does not become anarchy. Such a remarkable outburst as this needs a balancing section to restabilise the tonality; that is why, in this instance, Weelkes prolongs the *alla breve* section into the second couplet line, which he sets in music of complete tonal clarity (Example 42*c*). At the same time, he maintains the policy of using identical material for the second couplet line and its ensuing fa-la by making this fa-la a slightly varied diminution of the preceding passage (Example 42*d*).

Strength and stability are the essence of the latter half of *Hence, care*, and the lift onto D minor is a powerful musical reflection of the 'force' of the text. The more animated final line is bound to the preceding by the strong 'sustained' harmonic foundation. As the fa-la is reached, the music slips cunningly back to the preceding fa-la, and closely recomposes the approach to the cadence of that section (Example 42*d* and *e*).

For many this pair is Weelkes' madrigalian masterpiece. Certainly there is no English madrigal that strikes harder at the listener. Thomas Tomkins was deeply impressed by its conception, and not only modelled his own

Ex. 44

Too much I once lamented[1] upon it, but even borrowed Weelkes' opening for this madrigal. But if none of Weelkes' madrigalian conceptions is more inspired, there is none that is more highly organised. A similar situation arises, though in a less exacerbated form, in the expressive dualism of the ensuing madrigal, *See where the maids are singing* (No. 6), and it is not surprising that this is the only other work in the volume to show a comparably intensive integration, achieved here both through textural correspondences and through direct thematic and recompositional relationships. Example 45 sets out the structure diagrammatically. The thematic kinship of the central *alla breve* section (Example 45*d*) to its flanking passages (Example 45*c* and *e*) is fictiously produced by the staggered entries of

---

[1] *Songs of 3, 4, 5 and 6 parts* (1622). Tomkins' madrigal pair, *O let me live for true love* / *O let me die for true love*, is also a tragic ballet.

two voices, but the identity is clearly audible in performance, and confirmed when Example 45d is forthwith overlaid by 45e. Although lacking

Ex. 45

the boldness of the *O care | Hence, care* pair, this madrigal technically and expressively does honour to its composer.

Why are you ladies staying? (No. 7) and *Hark! I hear some dancing* (No. 8) make up the other pair of this volume of five-voice madrigals. Both are short, spirited and extrovert, with a directness that is clear-headed, not simple-minded. There is a robust readiness to depict textual details, and the opening refuses impatiently to stay with the ladies in pseudo-anti-phony, and provides an impetuous response to the text's precept to 'run apace'. Semiquavers are called in to add extra velocity, and the madrigal is set off at a cracking pace. The texture clears as the fourth line of the lyric is treated upon a melodic point related to material from the madrigal's opening. The final couplet is set homophonically with a lucid antiphonal dialogue between various vocal groupings. The homophonic manner persists into *Hark! I hear some dancing*, which flanks the setting of the central four lines with related triple-rhythm sections which treat the first and final lines. Before all this begins, the exhortation 'Hark!' is presented in an effective piece of musical *pointillism*, a device which Weelkes was to use again at the opening of two of his *Ayres*, published in 1608.[1] A blatant pair of consecutive unisons between the tenor and bass at one point[2] does not destroy the overall impression of technical precision which this work gives. Altogether this madrigal pair is clear, economical, and especially attractive for its rhythmic life.

After the compressed or highly characterised expression typical of the preceding works, it comes as quite a jolt to return to a straightforward application of a single subject in regular imitative entries. This happens for the first two lines of *Lady, the birds right fairly* (No. 9), and the result sounds strangely old-fashioned. The structure of the first two lines is altogether looser, and the music, though bright, is quite abstract, despite the temptations to musical characterisation offered by the text. Characteri-sation does begin with the appearance of the mixed aviary of lines three to four, and the treatment of line five is as striking as it is brief. The BACH motif in the top voice part seems to have fathered the melodic point of the final line (Example 46); the unusual diminished fourth at its core maintains the tension created in the *alla breve* section.

Ex. 46

a

then why sleep ye?

b

To love your sleep it may [not be]

---

[1] *Come, let's begin to revel't out* (No. 1) and *Ha! Ha! This world doth pass* (No. 19). Two other works from the same volume (*Tan ta ra! cries Mars* (No. 7) and *Strike it up, tabor* (No. 18)) also benefit directly from the setting which Weelkes accords the 'nimble morris prancing' in *Hark! I hear some dancing*.

[2] EMS11, p. 42, bars 1–2.

Two features of special interest appear in the last five-voice madrigal, *As wanton birds* (No. 10). The first of these is the use of a kind of rudimentary and constantly evolving ritornello. It is always homophonic (or virtually so), and the prototype is the work's opening bars. As the successive homophonic incidents occur, so the common feature emerges of a top line founded upon E with two shallow peaks rising to F, the second produced by crossing of the upper voice parts (Example 47). As a 'ritornello' its use is at first very tentative (Example 47*b*), but later applications are clearer, as though the structural idea grew upon Weelkes as he proceeded through the madrigal.[1] As used in this work the idea would pass unnoticed, but nevertheless it seems that we may have here the source of a device which Weelkes was to employ much more positively in *Like*

Ex. 47
[*summary outlines*]

a [As wanton birds]

b [So I, whom love]

[Do now with joy]
c

d [a happy day]

e [Long may he live]

two proud armies (the first of the six-voice madrigals), even more purposefully in the full anthem, *Hosanna to the Son of David*, and which was to reach its most fully developed expression in the chorus variations of the verse anthem, *Give ear, O Lord*. It was typical of Weelkes, the transitional

[1] Even the setting of 'whose sane bright beams' reflects the 'ritornello' as far as its limited length will allow. No doubt the presentation of this piece of text in 'white' notes is a piece of 'eye music'.

composer, that he should combine this novel repetitive device with the constantly unfolding flow of musical thought which came naturally to the Renaissance polyphonist.

Between the 'ritornello' incidents of *As wanton birds* are sections which are more contrapuntally orientated, and thematic relationships are detectable between three of these (Example 48). The second novel feature in this madrigal is the setting of the final line. This marks the first appearance in Weelkes' work of an extended section based upon a single point

Ex. 48

(Example 49) so constructed that it permits concentrated exact imitation at the unison or octave, thus producing a point-saturated texture. The saturation in this madrigal is not as complete as in some of the later ones; nevertheless, its thirty-nine entries build a mightily impressive paragraph, and the final homophonic passage confirms the blessing of long-

Ex. 49

evity upon those who honour Phillida. This is a splendid conclusion, not only to this madrigal, but to the whole half-volume.

The level of achievement in these ten five-voice works is not only higher, but more consistent than in the two earlier volumes. Admittedly *Take here my heart* and *Lady, the birds right fairly* can be considered only partial successes, but the remaining eight are all first-rate. These may be divided into two distinct groups. One is made up of the 'disappointment and despair 'division, *O care / Hence, care* and *See where the maids are singing* (Nos. 4–6), all in the minor mode, all personal in expression and using considerable or extreme contrast between *a note nere* and *alla breve* manners, and all countering this dichotomy with a very intensive musical organisation achieved through thematic, variational and recompositional techniques. The remaining five works are more objective, more brilliant, laconic and lucid in structure, often contrasting a dynamic homophony with an athletic contrapuntalism. Four of these pieces are in the major mode.[1] Three enhance their brilliance by the use of passages in triple time; in two this device helps to clarify the structure.

In the six-voice madrigals less use is made of the vocal network which impresses through the orderly independence of its constituent voices. This is replaced by a more resonant fabric, epitomised in the point-saturated texture, such as has already been encountered at the end of *As wanton birds. Like two proud armies*, the first of the six-voice works, not only uses this same device for its conclusion, but further develops the 'ritornello' tendency of the concluding five-voice madrigal, for it employs three times a simple motive (a tonic-subdominant-tonic progression) as the central incident to closely related passages. A diagram is the clearest means of making the structure clear (Example 50). During the treatment of the first two lines the 'ritornello' emerges (Example 50*b* and *c*); on its third appearance (Example 50*d* and *e*) it is expanded, for its antiphonal potentialities make it apt material for treating the accusations and counter-accusations of the fourth line ('the one claims the crown; the other says 'tis treason'). The flanking third and fifth lines use related but transformed melodic material (Example 50*f* and *g*). The melodic point of the final line (Example 50*h*) seems to summarise the thematic content of the whole work, and is used to build a saturated texture over a tremendous augmentation in the bass.

Kerman has noted that 'the bellicose beginning is derived from a famous madrigal by Alessandro Striggio, *Non rumor di tamburi*, which Watson translated as *Love hath proclaimed war, by trumpet sounded*'.[2] Nevertheless the result is a splendidly Weelksian conception. The musical imagery of the madrigal is most apt, with much use of close, contentious dialogue between one soprano/bass pair and the other, and, at the instigation of 'thundering', as graphic a passage as any in Weelkes' work. The massiveness of much of the music, and the intensive integration results in a work of quite baroque monumentality.

---

[1] The odd one out, *As wanton birds*, is on a more extended scale because of its massively extended conclusion.

[2] J. Kerman, *The Elizabethan madrigal*, p. 231.

Ex. 50

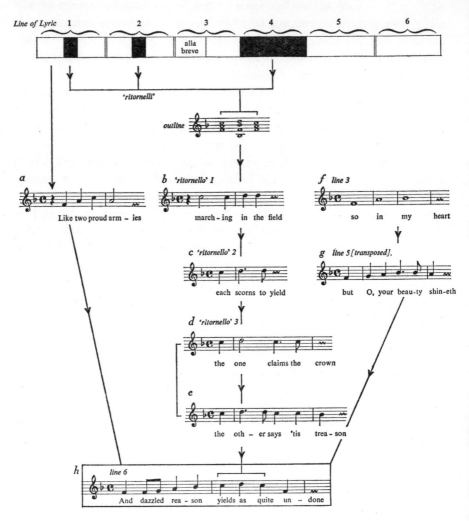

The appearance of 'satyrs' in the lyric of *When Thoralis delights to walk* (No. 2) seems to have recalled to Weelkes his own *Three virgin nymphs* of 1597, for he employs here the same device of an augmented and varied repetition of the opening section. In the present madrigal it is rather differently managed, for the repetition offers a contrapuntal treatment of the simple initial idea, followed by a twofold statement of the original cadence, instead of a single cadential augmentation as in the earlier work (see Example 15). The satyrs leap aptly upwards on triads; indeed, all the important melodic ideas of the piece are shaped around a triadic structure so that they can be used repeatedly in the normal and inverted forms to build highly saturated textures deployed on broad harmonies. The whole piece culminates magnificently in one of the two most extended of Weelkes' point-saturated textures, some two score repetitions of 'Long mayst thou live, fair Thoralis' pealing out over an eightfold augmentation in the bass.

The only rival to this conclusion is the final section of *As Vesta was descending*, Weelkes' contribution to *The Triumphs of Oriana*, printed in the following year (1601); this seems the appropriate point at which to digress to examine this madrigal. This saturated paragraph uses a melodic point very like the final 'conflated' point of *Like two proud armies* (Example 50*h*), but deploys it upon the scale of the conclusion of *When Thoralis delights to walk*. The whole piece is in Weelkes' best manner. It grasps at the numerous opportunities for musical symbolism, especially in the central couplet, where 'two by two', 'three by three', 'together' and 'all alone' determine the number of voices to be used for setting each particle of text. This madrigal is not remarkable for its thematic relationships, but bases its structure upon a mirror scheme (Example 51). The work's growth is carefully calculated; the initial entry of the two lowest voices is long delayed, and the concluding peroration is as splendid as any Weelkes ever wrote. Elizabeth I (or whoever was concealed behind the mask of Oriana) was well honoured in this tribute.

Returning to the six-voice madrigals of 1600, we encounter a madrigal pair, *What have the gods?* (No. 3) and *Methinks I hear* (No. 4), which show a structural organisation as thorough as that of the *O care / Hence, care* pair. The identical last line of each lyric prompts musical similarities between the two madrigals' final sections, but passages related to these are also used to set the central line of each madrigal. These four full six-voice sections are the cornerstones of the whole structure; their common features are a homophonic A major-D minor/major progression, and an ensuing passage founded upon a common melodic point. Weelkes, the resourceful contrapuntist, applies these ingredients freely in each case, but the relationships are still positive.

Other relationships, some quite tenuous but others very firm, articulate a more elaborate scheme within each madrigal. That of *What have the gods?* is abaCcdC, the capitals representing the central and final sections related in both madrigals. Example 52 deploys the structure diagrammatically; most of the relationships can be grasped from this. It is, however, especially worth noting the *alla breve* section (b), which contains a high proportion of dissonance, all the more pointed for being set in such a lean texture. This passage repeats the unusual cadential formation which

Ex. 51

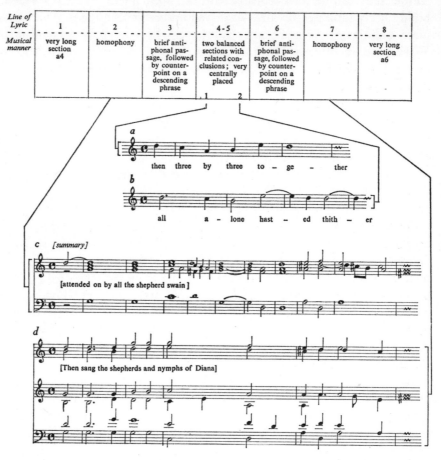

Line of Lyric	1	2	3	4-5	6	7	8
Musical manner	very long section a4	homophony	brief antiphonal passage, followed by counterpoint on a descending phrase	two balanced sections with related conclusions; very centrally placed	brief antiphonal passage, followed by counterpoint on a descending phrase	homophony	very long section a6

a

then three by three to - ge - ther

b

all a - lone hast - ed thith - er

c [summary]

[attended on by all the shepherd swain]

d

[Then sang the shepherds and nymphs of Diana]

had already appeared in *Phyllis, go take thy pleasure* (1598) (see Example 35).

The structure of *Methinks I hear* should also be clear from the diagram of Example 53. The underlying scheme in this case is abC(x)CbaC. The lower of the two subjects of the opening (Example 53*a* and *b*) is ubiquitous but ambivalent, the modified form in 53*b* being a retrograde inversion of the upper subject, and especially prominent; it shapes the bass conclusion of the opening section, and forthwith provokes the lower of the associated subjects of the next section (Example 53*c*). Together with new superimposed material (Example 53*d*) it inaugurates the penultimate section, and in the final cadence attempts a combination of this new material with the subject which had accompanied it at the madrigal's opening (Example 53*g*). Weelkes was to use a similar procedure in some of his anthems, where the final 'Amen' may summarise certain of the ideas which had been used earlier in the piece.

Madrigal singers seem to have neglected these two works. Their musical imagery is not as passionate as that of *O care | Hence, care*, nor as extravagant as that of *Thule | The Andalusian merchant*, and this may account for their lesser popularity. This neglect is a pity, for the whole

Ex. 52

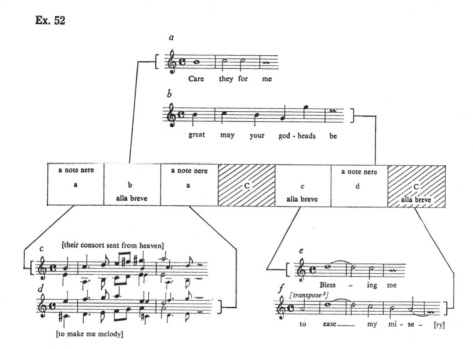

conception is splendid, well worthy to keep company with these other two pairs. Unfortunately it is not possible to feel the same unqualified enthusiasm for *Three times a day* (No. 5). Though the treatment of dissonance is clean, the texture is not always satisfactory in the fuller sections, and the handling of the vocal lines is sometimes unsure. Nor is the continuity easy in the last two *a note nere* sections, which both fall away into note spinning. These factors, coupled to its unusually low tessitura and the reappearance of a canzonet structure, give it the flavour of an earlier vintage. However, the canzonet scheme is disguised, for new material appears on both occasions where a conventional repeat is expected to begin, and the original section is only rejoined at a later stage. Even then, in the initial repeated section, the conclusion itself is varied (Example 54). The rest of the work is made out of three *a note nere* sections followed by *alla breve* passages; the last two of these dual sections constitute the concluding statement and repetition of the canzonet scheme.

Ex. 53

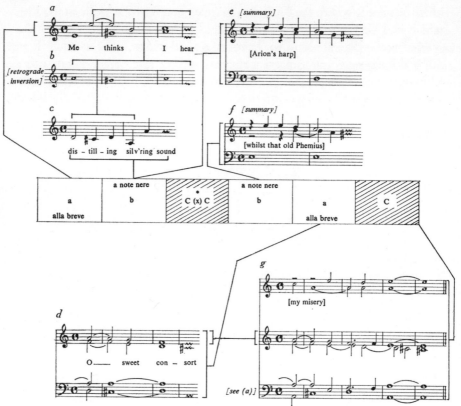

* x indicates new material accounting for nine minim pulses

Ex. 54

a

[Three times a day my prayer is. *Cadence only*]

b

[To gaze my fill on Thoralis. *Cadence only*]

Although it is an unequal work, the general level of achievement rises again with *Mars in a fury* (No. 6). The 'furious' running quavers of the opening are in Weelkes' best manner, and the pace of the setting is admirable. Aptly martial sounds proclaim the warrior's terrible advance, and heaven is accorded its proper vocal altitude. But disappointment comes at the end. Instead of an active response to 'Venus shall die', the treatment is uncharacterised. Perhaps Weelkes intended to suggest exhausted anger or glumness—after all, a warlike display was hardly the way to settle Venus. More probably he feared a sudden change would disrupt the work musically. Whatever the cause, the result is an anticlimax.

The level of achievement is fully restored by the madrigal pair, *Thule, the period of cosmography* (No. 7) and *The Andalusian merchant* (No. 8). The final couplet is common to both madrigals, and in each Weelkes uses the same music for these lines (with a final cadential adjustment). He also makes the opening paragraph of each alike in their prevailing dotted rhythm, and the points to the second lines are very similar (Example 55).

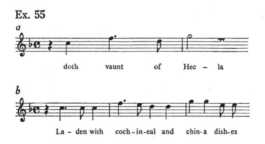

Ex. 55

It is possible to find other unifying features, but this is a madrigal pair to be heard first and foremost for its diversity of detail, for the brilliant, 'fantastic' and 'artificial' richness of its musical imagery. The opening paragraph of *Thule*, based upon a double subject, accumulates power not impetuously, as had the opening of *Mars in a fury*, but more broadly. 'Vaunting' is suggested by a strong leaping phrase (see Example 55a), and the boiling sulphureous fire of Hecla is graphically depicted in a solid texture of rolling quavers. The sudden change from volcanic 'fire' to 'frozen climes' is realised by an equally extreme change in musical manner —from polyphony to homophony, from powerful progress to smooth stillness, and by a harmonic move as striking as any in Weelkes' work. Trinacrian Etna's flames invoke a triple rhythm, the first to appear in the six-voice madrigals. It is tempting to rhapsodise upon these pieces of musical pictorialism, but the listener will find it easy enough to pick them out for himself. Nevertheless, one further passage does call for special comment—the weird chromatic setting of 'how strangely Fogo burns' in the second madrigal (Example 56). Tovey wrote with characteristic perception when he distinguished the chromaticism of this passage as being 'entirely different in conception . . . from the wonderful modulations of *Hence, care, thou art too cruel*, which are essentially diatonic but remote modulations, expressing no freak of nature but profound human emotion'.[1]

Ex. 56

[How strangely Fogo burns]

Chromaticism relies for its *emotional* impact upon the inflection it makes against a firm, perceptible diatonic background. The chromaticism of *Hence, care* is mingled with that most firm of diatonic formations, the perfect cadence (see Example 44). No goal could be more explicit than the final tonic; thus, when Weelkes denies the resolution onto the tonic, or shoots off in a new tonal direction, the new move is all the more striking. The listener is kept in a state of alternating tension and expectation of relaxation, and this dynamic assault upon his nerves becomes a subjective experience. Example 56 presents no such diatonic background; the chromatic passage, once entered, never promises a cadence. Chromaticism is not pulling against diatonicism, and the listener, remaining passive, can only wonder at the 'strangeness' of it all.

Thus, this madrigal pair is not one likely to arouse a very emotional response—at least, not in the way that *O care | Hence, care* may. It is all too

[1] D. Tovey, *Essays in musical analysis*, vol. 5, p. 12.

unusual, and the strange phenomena of the text and music finally tend to overshadow the human feelings expressed in the final couplet of each madrigal. Yet the listener surely cannot fail to wonder, and having once experienced its fascination, he cannot but return to it again and again to marvel. *Thule | The Andalusian merchant* is unique; it is, of all English madrigals, perhaps the most remarkable.

The old-fashioned ring of the lyric may have induced Weelkes to a more thoroughly contrapuntal manner in *A sparrow-hawk proud* (No. 9). The technique is clean, and the challenging manner chosen for 'to whom with sighs she said' is well handled. Admittedly the final section includes a large number of dissonant passing notes, but there is clear evidence that these little abrasions were deliberately sought by Weelkes. He derives this concluding section from the second fa-la of his ballet, *Farewell, my joy* (1598), but in the present madrigal he repeatedly uses a dissonant formation which he had consistently avoided in the earlier work (Example 57). The madrigal's lines are more plastic, and avoid the awkwardness and

Ex. 57

patent redundancy of some melodic incidents in the ballet; the working of this melodic point is altogether more accomplished. The contrapuntal manner of this madrigal is unfavourable to textual characterisation, and such a graphic point as might be made on 'sighs' is completely passed over. Still, this is a nice piece—the sort of work whose attractions will continue to grow when the more spectacular effects of some of the others have begun to pall.

An elegy, *Noel, adieu, thou court's delight* (No. 10), closes this volume of six-voice works. Weelkes published two other such compositions, *Cease now, delight*, the lament for Lord Borough added at the end of the *Ballets and madrigals* of 1598, and *Death hath deprived me of my dearest friend*, his tribute to Morley, likewise added onto a volume of madrigals, the *Ayres* of 1608. The earliest of these elegies, *Cease now, delight*, is also the weakest. Weelkes divides the six lines into two equal groups, and founds the musical treatment of the second half largely upon that already accorded to the first. After the introductory invocation, 'Cease now, delight', four divisions are discernible in each half.[1] This is an *alla breve* work, solemn in manner, but relying too heavily upon formulae. Thematically it is hardly distinctive enough for the scale of the piece.

Noel, adieu, thou court's delight improves greatly upon this. The subject must surely be Henry Nowell, the prominent Elizabethan courtier who died in 1598; he was well served for memorial elegies, for Morley also composed one upon him. The proportion of accented quaver and crotchet passing notes marks this as an early work, but the norm of dissonance is the highest of any piece by Weelkes, and such momentary asperities as do occur only enhance the affective sorrow of the elegy. To the same end, *a note nere* and *alla breve* passages are in particularly strong contrast. *Noel, adieu* is a sprawling work, lacking in conciseness, but countering diffuseness by the strong family kinships of the greater part of the thematic material (Example 58), and by repetitions and recompositions.[2] The exceptionally astringent dissonance of the piece includes several simultaneous false relations, and effective use is made of various permutations of an augmented triad plus a suspended perfect fifth (Example 59). Weelkes certainly wrote tauter pieces, but *Noel, adieu* contains some of his most profoundly affecting music. No man could reasonably hope for a more distinguished musical memorial.

It was Weelkes' fellow elegist, Morley, who was the recipient of his third and final panegyric, *Death hath deprived me of my dearest friend.* This, seemingly the last of Weelkes' six-voice madrigalian compositions, is an altogether more sculptured work than its two predecessors. The opening is the same as that of the final broken-voiced paragraph in Weelkes' own *O my son Absalom*, but the elegy quickly takes its own independent course, and unfolds some of Weelkes' very best music—profoundly sad, and the more moving for its restraint. The gentle chromatic change on 'dead' is particularly beautiful, and 'laid in grave' draws

---

[1] The cross-relationships appear thus:
(the barring, according to EMS10, is given in brackets)
Introduction (1–10)

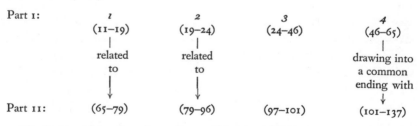

[2] For instance, bars 58–73 (according to the barring in EMS12) quote, or are derived from material in bars 10–12, 42–46, 46–48 and 25–28. Bars 118–127 are a compressed recomposition of bars 99–116 (omitting bars 101–2 and 109–14).

Ex. 58

a

No - el, a - dieu, thou court's de-light

b

our pleas-ure dies out-right

c

When thou in dust art laid

d

time helps some grief

e

up - on whose locks the grace[s]

f

now thou___ art dead

g

for___ who___ can joy

h

be - dew___ my notes [his death - bed with your tears]

i

No___ time___ your grief out - wears

Ex. 59

the voices down into their darkest and most subterranean register. 'Until the world shall end' is treated to a piece of musical pictorialism as startling as any moment of *Thule | The Andalusian merchant*. Lord Borough, that 'great lord of greater fame', may have looked enviously at Weelkes' homage to the 'court's delight', Noel—but it was Morley who had cause for the deepest satisfaction. Surely his distempered and querulous spirit must have been mollified to find that it was to *him* that his friend and fellow elegist offered his most deeply felt tribute.

Weelkes' madrigal volume of 1600 is one of the finest achievements of this great period of English composition. If the foregoing examination has seemed more concerned with exposing the structural features of these madrigals than with rhapsodising upon their musical beauties, it is because the latter can commend themselves forcefully enough to the listener with-out the critic's advocacy. Unlike many of the best English madrigals, the vivid expression of some of Weelkes' finest works makes them as compelling to the listener as to the performer. Indeed, the instrumental character of some of his writing, and his practice of making the vocal lines of some sections subordinate to the requirements of resonant texture, render some of his passages vocally less grateful to the performer than, say, the melodic strands of madrigals by Morley or Wilbye. But while we are admiring the power and originality of Weelkes' achievement, it is also worth reflecting that, except for the last piece, all that has been studied in these last three chapters represents some four or five years' work by a very young composer. For all their inequalities, these three volumes are one of the most remarkable beginnings to any creative career in English cultural history. But it remained only a beginning. The inherent conservatism of English musical taste, and changing musical fashion have already been suggested as causes of this, but there were perhaps even more positive reasons why Weelkes ceased to compose madrigals. The most immediate was the demand for church music which must have resulted from his appointment to the musical staff of Chichester Cathedral in 1601 or 1602; another concerned his ambitions for the future. Madrigalian composition would find quicker recognition and favour among wordly amateurs than ecclesiastics. The B.Mus. degree which Weelkes acquired in 1602 was a step towards high musical respectability, but if he aspired to an appointment in the sovereign's Chapel Royal, it would still be necessary to prove that he could offer music which could worthily adorn the Chapel. So far, all his creative efforts had evidently been absorbed by madrigals; now he needed to furnish substantial proof of his worth as a composer of church music.

Evidently Weelkes did briefly attain, or came very near to gaining, an appointment as a Gentleman of the Chapel Royal. As was noted earlier, his name never appears in the records of the Chapel, but he styles himself 'Gentleman of His Majesty's Chapel' on the title page of his *Ayres* of 1608. This slim volume was to be his only other madrigalian publication. If it does not fulfil the promise of the earlier volumes, it nevertheless contains some hearty, and occasionally very beautiful music. It offers enough to make a short chapter on it more than a simple matter of duty.

VI. THE AYRES OF 1608

The title which Weelkes gave to his last madrigalian publication—
"*Ayeres or phantasticke spirites*" *for three voices* (1608)— was not
entirely fanciful. The absolute supremacy of the madrigal in England had passed with the 1590s, and by 1608 the lute-accompanied solo
song was firmly rivalling it in popularity. The expressive range of these
songs was wide, extending from the most elaborate and intense of John
Dowland's great declamations to the simpler periodic dance structures
which Dowland also offered, and the unaffected but irresistible ayres of
Philip Rosseter and Thomas Campion. Rosseter had cited poetic analogies
to justify the simplicity of his own and Campion's compositions: 'What
epigrams are in poetry, the same are ayres in music, then in their chief
perfection when they are short and well seasoned'.[1] Simplicity is also a
strong feature of the compositions in this last volume of Weelkes, for
although these ayres are purely vocal compositions after the fashion of the
madrigal, many of them have abandoned almost all pretence to a contrapuntal style such as Weelkes had used in the three-voice compositions of
his own first volume. Many of the pieces are largely or even completely
conceived in two parts, the middle voice merely chaining itself in parallel
thirds or sixths with one of its companion voices (*Some men desire spouses*
(No. 3) and *Late in my rash accounting* (No. 13) are the two most extreme
instances). Thus the centre of melodic interest is firmly in the uppermost
voice part, which is supported by the bass of the lowest part; the whole is
not 'long, intricate, bated with fugue',[2] but often presents a consistently
homophonic impression.

The abandonment of contrapuntal procedures has, however, deprived
many of these pieces of a fundamental means of growth. To compensate
for this, Weelkes has called in multiple sequences founded upon a small
fragment, perhaps no more than two crotchets long, as in this extract
from *Lord, when I think* (No. 15) (Example 60). This sequential practice

Ex. 60

[what a paltry thing is a glove, or a ring, or a top of a fan]]

---

[1] From the preface of Rosseter's *A Book of ayres* (1601).　　　[2] *ibid.*

119

was not new. Weelkes himself had used it before, and Morley had offered him ready examples of it; nevertheless, its extensive application throughout this volume makes it one of the most striking new trends in this collection.

The narrower range of textures which results from this rejection of contrapuntal method has also helped to blur the distinctions between the familiar forms of madrigal, canzonet and ballet. All pieces employ repetition, but this seems designed more to compensate for their brevity than to establish a canzonet or ballet structure. Some pieces have two or more verses, and therefore would promise to be canzonets rather than madrigals; yet they have a musical repeat of one half only. Others use a single text like a madrigal, but repeat both halves like the truncated binary canzonet. Even the ballets in the collection are not all straightforward, for some place their fa-las in unorthodox positions.

Segregation into madrigals, canzonets and ballets is also made more difficult by the lyrics, which show a very wide variety, both in content and structure. There are some examples of typical madrigal verse, peopled with the stock nymphs and shepherds, and exuding the customary despairing but trivial lovesick sentiments; but two new trends are notable—topicality and cynicism. A good number of lyrics seem to refer to definite occasions, often involving dancing and alluding to real people (*Jockey, thine hornpipe's dull* (No. 2) and *Strike it up, tabor* (No. 18)[1] are only two examples). Nor are the lover's sentiments of verses like *Some men desire spouses* (No. 3) the conventional ones of the amorous Petrarchan (surely this, too, must be a topical piece). Bitterness and cynicism are apparent in *Ha! Ha! This world doth pass* (No. 19) and even more so in what was evidently the original *envoi* of the volume, *As deadly serpents lurking* (No. 23), which deplores the envious times which other Elizabethan composers (notably Morley) had bitterly castigated. So, too, there is disenchantment with the female kind in *No, no, though I shrink still* (No. 11) and *Lord, when I think* (No. 15). A rough native virility, which contrasts refreshingly with the more faded Italian conventions, is evident in some of these pieces, both in their earthy topical allusions and in their lively use of short, sharp lines of varying lengths. In *Four arms, two necks, one wreathing* (No. 14) a whiff of metaphysics may be scented.

Clearly many of these pieces were not composed specifically for a madrigal collection, but were occasional pieces which Weelkes incorporated to make up the volume. It is easy to believe that many of them belong to his Chichester period, for they have an earthiness which accords well with the convivial existence he seems to have had there; certainly their

[1] G. E. P. Arkwright pointed out that this composition uses the popular dance tune, *Watkin's ale*, at the words 'he did labour . . .' (see the Introduction to Arkwright's edition of Weelkes' *Ayres*, published as vol. 17 of *The Old English Edition*).

general tone contrasts sharply with that of the madrigals from the Winchester phase. There is some suspicion that not only the concluding six-voice elegy, *Death hath deprived me of my dearest friend* (No. 26), but also the preceding two pieces, *Donna, il vostro bel viso* (No. 24) and *The Nightingale, the organ of delight* (No. 25), were added after the general scheme had been completed, since not only are the other twenty-three grouped strictly according to mode and key signature, but the first and last of these are very much an introduction and *envoi* respectively.

Not every work demands specific comment, for this is an uneven collection; nevertheless, there are some fresh and often witty compositions in it and, at the heart of the volume, as beautiful a piece as Weelkes ever wrote. Of the seven ballets, three depart from the established pattern; two of these, *The gods have heard my vows* (No. 8) and *Ha! Ha! This world doth pass* (No. 18), have a single fa-la at the end of each complete stanza, and *Fa-la. Now weep, now sing* (No. 21) places its two fa-las near the beginning as flanks to an *alla breve* incident. All three of these ballets aim at some variety of manner, and the opening of *Ha! Ha! This world doth pass* offers a witty piece of Weelksian *pointillism*, but their achievement is obviously bounded by their brevity and textural slenderness. A feature of the fa-las of all these ballets is that none presents a contrapuntal network; indeed, some are thoroughly homophonic. *Some men desire spouses* (No. 3) is typical; as noted earlier, this is virtually a two-part composition. A multiple sequence occurs in its second half, but this device is applied more

Ex. 61

extensively in *Late in my rash accounting* (No. 13) (Example 61). Weelkes' own device of pseudo-antiphony is echoed in the repetition of brief fragments in *Four arms, two necks, one wreathing* (No. 14); numerous instances of this technique are to be found in this volume. So, too, it was

characteristic of Weelkes to integrate the two verse sections through the
virtual musical identity of the second lines of these. But the most
thoroughly integrated of all these ballets is the remaining one, *No, no,
though I shrink still* (No. 11), whose fa-las are identical, and whose verse
sections are closely related (Example 62).

Ex. 62

[No, no, though I shrink still]

Opening of second half   [Till then I will be glad]

A number of works in this collection show a thoroughly English
virility in both words and music, especially those which seem to allude to
specific persons, or which express hearty, convivial sentiments. These are
among the best works in the volume. The static bass at the opening of
Jockey, thine hornpipe's dull (No. 2) and *Strike it up, tabor* (No. 18) is
obviously provoked by the rustic dancing of the text, and the change
from triple to duple rhythm in the second half of each adds an extra
sturdiness. Both pieces employ multiple sequences, but these are even
more strikingly used in *Come, sirrah Jacko* (No. 6), especially at the end
of the first half with its lagging off-beat middle voice. This encomium of
tobacco is one of the most irresistible pieces in the whole volume. *The
Ape, the monkey and baboon* (No. 10) is also a good piece, more contrapuntally minded than these other items, and suggesting from the locale
of the lyric that Weelkes must have had some active contact with London
circles. *Since Robin Hood* (No. 20) is a less happy effort which completely
falsifies the punctuation of the text, for the musical break at mid-point
occurs in mid-sentence. The mention of 'tabor' leads to a musical setting
closely related to the opening of *Strike it up, tabor*. The allusion at the
opening to *Sellenger's round* may be coincidence.

Most of the remaining pieces present a more Italianate visage. The first
piece in the book, *Come, let's begin to revel't out*, is as attractive as any,
furnishing at its opening the other instance in this collection of Weelksian

pointillism. Its double representation of 'hills and dales' and 'echo' is orthodox, but still appealing. Neither *Tomorrow is the marriage day* (No. 4) nor *Upon a hill a bonny boy* (No. 5) stimulates special comment. *Tan ta ra! cries Mars* (No. 7) appears to be a patchwork composition, containing two especially clear identities with other works in its second half, which initially uses material already applied in *Jockey, thine hornpipe's dull* and then passes into a section used in *Strike it up, tabor*.[1] The text to which this section is fitted in the latter work ('to dance about the maypole') is more apt than that to which it is applied here ('But I, alas, lie weeping, for death hath slain my sweeting'). This work has also borrowed a good infusion of native virility. *Though my carriage be but careless* (No. 9) and *Lord, when I think* (No. 15) may be passed over, but *Say, wanton, will you love me?* (No. 16) is less facile, and *Alas! Tarry but one half hour* (No. 22) makes a still firmer impression, and is neatly integrated through the ubiquitous use of stepwise descending quavers. *As deadly serpents lurking* (No. 23) is serious, borrowing its opening from *O care, thou wilt despatch me* (five-voice madrigals of 1600) and hinting, in its second half, at the unusual cadential formation already encountered in *Phyllis, go take thy pleasure* (1598) and *What have the gods?* (six-voice madrigals of 1600) (see Example 35).

The four remaining pieces include two settings of Italian versions of lyrics which Weelkes had already set in English in his very first madrigal volume (see above, p. 73). *Donna, il vostro bel viso* (No. 24) is an affective piece which makes its expressive points efficiently without establishing itself as one of Weelkes' most distinctive compositions. The other Italian-texted piece, *I bei ligustri e rose* (No. 17), is more notable, is well integrated through thematic relationships between its two halves (Example 63), and culminates in a splendidly spanned *alla breve* paragraph. *The nightingale, the organ of delight* (No. 25) is in complete contrast, though

Ex. 63

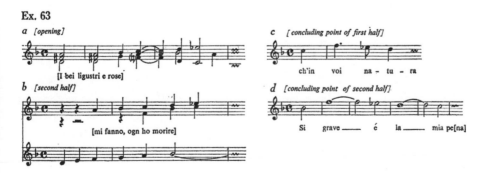

[1] This section had already appeared in *Hark! I hear some dancing* (five-voice madrigals of 1600).

Ex. 64

Ex. 65

curiously using a brief passage identical with an incident in *I bei ligustri e rose* (though now transposed into the major key). A further parallel with a section from *Our country swains* (1597) might arouse suspicions that this is another patchwork composition, but the whole piece is carried off most convincingly; it avoids the over-easy facility of the canzonet style, and concludes with a paragraph of cuckoo noises which shows Weelkes' musical wit at its healthiest.

But it is the remaining piece, *Ay me, alas, hey ho! Thus doth Messalina go* (No. 12) that is the gem of the collection. It is less out-of-doors music, and more refined than *The nightingale*, and appears at first to be simply a binary composition; nevertheless, there are indications of a ternary structure, for halfway through its second half there is a return of the music that had followed the initial exclamations (Example 64). There are further general affinities between this final section and the whole of the first half, for they are subtly but effectively integrated by the descent through four adjacent notes either in the outlines of the melodic material, or in the broader outlines of each section (Example 65).

The piece has a flexible rhythmic life and some nice expressive touches, especially in the setting of 'up and down the house a-crying': the musical symbolism on 'up and down' is conventional, but the arrival on a *musica ficta* A flat in the course of a move from G minor to D minor is delicate, yet telling.

No more need be said of this volume. After Weelkes' earlier collections it comes as a disappointment; it is unambitious and its technique is much enfeebled. Nevertheless, it does make a small new contribution to the range of Weelkes' output through the more virile topical offerings–and we must have permanent gratitude for works like *I bei ligustri e rose* and *Ay me, alas* which continue the Italianate line of the earlier works. With this collection Weelkes the madrigalist fell silent.

VII. WEELKES' MADRIGAL STYLE: II

Morley and Wilbye: Sequence and Repetition

It is now time to take a broader view of Weelkes' madrigals in order to regain some sense of perspective. Weelkes was a very individual composer, but he was certainly not the only English musician of his time to be increasingly concerned with matters of musical structure, or with the exploration of new territories of expression. To restore some sense of proportion, it will be useful to set his work alongside that of two of his greatest English contemporaries, Morley and Wilbye. Morley, as we have seen, was one of the most important formative influences upon Weelkes' style; Wilbye, on the other hand, was Weelkes' contemporary, and owed a debt to Morley every bit as large as that of Weelkes himself. His existence is really highly convenient, for he was of Weelkes' own age, grew up within the same general musical environment, entered publication at the same time, and straightway established himself as a composer of Weelkes' own stature, though one who used their common musical heritage quite differently.

Much has been written in this book of Weelkes' use of various types of repetition, and it is possible to make a revealing comparative study of these three madrigalists simply by examining the way in which each of them used this device. Repetition could serve either a structural or an organic purpose. Its structural use appeared in conventional repetitions like those of the canzonet or ballet, or else when the restatement of an earlier section at some later stage created a long-range internal relationship. On the other hand, organic repetition was immediate reiteration, either at the same pitch or at another level (i.e. sequence), whose function was to expand. Organic repetition became of special value when the disintegration of Renaissance polyphony deprived the composer of a technique whose very nature was expansive. This point has been very firmly made in the study of some of the pieces in Weelkes' 1608 volume. Yet in this period when polyphony seems to be finally doomed, the later madrigals of Morley, Weelkes and Wilbye all paradoxically display an intensification of counterpoint.[1] But from this paradox may come insight, since the different reasons for this reflect the fundamental divergencies in their musical outlooks.

Morley's earlier madrigals nicely demonstrate one balance in the relationship between the older polyphonic methods and the newer repetitive

[1] This discounts Weelkes' *Ayres* of 1608, which were an afterthought, and not a fulfilment of the trends apparent in his three earlier volumes.

procedures. Morley's use of the latter devices is still sparing, and in his first volume, *Canzonets . . . to three voices* (1593), less than half the twenty compositions use any genuine organic repetitions,[1] and some of these instances are quite trivial. Sequences are scarcely more common, and most are made from very short fragments, reiterated no more than three times. Of these, a number do not permeate the whole musical web, but are only part of a texture which is being continually modified. The 'dancing' sequences on the last page of *Arise, get up, my dear* (No. 20) show this most strongly, and indicate Morley's instinct to an 'unfolding' manner —an instinct that was not surprising in a composer who had been schooled by Byrd in the older, pre-madrigalian polyphony. Hints of this engrained contrapuntal mentality emerge more strongly still in Morley's next madrigal collection, *Madrigals to four voices* (1594). The extra voice part afforded a texture which gave more scope for contrapuntal activity, and this may partially explain why sequences which are only part of an evolving contrapuntal texture are the commoner type in this collection. Nevertheless, sequences are now less common than repetitions, and there is more definition between those repetitions which are exact, and those which are modified. The average length of the repeated units is markedly shorter than in the 1593 volume (about three-quarters are made out of units of two bars or less) and their value as an arresting effect is more firmly grasped, for some repetitions are clearly devised primarily to entice the ear. Two ideas appealed to Morley so much that he used each in two different madrigals.[2]

There is no need here to trace these features in Morley's two volumes of 1595. In his last madrigal volume, *Canzonets . . . to five and six voices* (1597), a marked return to contrapuntal processes is sometimes apparent. On the one hand there is the expansion of the decorative, purely madrigalian counterpoint, such as the fifteen bar web which ends *I follow, lo, the footing* (No. 17); on the other there is what sounds like a resurgence of the older polyphonic manner in, for instance, the setting of 'and she like to the eagle' in *False love did me inveigle* (No. 2). This latter tendency is regrettable, for the heavy melodic manner and the less articulate harmonic

---

[1] In this study the difficult question has sometimes arisen: 'When is a repetition not a repetition?' For instance, there are some occasions where an effect of repetition arises from consecutive contrapuntal entries at the same pitch, while the texture beneath unfolds freely. Likewise, the melodic point itself may be sequentially constructed, thus producing sequential over-tones in a texture of freely unfolding counterpoint. In this discussion, reference is made only to those repetitions or sequences which *seem* to be deliberate. Instances of the former type of 'surface' repetition, for instance, seem to be only incidental in many of Morley's madrigals, but quite deliberate in certain of Weelkes'.

[2] See *Why sit I here complaining?* (No. 3) ('with sobs and groanings'), and *Lady, why grieve you still me?* (No. 6) ('O no, you love me'); *Clorinda false* (No. 2) ('adieu, adieu, then'), and *Besides a fountain* (No. 14) ('I die, I die, quoth he').

foundation results in stodginess. This increased contrapuntalism is accompanied by a recession of organic repetitions and sequences. Exact organic repetitions have disappeared, and such sequences as do occur are always heavily modified in some way, or are set against a constantly evolving contrapuntal background; thus in all cases some progress to new music is maintained. If we are to believe the assertion in the preface to his very last publication, *The First book of ayres* (1600), that all the songs in it 'were made this vacation time', then towards the end of his life Morley sometimes turned completely to the older manner, for songs like *A Painted tale* or *Who is it that this dark night?* revert to the manner of the viol-accompanied song.

There are many more instances of organic sequence and repetition in the thirty works that make up Wilbye's *The First set of English madrigals* (1598) than in all the sixty-one compositions in the three volumes by Morley which have been under discussion. If for Morley these devices had been a useful adjunct to his technique, for Wilbye they were fundamental, and because of his wider and more differentiated use of these procedures, it will be as well to particularise the main types of organic repetition that can be distinguished in his madrigals. There are three distinct kinds:

1. The *internal* repetition, usually made from a unit of one or two bars (or even less), which occurs within a musical phrase or section. The multiple sequences of Weelkes' *Ayres* of 1608 are of this type (see Examples 60 and 61).

2. The *block* repetition. This involves the repetition of a more extended whole phrase or paragraph (usually some three to six bars long), ending with a clear cadence which may be modified or completely changed in the reiteration. A block repetition may be treated in a variety of ways; either it may be very literally repeated, or it may be modified so that the repetition offers a re-arrangement of the voice parts to give it a new complexion, or it may be elaborated by fuller scoring: or it may go even further, and provide contrapuntal embellishment from extra voice parts.

3. The *dovetailed* repetition. Here the statement is contrapuntal, and the restatement is dovetailed into it to make a continuous contrapuntal complex. The dovetailed repetition can produce something of the breadth and solidity of the older polyphonic manner.

The six three-voice works which open Wilbye's first volume make the least use of organic repetition and sequence (three ignore these devices completely). Significantly these are the most Morleyish pieces in the collection—already very polished, but hardly distinguishable as Wilbye's work. These procedures are used much more frequently in the following six madrigals for four voices, which are altogether more characteristic.

Indeed, repetition and sequence expand *Lady, when I behold* (No. 10) by one third (this is discounting the conventional canzonet repetitions of the piece). There is only one instance of the dovetailed repetition in these four-voice madrigals,[1] and the ten or so other examples are block repetitions, mostly with little or no modification. Throughout this whole collection Wilbye is attracted to repetition as much for its effectiveness as for its expansive possibilities, and the dovetailed repetition, which is the least arresting type, is not common. One other point is well worth noting: sequence is much less important than repetition in this first collection—a significant feature in the light of Wilbye's practice in his second volume.

From the beginning Weelkes also had an ear for the effectiveness of repetition and sequence, but otherwise his use of these devices shows a purpose quite different from Wilbye's. The three-voice works of his first volume (1597)—works which are so much less polished than Wilbye's three-voice madrigals, but so much more characteristic of their creator—mostly use the short internal repetition or sequence; in addition (and in direct contrast to Wilbye's early practices) sequence is employed more than repetition. Often the literal repetition or sequence appears only on the surface of the music, and is achieved through the alternation of the upper two voices. Example 66 is the first instance to occur in the col-

Ex. 66

[each chirping bird records a piping voice]

lection. Here already is the most rudimentary embryo of pseudo-antiphony, which was to become Weelkes' favoured procedure for creating the short internal repetition. But even pseudo-antiphony, that most blunt type of repetition, was produced by contrapuntal means—a very simple form of double canon. As has been emphasised already in this book, this instinct to think contrapuntally was fundamental to Weelkes' work from the first, and it was this fact that made his approach to the whole matter of organic repetition quite different from Wilbye's. Compare the extracts from the two composers' six-voice madrigals which are given in Example 67. Weelkes achieves a continuous contrapuntal evolution, overlapping

[1] The setting of 'Coral and Ambergris, sweeter and dearer' in *O fools, can you not see?* (No. 8).

the repetitions on the surface of the music, and preventing the cadences from interrupting the continuity of the paragraph. Wilbye makes a clear cadential break between statement and repetition, and then assigns the

Ex. 67

a   WEELKES: If beauty be a treasure (1597)

[Sweetheart, enjoy your pleasure]

b   WILBYE: Of joys and pleasing pains (1598)

[All day long I my hands, alas, go wringing]

exact restatement to the other three voices, extending two of the initial three in decorative countermelodies. The addition of such counterpoints was a stroke which he sometimes applied quite ravishingly in his second madrigal collection.[1]

[1] There is a good instance in *As Matchless beauty* (No. 15) ('Thou diest in him' when set à 4), but the most beautiful of all is that in *Draw on, sweet night* (No. 31) ('Sweet night, draw on, O sweet night, draw on'), where he adorns the music with which the work had opened.

The fact is that, despite the instances of pseudo-antiphony, repetition in Weelkes' first madrigal volume was largely a decorative addition, incidental to the progress of the music rather than the source by which it grew. The very great majority of repetitions were of units two bars or less in length; when larger units were used, they were more likely to be treated sequentially, so that there was some advancement of the music. This unwillingness to hold back the progress of the music was a perfectly natural attitude in a contrapuntally-minded composer, and is completely consistent with the 'evolving' devices of variation and recomposition which Weelkes instinctively used to articulate structure. It was equally consistent that Wilbye should have used literal repetition in the same way as a structural device. In Weelkes' first collection there is only one instance of exact repetition being used in a context where there was no conventional precedent for it,[1] but such unwonted structural landmarks are to be observed in about one quarter of the madrigals of Wilbye's first volume.[2]

Wilbye's use of pseudo-antiphony in his later collection, *The Second set of madrigals* (1609), is a positive sign of Weelkes' direct influence.

---

[1] This occurs at the end of *Ay me, my wonted joys* (No. 9).

[2] Repetition is used to create a tangible unity between the halves of two of the madrigal pairs in the volume. In the case of one, *Of joys and pleasing pains | My throat is sore* (Nos. 26–7), the text ('And still the close points to my first beginning') prompts Wilbye to set the final two lines to the music which had already adorned the opening couplet, thus affording a neat musical frame to the whole double composition. But there was no real compulsion to take the occurrence of 'treasure' at the centre of each lyric of the madrigal pair *What needeth all this travail? | O fools, can you not see?* (Nos. 7–8) as a cue to use the same half-dozen bars at the centre of each, nor is there any extra-musical reason why the last ten bars of *Sweet love, if thou wilt gain* (No. 23) should be largely compounded from two quotations from earlier incidents in the piece. Other brief unconventional repetitions occur in *Adieu, sweet Amaryllis* (No. 12) and *Why dost thou shoot* (No. 30); a larger one is to be found in *And though my love abounding* (No. 15), the overall structure of which is ABBCDD. In view of the clarity of these unconventional repetitions, it is interesting to note that, when observing the conventional repetition, Wilbye frequently tries to make it less blunt, or even to disguise it altogether. This may be done by dovetailing; the most striking example is the opening section of *Thus saith my Cloris* (No. 11) where the overlapping is so complete that the listener may not even realise that any repetition has taken place. At other times Wilbye interpolates some new material before proceeding to the repetition; he does this at the beginning of *I always beg* (No. 16), and then uses this new prefix to launch *If love commands* (No. 17), the second half of this madrigal pair.

Like Weelkes, Wilbye makes some use of less exact relationships between whole segments of a madrigal. Such cross-references can be traced between the respective halves of the madrigal pairs, *I fall, O stay me | And though my love* (Nos. 14–15) and *I always beg | Thus love commands* (Nos. 16–17). Like Weelkes, Wilbye is sometimes inclined to employ an underlying mirror scheme. Textural differentiation articulates such a plan in *I fall, O stay me*, in which three five-voice sections are separated by two interludes, in each of which a passage for three upper voices is echoed by the lower three. So, too, the setting of the final two lines of *Alas, what a wretched life* (No. 19) 'reflect' the material of two passages near the opening.

Of the two instances of this device in Wilbye's earlier volume, one had been prompted by the text,[1] but in his second volume about half the internal repetitions are conditioned by pseudo-antiphony, and there are half a dozen genuine instances of the device. Nevertheless, it was not the sort of effect to have any very great attraction for him, and his use of it is comparatively sparing. His ear, even in six-voice madrigals, was generally inclined to finer and more varied textures. But, apart from the common factor of pseudo-antiphony, their mature madrigals confirm the divergent trends of the two composers' respective first collections. In Wilbye's second volume the importance of repetitive procedures is even greater than in his earlier collection. This is apparent both in the wider use of these techniques and sometimes in the greater scale of their individual applications.[2] Nevertheless, the most important new trend in the whole volume is the greater use of organic sequence instead of organic repetition. In this second collection there are twice as many internal sequences as repetitions, and these sequences may be quite prolonged. Still more numerous are the block sequences and repetitions, and here the shift is even more drastic, for, in relation to the number of block repetitions, block sequences have increased sixfold over those of the earlier volume.

One specific instance of the use of these devices will be more illuminating than an infinity of generalisations. About one third of *Draw on, sweet night* (No. 31) is made up from the *reiterations only* of organic sequences or repetitions—a really sizeable portion of the whole piece. In addition to these, there is a structural recomposition[3] (as model as any in Weelkes' work) and structural repetitions. This madrigal's complex structure may be more easily grasped from a diagram (Example 68).

It is not difficult to understand why Wilbye came to make so much more use of sequence. Repetition can only inflate; sequence, by trans-

---

[1] The setting of 'My echo calls me wretched' in *I always beg* (No. 16); the other occurs briefly in *Lady, when I behold* (No. 24) ('the roses sprouting'), one of the very best pieces in the collection. Perhaps it was one of the last to be written, and was composed with a knowledge of Weelkes' work; it is significant that it is texturally by far the densest of the six-voice madrigals of Wilbye's collection.

[2] Indeed, the boundary between the structural and the organic repetition is sometimes blurred, for when organic block repetitions or sequences are built from large units (say, eight or more bars), they cease to comprise just brief incidents and instead generate substantial segments, large enough and sufficiently characterised to serve as real structural landmarks. For instance, there is the ten-bar two-fold sequence over a sustained bass in *Change me, O heavens* (No. 11) which serves as a very symmetrical centre to the flanking passages which are less sustained harmonically. An even more positive instance is the thirteen-bar three-fold repetition at the centre of *Yet, sweet, take heed* (No. 18) which forms a clear central area flanked by full five-voice contrapuntal sections.

[3] In addition to the obvious similarities in the uppermost voice parts of each extract from sections 1*b* and 5 of Example 68, note how the bass duet which starts in bar 5 of the extract from 1*b* is taken up in bar 3 of the quotation from section 5. Note also the upward octave leap (D-D) and ensuing stepwise descent in a middle voice from each extract.

Ex. 68

[summary]

[Draw on, sweet night]

[outlines only]

[That do arise from painful melancholy]

[outlines only]

[And while thou all in silence dost enfold]

1a	1b	2	3	4	5	6
Draw on, sweet night...	That do arise...	My life so ill...	Sweet night, draw on	My griefs	And while thou all...	I then shall have
3 x 7 - bar sequence on D, G, D.	contrapuntal passage gathering power	2 x 4 - bar free sequence on identical bass; then counter-point upon sequentially made Point; first F ("rel. major") has strong pull, then D	2 x 4 - bar sequence sandwiched between identical 2 bars; then 2 x 3 - bar sequence. ALL BASED ON 1a.	2 x 4 - bar sequence; then related 2 x 5 - bar sequence with 5-bar related insertion.	contrapuntal passage founded on same point as 1b, gathering power; D established as tonal centre.	3 x 4 - bar repetition (close variant of opening of 2) with brief interpolation and coda; firmly centred on D

[My life so ill through want of my complaining]

[I then shall have best time for my complaining]

[My life so ill through want of comfort fares]

ferring the repetition to a new level, can really expand the music and can be maintained for a longer stretch. Wilbye found these repetitive devices invaluable as an alternative to organic counterpoint, since contrapuntal thought was never for him the deep-rooted instinct it was for Weelkes, despite the intensification of the contrapuntal element which is apparent in this second collection by Wilbye. His counterpoint was richer and more sinewy than Morley's, but even in his most selfconsciously contrapuntal passages (as, for instance, in much of *Love me not for comely grace* (No. 12)) the texture lacks the rhythmic turbulence which is the life and soul even of such predetermined textures as those which conclude Weelkes' 'Oriana' madrigal, *As Vesta was descending* or *When Thoralis delights to walk* (six-voice madrigals of 1600).

The increased contrapuntalism in the later madrigals of the three composers signified different things. For Morley it was largely a regression to his own older practices, for Wilbye it was an enrichment of his language, for Weelkes the fulfilment of his technique. With this innate contrapuntal outlook, Weelkes had nothing like Wilbye's need of repetition or sequence, and this was reflected in his comparative neglect of these devices in his mature madrigals of 1600. In these he used straightforward structural repetition little, and confined the short organic repetition mostly to pseudo-antiphony and associated techniques. Block repetitions turn up in only a quarter of these madrigals, and block sequences outnumber them by nearly two to one. Like Wilbye, Weelkes made more use of sequence than repetition; yet, unlike Wilbye, he hardly used the literal sequence, except in the *Ayres* of 1608. It was absolutely natural that when he did employ sequence, he should incline to fuse it with counterpoint, and there are some instances where the internal sequence emerges in the contrapuntal paragraph. On the other hand, there is no instance in Wilbye's madrigals of sequential elements distributed as in Example 69, so that the individual voice parts are mostly unsequential, and so that the texture gives the appearance of ever-changing polyphony.[1]

At times Weelkes used the more extended unit as the foundation of a contrapuntal section, as in the great peroration of *As wanton birds* (five-voice madrigals of 1600)—a four-fold, dovetailed sequence, with an extra bar interpolated after the first sequence.[2] Thus great breadth is allied to clear shape. The setting of 'Laden with cochineal and china dishes'

[1] There is also an instance during the final fa-la of *O care, thou wilt despatch me* (five-voice madrigals of 1600) and another in *A sparrow-hawk proud* (six-voice madrigals of 1600 ('O set me free')).

[2] See also the setting of 'And dazzled reason yields as quite undone' which concludes *Like two proud armies* (six-voice madrigals of 1600). This paragraph continues by applying a one-bar sequence to build a climax, but avoids shortwindedness by organising two voices in interlocking two-bar spans.

Ex. 69

from *The Andalusian merchant* (six-voice madrigals of 1600) shows an even subtler interpenetration of counterpoint and repetition/sequence, being made from three statements of the same tight series of entries, each time reallocated among five of the six voices (one voice always remains outside the system). But in the end, the impression of continuous flow is dominant, and the listener is scarcely aware that any sort of repetition has taken place. The device has given the counterpoint the utmost cogency, but it has not been elevated to a conscious expressive importance in itself.

Weelkes' contrapuntal technique was his greatest asset when he turned his creative gifts to church music. It was virile and resonant, and ideal to erect textures which could fill a large building with sounds befitting a public act of worship. Yet it could be very compact—an invaluable quality for really good liturgical music. There was therefore no need to seek out a new manner, and Weelkes' best church music is in direct line with his madrigals. But before turning to this music, we will pause to examine his few remaining secular vocal works and instrumental pieces.

VIII. THE MISCELLANEOUS WORKS

Apart from the published madrigals and the manuscript church music, very few compositions by Weelkes have survived. We have only a ballet, a setting of *The Cries of London* for solo voice and four viols, four pieces for keyboard instruments, and a handful of viol compositions. The list (with sources) is as follows:

Grace my lovely one, for five voices (BM. Add. MSS 17786–89, 17791)
   The source, reproduced in facsimile in the prefatory section of MB23, can no longer be traced (see footnote, p. 17)
The Cries of London (BM. Add. MSS 18936–9, 29427, 37402–6)
Two Voluntaries, [for organ] (N.Y. Public Library, Drexel MS 5612)
Pavane, for keyboard (N.Y. Public Library, Drexel MS 5612)
Galliard, for keyboard (BM. Add. MS 30485)
Pavane [No. 1], for five viols (BM. Add. MSS 30826–8 and RCM. MS 2049)
Pavane [No. 2], for five viols (BM. Add. MSS 17786–9, 17791, and 17792–6)
[*Pavane* No. 3?]; three parts of an instrumental piece (RCM. MS 2049)
Lachrimae, for five viols (BM. Add. MSS 30480–4 and 30826–8)
[*Fantasia*] 'for 2 basses', for six viols (BM. Add. MSS 17786–91)
In nomine, for four viols (Bodleian MSS Mus. Sch. d212–6)
Two *In nomine*, for five viols (Bodleian MSS Mus. Sch. c64–9 and d212–6).

A fourth pavane for five viols is ascribed to Weelkes in BM. Add. MS 17792, but in the other four part-books of this set it is credited to [Richard] Micho. Since it occurs between two other pavanes unanimously assigned to Micho, Weelkes' authorship of it seems highly improbable. In style it seems to be spurious too, for it lacks the gravity of the authentic pavanes, being more short-breathed and restless.

Grace my lovely one, described in one source as 'Sir Francis Steward, his Canzonet', is in fact a very unremarkable ballet. Its second fa-la virtually cribs its opening from the first fa-la of Morley's *My bonny lass*, a source which had also served Weelkes for another ballet, *We shepherds sing*. Nevertheless, it was characteristic of Weelkes to relate the two fa-las through the long step-wise descent which is the backbone of both.

The Cries of London is an altogether more interesting piece. It exists in two forms, one of which is an expurgated version that has censored the somewhat hearty description of the missing mare. Which came first is impossible to determine, though the shorter one is notably more symmetrical, and it offers the preferable alternative when the two versions diverge for a couple of bars near the opening.[1] Weelkes splits the piece into five distinct sections, three substantial polyphonic sections in duple time being intersected by two shorter triple-time passages which incorporate popular (or pseudo-popular) melodies, simply harmonised. Deering, too, used this division in his *Cries*, though Gibbons set his throughout in duple-time polyphony. Weelkes differs from both in scoring his for only one voice – a treble. Most of the counterpoint is accomplished, though the greater complexity in parts of the final section leads to a few bumpy moments. Weelkes' taste for dissonance is indulged in some notable contrapuntal collisions and one blatantly unresolved suspension (at * in Example 70).

Ex. 70

Despite the very earthy incident of the lost mare, the work slips smoothly into a final 'Alleluia', thus emphasising the expressive neutrality of this archaic manner.

The two four-part *Voluntaries* for organ occur consecutively in their sole source, and Weelkes' name is attached only to the second one; nevertheless, everything about the style of the former suggests him as the composer. This is especially true of the opening (Example 71), which is

Ex. 71

---

[1] There are further significant differences between the two versions, one at the end of the first triple-time passage (two bars) and the other, a much more substantial one, in the central duple-time section, which acquires an extra half-dozen bars in the longer form.

very like the introductory organ bars to a number of the verse anthems (especially *Give the king thy judgements*). After the initial ten bars, this *Voluntary* settles down to meditate intently upon the same four-crotchet point for its remaining thirty or so bars, but the other *Voluntary* uses three distinct points successively, of which the last was a particular favourite with Weelkes (see Example 116*b*). From this he generates some thoroughly characteristic music which he builds to a simple but impressive climax. Both *Voluntaries* are brief and dignified, and raise regrets that Weelkes has not left us more pieces of the same type. Neither of the other two keyboard pieces, a *Pavane* and a *Galliard*, is elaborate, though the repetition of each of the three strains of the latter involves some rapid keyboard figurations. The *Pavane*, likewise in three sections, does not vary its repetitions. Its opening is worth quoting (Example 72), partly as a sample of its music, but also because it was wrongly transcribed in the printed edition.[1]

Ex. 72

The second strain of this *Pavane* is composed in an *alla breve* manner, and Weelkes applied this style throughout all three sections of his piece for five viols to which the name 'Lachrimae' is appended in both sources. Music in this manner can never be entirely ineffective, but the piece relies too heavily upon cadential formulae, and its five-voice texture is scarcely ever relieved by rests. The title 'Lachrimae' seems to have been wrongly assigned, for the piece bears no relation at all to Dowland's song, *Flow, my tears*. It is much more likely that *Pavane No. 1*, which follows it in one of the sources, should bear this heading, for not only does it open with the same melodic descent as Dowland's song, but the third section opens with a very close derivative from the corresponding section of the same song. Just as interesting is the obvious relationship of the whole of this third section to the central portion of Weelkes' own anthem, *Alleluia! I heard a voice* ('and to the Lamb for evermore'); this passage in the pavane sounds exactly like a preliminary sketch for the first six bars of the anthem's

---

[1] *Weelkes, Pieces for keyed instruments* (edited by Margaret Glyn). The editor stated that 'the first chord is obliterated in the MS', but it is nevertheless possible to discern enough to render a reasonably reliable version of the first one and a half bars.

middle section (Example 73). In style both this pavane and *Pavane No. 2* are restrained, but with ample evidence of Weelkes' liking for strong passing dissonance. This second pavane is a most accomplished piece

Ex. 73

a DOWLAND: Lacrimae

Hark, you sha — dows   that in dark — ness   dwell

b WEELKES: Pavane 1 *[transposed]*

c WEELKES: Alleluia!

and to   the Lamb for ev- er - more,   ev - - er - more

which, by opening its third strain with a brief variant of its first bars (Example 74), calls to mind the internal headmotif technique which Weelkes used in a number of his verse anthems (see below).

Ex. 74

a *[Opening]*

b *[Strain 3]*

Weelkes' only six-voice instrumental piece is a composition 'for 2 basses', a short piece which Reese described as 'a singularly eloquent and stately composition', confirming his high regard for the piece by printing it in its entirety in his monumental book on Renaissance music.[1] The remaining three viol compositions are all *In nomine* settings. One of these, a four-part setting, is preserved in a single source only, which is clearly unreliable, though it is sufficient to confirm the high degree of dissonance characteristic of Weelkes' viol music. Three quarters of the piece is made up of the most intensive working of a simple four-note point, but the

Ex. 75

result is an academic concentration which contrasts unfavourably with the freedom of the other two *In nomine* settings. Unlike the four-part setting, which had introduced the *cantus firmus* forthwith, both the five-part settings start with a set of imitative entries which precedes the appearance of the *cantus firmus*. One derives its point from the *cantus firmus* itself, though subsequently it passes to new material, and maintains the flow fairly continuously with much interchange of ideas between the four free parts. A characteristically Weelksian touch is the delay of the first entry of the bass voice until over a quarter of the way through the piece. Whereas the four-voice *In nomine* setting had built its climax through a contrived intensification of the rhythmic counterpoint, this work broadens into a more sustained, rather *alla breve* manner near the end, which emphasises Weelkes' expressive intent in this piece. The other five-voice *In nomine* setting is also very expressive—as the opening, with its extremely dissonant entries, attests (Example 75). Neither of these works has the melodic luxuriance of string compositions by Gibbons, but both are valuable additions to the treasury of early seventeenth-century consort music.

[1] G. Reese, *Music in the Renaissance*, p. 872.

IX. THE FULL ANTHEMS

One of the charms of Weelkes' madrigals is their certain chronology which provides a firm foundation for the study of their evolution. But as we turn to the church music, the narrative loses its ready-made order. It is not simply that we have no precise knowledge of the dates of composition of any of these pieces. Even if we knew exactly when each of them was written, it is very unlikely that their chronology would explain the wide, even bewildering variety of styles in the full anthems. Indeed, the innocent listener might well be tempted to question Weelkes' authorship of some of these anthems. Can three such different pieces as, say, *Lord, to Thee I make my moan, Laboravi in gemitu meo* and *Alleluia! I heard a voice* really be the work of the same man? Are the seemingly less characteristic anthems in general of lower quality than those which are more readily recognisable as his work? The answer to both these questions is quite definitely yes—yet it would be a mistake to interpret the great variety of these anthems as a sign of stylistic vacillation. Weelkes had not lost his creative direction, nor were his creative powers necessarily enfeebled; he was simply responding to the very broad demands which early seventeenth-century English society made upon the composer of church music.

The origins of this situation lie in the Reformation. Though it has become almost axiomatic to condemn the influence of the Reformation churchmen in England as basically bad for music, it is quite possible to challenge this judgement. Their immediate influence had drastic, even disastrous results, but in the long run their demands and pressures were to produce some very real benefits, though in ways they could never have foreseen, and certainly never intended. The aims of these early reformers were admirable in that they sought to bring God and his Word into the lives of ordinary people to a degree which had before only been enjoyed by the religious 'professionals'. The highly evolved, esoteric art of pre-Reformation polyphony had been music for initiates, and could have little to say to the less exclusive members of God's Church. The simplicity which was demanded of the new vernacular church music may ostensibly have been intended to ensure audibility of the text, but it was just as much a question of confirming[1] a musical language which could address

---

[1] It is important to note that simple, virtually syllabic examples of church music exist from pre-Reformation times, and that the more progressive composers on the Continent already knew this style well.

itself in sufficiently simple terms to the worshippers of the expanding middle classes. These classes were an ever-growing force to be reckoned with in Church and State, and this new, simpler type of church music was to be, at least in part, music for them. This fact was to be of immense importance for the whole future of English music, for works in this style came to serve not just as an ornament for public worship, but as an accompaniment to private devotions—and as a source of recreation. Through such music the new classes started to develop a taste for more sophisticated music, and also to acquire the necessary skill to perform such music for themselves. Without this preparation the English madrigal could never have proliferated as it did in the last years of the century.

In the study of church music itself, this 'secular' function has often been insufficiently weighed. It meant that 'church' music from the middle years of the sixteenth century had a quite independent and extensive existence outside the walls of the church. The elaborate polyphony of composers like Fayrfax and Taverner could never have served this extra-mural purpose, for it would have been technically and expressively beyond the grasp of all but a few; nor are there any signs of an alternative tradition of purely secular music strong enough to have stimulated and fed the incipient musical aspirations of the middle classes. Indeed, it is doubtful whether thoroughly secular music would have been acceptable to some sections of the community, for there was a strong strain of puritanism in English society at this time which bred a distrust of things of this world. At the same time, this puritanism ensured an extra engagement between religion and everyday life, and thus fostered further a demand for 'religious' music for private use. Its most tangible influence is to be traced in the long line of psalter publications which started *c*. 1548 with *Certain psalms . . . drawn into English metre* by Thomas Sternhold, and which were certainly not intended to furnish material for public worship, but were to serve an extra-liturgical purpose. Sternhold's psalter had no music, since the metrical jingles he provided were designed as substitutes for the less chaste lyrics of popular tunes of the day. Later psalters included their own music, and the development of Elizabethan musical literacy can be traced in the progressive musical complication and sophistication of successive publications.

It is equally important to remember that, while this new ground was being broken, the line of more highly evolved Latin church music still continued. The reformers had restricted but not stifled it, and it was still permissible to say and sing the service in Latin in the colleges of Oxford and Cambridge, Eton and Winchester, as well as in certain royal chapels; indeed, a Latin translation of the second Prayer Book was actually printed for their use in 1560.[1] The joint set of *Cantiones sacrae* which Tallis and Byrd published in 1575 is sufficient evidence that this highly evolved musical tradition was still alive, and was in fact still evolving, though the commercial failure of the volume is also proof enough that there was as yet no broad demand for elaborate music of this sort. By the end of the century things were very different. The raising of the level of Elizabethan musical taste, and the growing awareness of the attractions of continental styles enabled English composers to produce, and English performers to enjoy the hedonistic delights of the thoroughly secular madrigal. It was inevitable that this more sophisticated taste should make its demands upon music for worship, and should ensure a wide demand for more elaborate music for the Reformed Church. This music was striking, business-like, and quite as aware of the need to address man as to glorify God. Its musical quality could be first-rate, and the best anthems and Services of composers like Byrd, Weelkes, Gibbons and Tomkins could equal the achievements of pre-Reformation polyphony. English church music was now worthy of the attention of any musician in Europe.

Thus the early seventeenth-century English composer found himself in a situation highly favourable to the production of first-class church music, and Weelkes was to make full use of this. But the purpose of these preliminaries is also to emphasise the breadth of the demand for 'church' music, and the range of purpose for which it was composed—a range which is amply reflected in Weelkes' extant full anthems. During Weelkes' creative lifetime the demand for domestic 'church' music remained as strong as ever. Very simple pieces were still required by some circles, but others wanted more elaborate compositions, and many of the anthems composed for church use were also sung domestically. Certainly those who used such pieces were proof against the charge that we must face today—that we are prepared, Sunday after Sunday, to assail the Almighty with music we would never dream of using for our own entertainment. The English madrigal volumes contain a considerable number of works written upon paraphrases of texts drawn from the Bible (even occasionally upon the texts themselves), or else upon verse of high moral sentiment. Weelkes' own madrigal volumes contain no such pieces,[2] but among his manuscript 'full anthems' is a setting of *When David heard | O my son Absalom*, a text also set by both Tomkins and East, and published by them in their own madrigalian prints. This is a pointed reminder that Weelkes' manuscript works contain settings of religious texts which lie

[1] *Liber precum publicarum, seu ministerii ecclesiastice administrationis Sacramentorum, aliorumq[ue] rituum et ceremoniarum in Ecclesia Anglicana* [revised from the translation of A. Ales by Walter Haddon].

[2] We may discount the three elegies as being occasional pieces which were included in the volumes opportunely rather than by destination.

completely within the ambit of the madrigal. Indeed, in the case of a few pieces to be discussed, the term 'anthem' is really a misnomer. Nevertheless, for the sake of convenience, we will retain this term to cover all those works, either upon liturgical or biblical texts, or else expressing specifically Christian sentiments, which are not settings of canticles or other standard 'Service' texts.

After the orderly madrigal volumes, the extant sources for Weelkes' church music present a chaotic picture. With the exception of two pieces which Sir William Leighton printed in his *The Tears or lamentations of a sorrowful soul* (1614)—a volume undoubtedly designed to furnish sacred music for domestic use—none of it was published in Weelkes' own lifetime. All else that we still possess lies in various manuscripts which are themselves dispersed on both sides of the Atlantic. Many of these sources are defective, and sometimes between them can muster no more than a solitary part of a composition. The surviving traces of some other pieces are even more scanty—perhaps just a text recorded in some anthem book, or even nothing more than a title noted by some scholar working years ago in the field of English church music.[1] We cannot but grieve when we reflect upon all the other musical riches which must have perished without anything to record that they had ever been.

We have musical evidence of ten Services and some forty anthems. Of the Services, the only complete canticles are those for Mattins of the Short Service (No. 7); of the twenty-three verse anthems, only five are intact. It is a welcome surprise to find that the full anthems are in a far less imperfect state. Only one, surviving in a single voice part, is impossibly fragmentary[2], while thirteen are actually complete, and the remaining four may be convincingly reconstructed. It seems almost treacherous to open this closer examination of the full anthems by depriving Weelkes of

[1] In J. Clifford, *The Divine Services and anthems* (editions published in 1663 and 1664) there are texts of three otherwise unknown anthems by Weelkes:

Sing unto the Lord, O ye princes (1663 and 1664), evidently a full anthem

Let us lift up (1664), a verse anthem

Thy mercies great & manifold (1664), evidently a full anthem.

E. F. Rimbault listed the titles of three other anthems by Weelkes in *Musical Antiquarian Society*, vol. 8, II, 1843, namely:

Behold, how good and joyful

O Lord, preserve thee

O Lord, rebuke me not (see below, p. 145, footnote).

M. Foster, in *Anthems and anthem composers*, p. 45, gives the title of yet another anthem by Weelkes:

With all our hearts.

This, he claimed, was to be found in 'John S. Bumpus's unique collection, mostly MSS, in the composers' autograph'. In fact, this piece was probably by Tallis.

The surviving bass part of the First Service states that the anthem to be sung with this Service is *Thou art my portion, O Lord*. This also has not survived.

[2] *Teach me, O Lord.*

credit for one of 'his' most famous compositions. It is nevertheless inescapable that *Let Thy merciful ears* is not his work at all. Fellowes evidently assumed, without any authority, that, since it followed hard upon Weelkes' Short Service in Peterhouse sources, this unattributed anthem was also by Weelkes, but in sources in York Minster, Durham Cathedral and the British Museum it is positively ascribed to Mudd. Of the other full anthems, two also are probably not his work. One, a four-voice setting of *O Absalom my son*,[1] seems unlikely to be Weelkes' work unless it was a very early attempt at treating this text; the other, *Deliver us, O Lord our God*, is a more difficult case to which we will return in due course.[2]

There is no evidence which establishes either the dates of composition of these pieces, or their chronology. Stylistic analysis cannot help and, as for the sources in which the anthems are preserved, they can provide little evidence, since most of them were compiled after Weelkes' death. Nevertheless, these do give a few pointers to the latest date at which certain of these anthems could have been composed. It will be easiest if the sources[3] and anthems concerned are tabulated:

Tenbury MSS 807–11, compiled *c.* 1610
 Gloria in excelsis Deo. Sing, my soul, to God

[1] This is attributed to Weelkes in the list of contents of the only source (RM 23.1.4, the Cosyn Virginal Book, preserved in the British Museum); the piece itself has no name attached to it. Presumably the scribe knew of Weelkes' setting of the text, and assumed this version to be his work. Despite its restraint, this is a setting upon which many a minor composer of the time might have looked with some satisfaction.

[2] In addition to these works of doubtful authorship, there is a five-voice setting of *O Lord, rebuke me not* which Peter le Huray has tentatively suggested to be Weelkes' work. As Dr. le Huray put it in the note which he provided on this work for the *Musica Britannica* edition of Weelkes' anthems: 'There are six early seventeenth century settings of the text. Five of the composers are known: Browne, the younger Bullis, Byrd, Child and Tomkins. It may well be that the sixth composer is Weelkes. There are two sources of this anthem: BM Add. MSS 17792–7, and N.Y. Public Library, Drexel MSS 4180–5, two closely related MSS. In both sets of books *O Lord, rebuke me not* is the second anthem of a group of three; the first anthem, *All people*, is ascribed to Weelkes in the New York books, but is anonymous in those of the British Museum; the third anthem is *Christ rising*—anonymous in both sources, but ascribed elsewhere to the Salisbury musician, Edmund Tucker.

'The contents of many early seventeenth-century sources are arranged in a rough geographical manner. It is possible, therefore, that *O Lord, rebuke me not* is also by a musician who was living in the Salisbury/Winchester area, since it lies between anthems by Weelkes and by Tucker. In style and technique *O Lord, rebuke me not* is not unworthy of a musician of Weelkes' calibre.' Weelkes' authorship is also supported by the rich treatment of dissonance and the appearance, at the opening of the second section, of several bars very similar to the central section of *Alleluia! I heard a voice* and the third strain of the instrumental *Pavane* [*No. 1*]. Nevertheless, the dissonance treatment is sometimes rough, and if it is indeed Weelkes' work, it seems likely to be an early piece. It falls into four self-contained sections, of which the middle two are notably brief.

[3] All the information on the dates and provenance of the MS sources is drawn from P. le Huray, 'Towards a definitive study of pre-Restoration Anglican Service music' (*Musica Disciplina* XIV (1960), pp. 167 ff.).

Hosanna to the Son of David
Laboravi in gemitu meo
When David heard | O my son Absalom
Sir Wm. Leighton, *The Tears or lamentations of a sorrowful soul* (1614)[1]
O happy he
Most mighty and all-knowing Lord
BM. Add. MSS 29372–7 (*Tristitiae remedium*, a manuscript collection compiled in 1616 by Thomas Myrriell)[2]
Alleluia! I heard a voice
O Jonathan
Tenbury MS 1382 (1617)
O Lord, arise into Thy resting place.

One other full anthem, the doubtful *Deliver us, O Lord our God*, exists only in a later set of part-books, but appears to be dated the most precisely of all: '9th March, 1617' (*sc.* 1618). In fact, this is almost certainly not the date of composition (see below, pp. 152–3).

There is no full anthem which we can confidently say was composed *after* a certain year. It would be dangerous to suppose that a work which refers to 'the king' must necessarily have been written after the death of Elizabeth in 1603, since it was customary to alter the text of an anthem to accord with the title or name of the reigning sovereign. Weelkes' own *O Lord God almighty* survives only in sources which list the principal members of the royal family as 'King Charles, our gracious Queen Mary, our/and Prince Charles'. This version must have been made after 1630, the year in which Charles I's eldest son, the future Charles II, was born. Nevertheless, one wonders just how Weelkes would have contrived a comparable list of royalty if he had composed this piece with Elizabeth in mind.

The dual function of much church music of this period has already been emphasised, and the sources do offer some evidence of the purpose for which certain of Weelkes' full anthems were composed. The extant manuscripts may be divided into two categories,[3] with 'liturgical' sources –choir part-books and organ books–comprising one, and 'secular' sources the other. The first category takes in manuscripts which were compiled to meet the needs of cathedral and chapel choirs; such manuscripts contain not only anthems but also Service music–canticles, festal psalms, and so on. The 'secular' sources lack such essentially liturgical music, but may

[1] The texts of the pieces in Leighton's publication had been issued a year before in 1613; presumably the music to set them had been composed by then.

[2] It is possible that this Thomas Myrriell is identical with the man who was appointed precentor of Chichester Cathedral on 11th April, 1613, and who remained there until his death in 1629. He would therefore have known Weelkes well.

[3] See P. le Huray, *op. cit.*

include madrigals and other secular pieces alongside anthems. Such anthologies seem to have been compiled to satisfy the needs of a musical amateur or a group of enthusiasts. A study of how the surviving parts of each anthem by Weelkes are dispersed among the sources should therefore give at least some idea of whether any particular work was specifically liturgical, specifically domestic, or dual purpose.[1] It comes as no surprise to discover that *O Jonathan* and *When David heard | O my son Absalom* survive only in secular sources; this exclusiveness is the more significant, since all three pieces are extant in numerous different manuscripts. The sources also confirm that Weelkes' two full anthems which set texts praying for the sovereign were specifically liturgical works; both *O Lord, grant the king a long life* and *O Lord God almighty* also exist in several sources, but all of these are choir books. The remaining full anthems survive mostly in both liturgical and secular sources; in practice most of Weelkes' full anthems clearly served, or came to serve, a dual purpose.

Before examining the music, a word about the texts Weelkes used for his full anthems. Most are in prose, and were selected from a wide range of sources. There is the expected crop of Psalm extracts (of which only one is metrical), but as many are drawn from other sources, mainly biblical. One anthem sets a Collect; two other metrical texts have not been identified.

Since they cannot really be considered anthems at all, it will avoid confusion if we discuss *Most mighty and all-knowing Lord, O Jonathan* and *When David heard | O my son Absalom* first, before examining those anthems which are wholly or at least partly liturgical. The first of these is one of Weelkes' two contributions to Leighton's volume of 1614, where it appears among the songs 'of 4 parts with voices'. This placing is confusing; it must surely belong with the 'Consort songs', since it shows every sign of being in the direct line of the viol-accompanied solo song.[2] Only one voice part is texted throughout, and this uses no verbal repetition; the other parts have nothing beyond an incipit, though four of the five verses are printed below each part. Any attempt to deploy the text throughout these parts involves verbal repetition and awkward underlay. In common with the usual practice of the viol-accompanied song, the texted voice is the last to enter, and has rest groups between its separate phrases, while the other voices flow on without break. Imitation is focused

---

[1] It must be borne in mind that when, during the Commonwealth, there was a wholesale destruction of church music sources, it was naturally the books in use in church services which would have suffered more than books in private possession. The fact that a work exists largely or even exclusively in secular sources does not therefore mean it was not used also in church services.

[2] Nevertheless, the text of *Most mighty and all-knowing Lord* was printed in J. Clifford, *The Divine Services and anthems* (1664).

mainly in the upper parts, and the final area of the piece exhibits the greatest rhythmic activity. The neutral expressive tone confirms the archaic ancestry of this piece. Musically it is quite unremarkable.

O Jonathan and *When David heard / O my son Absalom* may be considered as sacred madrigals, in that their subject matter is biblical, but their musical treatment thoroughly madrigalian. Their expressive ancestry is far more Italian than English, and neither their musical manner nor, indeed, their texts would have readily commended them for use in an act of worship.[1] The expressive ambitions of *O Jonathan* are unmistakable, yet though its first two bars (Example 76) depict broken-voiced sorrow

Ex. 76

most graphically through staggered entries (similar in principle, but utterly different in effect from the *pointilliste* incidents in some of his madrigals), and though some of the succeeding music achieves high pathos, the conclusion ('passing the love of women') hardly fulfils the expectations roused by the opening. Weelkes manages the closing passage much better in *When David heard / O my son Absalom*. In addition to the four-voice setting attributed to Weelkes in the Cosyn Virginal Book, there are two printed settings of this text by English composers of this period.[2] Tomkins made one, and dedicated it to Thomas Myrriell, who included it in his *Tristitiae remedium* of 1616; six years later Tomkins himself was to incorporate it into his single volume of madrigals. Michael East was the other composer, publishing his version (which sounds as though it had knowledge of Weelkes' setting) in his *The Fourth set of books* of 1618. From the greater number of sources in which the lament itself (*O my son Absalom*) is preserved, we may gather that it was this half of Weelkes' composition which especially struck his early hearers, just as it may still impress us today, for the conclusion of Weelkes' setting is one of the

[1] Yet it must be noted that Tomkins' *When David heard / O my son Absalom* was to be printed in his posthumously published collection of anthems and Service music, *Musica Deo sacra* (1668).

[2] Settings of the same text by Bearsley, Milton and Ramsey also survive in manuscript collections.

most remarkable passages to be found anywhere in his work. Weelkes' extraordinary imaginative powers are nowhere more strikingly displayed than in this disjointed, silence-laden texture (Example 77); again we may note its kinship to his madrigalian *pointillism*, though the effect could not be more dissimilar. Tomkins' setting is more fully polyphonic, employing broad sustained lines of lamentation, contrasted with syncopated sobbing passages. Tomkins makes his points with expressive breadth, and achieves a powerfully contrapuntal climax; Weelkes is succinct and dramatic. By

Ex. 77

comparison East's setting seems prolix, having neither the rich intensity of Tomkins' broad lament, nor the swift forcefulness of Weelkes' response to the text.

Weelkes' true full anthems defy neat classification, though it is possible to discern certain basic types. There are simple ones which would have been especially apt for domestic performance, not merely because of their humble expressive and technical demands, but also because many of their texts are personal and penitential, reflecting upon the unworthiness of the sinner and the abundant mercy of God. Their music mingles sections of quite plain homophony with passages of simple polyphony, freely laced with the dissonances common in English music of the preceding century. Their restrained manner is the very opposite to that of the sacred madrigals. These simple anthems are the most traditionally English of all Weelkes' works, and their ancestry is readily traceable back to the earliest music of the Reformed Church; indeed, there is little or nothing in some of these pieces which could not have been composed half a century earlier.

At the other extreme are the 'festive' anthems—pieces which have a great sense of occasion, rejoice in textural sonority, and demand a substantial and highly skilled body of singers to do them justice. Some of Weelkes' festive anthems exploit a fully contrapuntal technique and, although filled with all the grandeur of the finest early seventeenth-century English church music, such pieces also stem from an older polyphonic manner, and show a more archaic treatment of dissonance. It is significant that these pieces show no convincing signs of internal structural relationships. In this they differ completely from some of Weelkes' other festive anthems, which have greater conciseness, a wider range of textural types, and a more selfconscious exploitation of brilliant sound.

Of all the full anthems, *Rejoice in the Lord* is the simplest. From the organ score and two surviving voice parts it is quite possible to make a convincing reconstruction of the whole piece, which appears to be for four voices. It sets the joyful text in a singularly unjoyful manner which could not outrage even the most tender sense of religious propriety. Its incomplete state is a matter for only qualified regret; it is the most innocuous—and the dullest—of the full anthems. A similarly negative impression is afforded by the opening bars of *O happy he*, but after the neutral start the piece improves sharply, and the final section creates a firm impression through its intensive imitation and more dissonant harmonic language. Weelkes reinforces the expressive restraint with something of the solidity of his more splendid anthems, and the result is a piece which is modest yet firm.

Lord, to Thee I make my moan is more positive still, partly because it is a somewhat longer piece, but also because the extra expansion encourages a gentle use of internal cross-references which give the whole a more precise focus. It has three clear sections and there is a close relationship between the openings of the second and third sections (Example 78*a*, *c* and *e*); each section then passes into a contrapuntal passage founded upon related points (Example 78*b*, *d* and *f*). Weelkes works the last of these with characteristic expansiveness after a quite beautiful melismatic effusion at 'my request'. Within its voluntary limitations this is quite a pleasant piece.

As a model for his five-voice anthem, *O mortal man*, Weelkes took a primitive four-voice piece of Scottish origin, setting the same text, and composed by about 1580;[1] it afforded Weelkes his 'canzonet' structure, as well as most of his thematic material. Example 79 suggests that Weelkes also took his cue for diminution in the central section from the rather curious acceleration of note values in the Scottish setting, though sudden little convulsions of this sort appear, sometimes rather uncomfortably, in a number of his verse anthems. Yet the most instructive comparison can be made between the final sections, for Weelkes takes the rhythmic structure

---

[1] Printed in *Music of Scotland 1500–1700*, edit. K. Elliott and H. M. Shire (published as *Musica Britannica*, vol. 15), p. 161. The earliest source listed for this piece is *The Art of Music collected out of all ancient doctors of music* [c. 1580], now in B.M. Add. MS 4911.

of the melodic point of the Scottish setting (Example 80*g*), but applies it to the contour of his opening point (*a*), concluding with another point which is the same as Example 80*d* (there is no corresponding point in the Scottish setting). Thus Weelkes establishes a ternary scheme completely absent in the model.[1]

Ex. 78

O mortal man concludes with a fine Amen; so, too, does *O Lord God almighty*—an even longer and finer Amen, as far as can be judged from the imperfect musical remains of this Collect setting. This anthem appears to be for five voices and, being a fully liturgical work, avails itself of the possibilities of antiphony between the *cantoris* and *decani* sides of the choir. As a whole it lacks the cohesion and arresting rhythmic changes of *O mortal man*, although the considerable breadth of certain sections is admirable (notably the broad simple arch of 'through Jesus Christ our Lord', and the Amen).

Self-quotation was a favoured practice of Weelkes. A few instances have already been noted in the madrigals, and it occurs more frequently

[1] The fact that bars 40–43 of Weelkes' *O mortal man* turn up in a slight re-arrangement in the second fa-la of *Now is my Cloris* in the *Ballets and madrigals* of 1598 must raise the question: was the anthem in fact composed before 1598? It seems as probable that the use of this particular thematic point in *O mortal man* may have recalled to Weelkes his application of it in his ballet, and he resolved to adapt the fa-la to a new context.

in some of the anthems. It is even more frequent to find such relationships between Services and anthems, and there will be a good deal to say of this in due course. Momentary coincidences with other passages in Weelkes' own works occur in both *O mortal man* and *O Lord God almighty*,[1]

Ex. 79

a SCOTTISH VERSION

[Beseikand ay his hev'nlie majestie with force to fight against the flesh]

b WEELKES

[Beseeching aye His heavenly Majesty Of faith and force to fight against the flesh]

but there seems to be an especially close relationship between *O how amiable* and *Deliver us, O Lord our God,* for in one place they virtually share four and a half bars,[2] employ elsewhere a mutual set of entries on essentially the same point,[3] and in yet another section the two works have material in common.[4] This might cause some hesitation in denying Weelkes the authorship of *Deliver us, O Lord our God* but, in view of the regularly accepted practice of borrowing ideas from other composers, it does not really weaken the claim of William Cox to be the composer of

[1] Compare *When David heard,* bars 39–40 with *O Lord God almighty,* bars 33–34 and 37–38. The same brief passage is to be found in both the *Magnificat* and *Nunc dimittis* of the Second Service.

[2] Compare *O how amiable,* bars 32–34 and 35–38 with *Deliver us, O Lord,* bars 42–44 and 45–47.

[3] Compare *O how amiable,* bars 21–25 with *Deliver us, O Lord,* bars 13–17. Unfortunately the imperfect state of *Deliver us, O Lord* makes it impossible to assert an absolute identity, but the third entry in *O how amiable* fits perfectly into the incomplete texture of *Deliver us, O Lord* (this means delaying by one bar the entry of the reconstructed alto part offered in bars 14 ff. of this anthem in MB23, p. 12).

[4] Compare 'Blessed is the man that puttest his trust in Thee' in *O how amiable* with the Amen of *Deliver us, O Lord.*

Ex. 80

this anthem. The uncertainty over the authorship of *Deliver us, O Lord* arises from the inscription in the sole surviving source: ' "5 p[ar]ts. Mr Will: Cox. his Anthem. Thomas Weelkes. 9 March. 1617".'[1] This William Cox was probably identical with one of the canons of Chichester Cathedral, who may in turn have been the chorister who was admitted into the Cathedral choir in 1582, and who was replaced in 1588. The inventory of the cathedral music books, taken in 1621, lists 'Mr. Wm. Cox his anthem', and also discloses that Weelkes had copied music for the cathedral. These may be the crucial clues. Probably Weelkes was commissioned to make a copy of Cox's anthem; having completed the work he signed and dated it as a record of work done. John Barnard, whose part-books are the only surviving source for this anthem, later copied not only the music but also the subscription, and thus caused our present confusion. The quality of the piece does nothing to settle the question of authorship, since it is quite unremarkable and could well be the work of a second-rank composer.[2]

This anthem raises a problem of performance. Just before the final Amen, a four-bar 'Verse' is interpolated. Unlike the two brief solos for a male voice in Weelkes' own *Alleluia! I heard a voice*, this solo in *Deliver us, O Lord our God* cannot be made to sound convincing as it stands, for

[1] Only four voice parts survive (although one of them divides in the Amen to make a five-voice texture).

[2] It is perhaps worth observing the similarity to Gibbons' setting of the same text at the opening of the second half: 'Blessed be the Lord God of Israel'.

it is obviously an harmonic bass part. Since one voice is missing from the source, this section could be a duet, though it is difficult to imagine this sounding convincing. It seems more likely that the singer was co-operating on the bass line with an obligatory organ part, and that this particular 'a capella' anthem could not be performed without organ accompaniment.

O how amiable requires little comment. It is a good piece which reserves its finest musical moment until the Amen. Both *Deliver us, O Lord our God* and *O how amiable* have approached more closely a polyphonic manner, not only in their fully imitative openings, but in their more consistently maintained contrapuntal progress. Nevertheless, their style still seems to be essentially an elaboration of the simple contrapuntal manner of the earlier music for the Reformed Church; on the other hand, the contrapuntal manner of *Laboravi in gemitu meo* stems from the broader, more truly polyphonic technique of the continuing tradition of Latin church music. There is no question of mere pastiche, for Weelkes has fertilised the technique with something of the intense expressive response to the text characteristic of some of his finest madrigals. The texture created by the five extant parts of Weelkes' setting is clearly incomplete, and the fact that his thematic material is modelled upon that which Morley had devised for *his* six-voice setting of the same text encourages the opinion that Weelkes' *Laboravi* is likewise for six voices. Weelkes follows Morley's example in splitting each complete phrase of text into fragments of one or two words only and allocating a clear point to each, so that each section may be wrought from two or even three different thematic ideas used simultaneously. The result is variety combined with thematic concentration. If nothing of Weelkes' church music so far discussed has raised the same sort of enthusiasm as the best of the madrigals, *Laboravi* certainly does. Its conservative technique, as well as the conditions created by its relationship to an earlier setting, would not have encouraged the use of techniques which integrate the structure, and there are no convincing signs of any in this work.

Laboravi is Weelkes' only setting of a complete Latin text. This, coupled to the parodistic features of the melodic material and the conservative basis of the style, favours the view that it was Weelkes' B.Mus. exercise and was therefore composed in 1602. Its display of skill in tackling the older compositional discipline might be designed to commend it to the academic mind, and its re-working of material which Morley had already used most splendidly might be a deliberate demonstration that Weelkes could handle this material as profitably as the older composer. Yet the differences are more revealing than the similarities. Morley's texture is finer and constantly changing; compared to Weelkes' more

consistently dense web, it sounds almost delicate. The expressive tempera-
ture of Weelkes' setting is higher than Morley's, the growth of the opening
paragraph is more deliberate and massive, and the treatment of 'lacrimis
meis' is more dissonantly affective than Morley's tender pathos.

Among Weelkes' anthems the natural companion to *Laboravi* is *O
Lord, arise into Thy resting place*, the first work of his we have so far
encountered for as many as seven voices. Like *Laboravi*, it is fully polyphonic. It employs its broad, distinctive points to generate strong yet
concentrated polyphonic paragraphs which cumulate seamlessly into a
massive final 'Alleluia', as grand and richly detailed a conclusion as any
anthem could wish to have. Like *Laboravi* it has tangible relationships
with a work by another composer. This time it is Tomkins' *O sing unto
the Lord* (also for seven voices); unfortunately there is no way of knowing
who was the creditor and who the debtor, since the earliest source of both
anthems is the same. Tomkins employs exactly the same series of initial
entries as Weelkes, though his version of the point is less clearly profiled;
his setting reflects the same repeated plagal progression at the end of the
first paragraph,[1] and some of his other melodic material seems to be related to points in *O Lord, arise* (Example 81). In their final 'alleluia'

Ex. 81

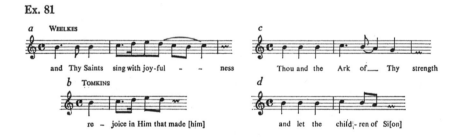

sections the two works draw together again. Tomkins opens his with the
same point as Weelkes (but with an extra initial note), and for some half
dozen bars proceeds quite differently; then the two settings slip into
parallel, and one 'alleluia' becomes largely a parody of the other (Example
82). Tomkins' *O sing unto the Lord* is a splendid piece, but Weelkes' *O
Lord, arise* is even finer, except perhaps in the final 'alleluia', where
Tomkins is Weelkes' peer (though Weelkes' stronger contrapuntal proclivities are fully extended to produce a particularly impressive final page).

O Lord, arise makes less simultaneous use than *Laboravi* of two or
more points to raise a contrapuntal paragraph (though there is a notable
exception in the setting of 'Save Thy people, good Lord / and bless

[1] Compare *O Lord, arise*, bars 11–13 with *O sing unto the Lord*, bars 17–19.

Thine inheritance'). For all their common contrapuntal outlook, these two works are expressively poles apart. A meditative mysticism breathes through the undulating melismas of the Latin setting; *O Lord, arise* has tauter, more syllabic lines and a more strongly measured pulse which

Ex. 82

Skeleton of parody

a WEELKES

generate a majestic extroversion. Here, as in Byrd's best English anthems, the streams of Latin and English church music have converged.

Weelkes' remaining five full anthems may also be classed as festive anthems, although the consistent contrapuntal manner of *O Lord, arise* is not employed throughout, and two of them are barely half the length of that work. *O Lord, grant the king a long life* is the only other of Weelkes' full anthems for seven voices. Structurally it has three main divisions, the first two opening with a quasi-homophonic passage leading into imitative sections founded upon related points (Example 83). The concluding division draws the end of the text and the Amen (a truly splendid one) into one broad unit.

Ex. 83

a

that his years may en – dure

b

that they may pre – serve [him]

Of the other four full anthems, three incorporate a Latin acclamation as well as an English text, opening with the acclamation and later repeating the Latin fragment to identical or related music. Two, *Gloria in excelsis Deo! Sing, my soul, to God the Lord* and *Alleluia! I heard a voice* are frank ternary structures. The former, for six voices, employs two identical settings of 'Gloria in excelsis Deo' as flanks to the English-texted centre. The counterpoint is close-knit, and there is a marked kinship between certain of the thematic points (Example 84). The most striking single

Ex. 84

a

in ex – cel – sis De – – o

b

Lay the an-gels' choir a[broad]

c

in their high – est ho-ly day

d

un-to praise's high – – – – [est part]

moment in the piece is provoked by 'to tune [thy heart]' which Weelkes treats to a simple chromatic progression which is as apt musically as it is symbolically (Example 85). The whole anthem is a brilliant and vigorous paean of praise, after which the sustained Amen comes as a most heart-easing contrast.

Ex. 85

[Crave thy God to tune thy heart]

The Amen of *All people, clap your hands* serves a completely different purpose—not to contrast, but to summarise. This anthem has a number of passages seemingly related to incidents in other works by Weelkes, but, despite its 'patchwork' appearance, it is a convincing piece. The anthem has two clear (and rather similar) homophonic moments, one at the opening and the other halfway through, and each is followed by two contrapuntal sections. These two halves are drawn together in the Amen, which is founded very overtly upon two preceding incidents, one from each half of the anthem (Example 86).

Ex. 86

[Praise the Lord with harp]   [sing loud unto the Lord with a joyful voice]

[Amen]

A similar procedure is used in *Alleluia! I heard a voice*. This five-voice anthem, like *Gloria in excelsis Deo!*, is a ternary structure and the main portion of the English-texted centre is a broad contrapuntal paragraph upon a vigorous point (Example 87*a*). At the very end, after the due repetition of the 'alleluia' paragraph, Weelkes prolongs this section, passing finally into a short coda employing a compressed version of this point (Example 87*b*).

Ex. 87

a

and to the Lamb for ev - er – more

b

al – le - lu - i - - ia!

Alleluia! is especially notable for its harmonic purposefulness. In *Gloria in excelsis Deo!* the harmonic vocabulary of the acclamation paragraph had been constricted to centre around the tonic A; in *Alleluia!* the acclamation is deployed upon a series of cadences mostly a fifth apart (D–A–D–G–C, A–D), thus gaining a far greater sense of purposeful progress. The same forward progress is continued in the English-texted centre; indeed, the setting of 'and to the Lamb for evermore' follows exactly the greater part of the same harmonic course (D–G–C–A–D) as the 'alleluia' which precedes and follows it. *Alleluia!* is the most singleminded of all Weelkes' full anthems.

The most notable single incident in this anthem is the introduction, which combines a bass solo with impatient alleluias which can scarcely contain their compulsion to praise until the appointed moment. Even their 'official' eruption in bar 7 is premature, overlapping the end of the bass solo; it is a tiny detail, telling out of all proportion to its simplicity (Example 88).

Alleluia! is unique among all the anthems of this period in that it exists both as a full and as a verse anthem. The latter version survives in sources in Durham Cathedral, which date from well after Weelkes' death. On purely musical grounds it seems doubtful that this version was ever Weelkes' real intention for the piece, even though the opening bass solo sounds more normal when accompanied by the organ. In performance the verse version is less effective, for the organ part demands a more discreet pace than the music will permit if its full joy is to be realised. But against this must be set the use of a dozen bars of the 'Alleluia' paragraph as part of the Gloria of *Nunc dimittis* in the Fourth Service, which is a verse

Ex. 88

Service with obligatory organ part. The question of which version is the original is therefore wide open.

Hosanna to the Son of David differs from both *Gloria in excelsis Deo!* and *Alleluia! I heard a voice* in placing its acclamation 'hosanna' not only at the beginning and end, but also in the centre. Nor are the musical repetitions exact in this anthem; instead Weelkes employs a single clear harmonic progression (Example 89) as a foundation for each acclamation, treating it to a different contrapuntal network on each appearance. The procedure is a further development of the 'ritornello' technique employed in the madrigal *Like two proud armies*; the harmonic foundation is the

Ex. 89

same in both madrigal and anthem. The rest of the work is magnificently exultant, offering some of the most close-knit counterpoint to be found anywhere in Weelkes' work. A comparison with Gibbons' more expansively contrapuntal setting (also for six voices) does much to clarify the difference in character between the two composers.

As noted at the beginning of this chapter, the listener who reviews the whole list of Weelkes' full anthems must be struck by the range of these works. In counterpoint alone there is the broad polyphony of *Laboravi in gemitu meo* on the one hand, and the intensive, virile counterpoint of *Hosanna to the Son of David* on the other. There are polyphonic works which follow Renaissance precedent by deploying a succession of paragraphs related only through the logic of the text; there are integrated works which contrive inner musical relationships with a variety of intensity and by a variety of means. There are simple homely pieces and majestic festive pieces. But the best of the full anthems—works like *O Lord, arise, Alleluia! I heard a voice, Gloria in excelsis Deo!* and *Hosanna to the Son of David*—are easily recognisable as products of the same mind that had fashioned the great madrigals of 1600.

X. THE VERSE ANTHEMS

Weelkes' verse anthems have been the most sadly neglected of all his works. Even Fellowes, in the six pages he devoted to Weelkes' Services and anthems in his book on English church music,[1] never breathed one hint that he ever wrote a single verse anthem. In fact, not only are there musical remains of more verse anthems by Weelkes than by either Byrd or Gibbons, but they actually exceed in number Weelkes' own full anthems—twenty-three verse anthems (four of these make up two pairs) as against fourteen or fifteen full anthems.[2] To be fair, only five of these twenty-three are complete, and the majority are so fragmentary that no more than a partial idea of their full effect may be gained. This has discouraged the potential performer from investigating these works, but the scholar may find their remains very illuminating. Even though four exist as only one, two or three voice parts, these sparse fragments may afford information about the proportions and certain structural features of these works; still more ample intelligence upon such matters is yielded by the organ scores of eleven others (one of these also has the imperfect remains of its vocal parts). These fifteen anthems are too fragmentary for any authoritative reconstruction of their missing parts to be made, but this exercise is both possible and profitable in the case of a further three.

Eight, therefore, are complete or may be restored with fair reliability, and these will require more individual attention. As for the rest, there is little point in attempting separate examination of these. To be honest, we do not appear to have suffered any very great artistic loss in the imperfect state of some, but at least we should look at some of the more general features of both complete and incomplete works. It will also be profitable to broaden the examination and contrast Weelkes' attitudes and practices with those of Byrd and Gibbons. Such a comparative study reveals that in certain respects, especially in the vocal style of the soloists, Weelkes' verse anthems are strongly conservative; in other features, notably in matters of structure, they are strongly progressive.

[1] *English cathedral music from Edward VI to Edward VII*, pp. 93–99. On pp. 88–89 Fellowes observed that the work of Weelkes and others of the time 'seems to show that the drift towards the verse anthem did not become pronounced for another fifteen or twenty years'. It is rather a shattering fact that not a single verse anthem by Weelkes was ever printed until 1966.

[2] This reckoning discounts the sacred madrigals, *O Jonathan* and *When David heard | O my son Absalom*, and the consort song, *Most mighty and all-knowing Lord*.

Only one of Weelkes' verse anthems, *An earthly tree*, is structurally of the older 'transitional' type. Although it survives solely as an organ score, there can be little doubt that it sets the same text that Byrd had once treated, for it is designed as a single large verse 'for two counters [i.e. countertenors]' with chorus, all to be performed '3 times over'. Byrd had printed his setting (with a chorus, *Cast off all doubtful care*) in his *Songs of sundry natures* (1589), and had described it as a 'carol'—that is, a number of verses which alternate with a choral burden. There is no feeling of any musical interdependence between verse and chorus, and their musical conjunction seems fortuitous. But if Byrd's *An earthly tree | Cast off all doubtful care* and its companion in this volume, *From Virgin pure | Rejoice*,[1] are transitional pieces, the third verse anthem in the *Songs of sundry natures*, namely *Christ rising | Christ is risen*, is a fully developed example of the form. The essence of the true verse anthem is the intimate and integral collaboration of verse and chorus to form the piece. To use the chemical analogy: it is not a mixture, but a compound. Byrd's *Christ rising | Christ is risen* is just such a fully compounded specimen. Some choruses do simply maintain the musical progress with new material which sets the next piece of text, but there is a very real sense of musical continuity. Other choruses virtually repeat the end of the preceding verse, or take over material from the verse to elaborate it into a further extensive paragraph, and there is a firm grasp of the effectiveness of verse-chorus alternation, and of welding verse and chorus together. Such a work demonstrates that, years before Weelkes started composing, the verse anthem was a fully evolved form.

In due course we will pursue further the examination of structural matters. But first we should pause to consider the style of the verse sections, for the phenomenon of a solo vocal line or lines, accompanied by an independent instrumental part, is something we have not before encountered in Weelkes' work, except in his brief consort song, *Most mighty and all-knowing Lord*, and his *Cries of London*. In the choruses of the verse anthem the role of the organ (or, alternatively, a consort of viols) was merely to double the voice parts, but in the verses it provided a quite independent though undemonstrative accompaniment to the soloist(s). Early seventeenth-century organ scores were not usually written out in full; they offered consistently the top and bottom of the music, but gave only fragmentary indications of important inner parts, such as sections of the part(s) for the solo voice(s) in the verses, important leads in the choruses, or parts which had to be shown to obviate

---

[1] In this composition (for a solo voice) there is a brief thematic relationship between verse and chorus, but this is not a relationship really strong enough to counter their essential irrelation.

incompatibility between the vocal lines and the organist's filling-out of his part.

There is no need to comment further on the organ's role, but the matter of the solo vocal style requires a more detailed examination. One of the areas of musical activity in which the Englishman of about 1600 must have been aware of rapid developments was that of solo singing. For generations England had produced splendid choral singers, a fact well recognised on the Continent, but there is nothing to suggest that we had any comparable soloists. The typical solo vocal line of Elizabethan music delivered the text deliberately, even stolidly; the range of the line was small, and the whole effect cautious. However, the cultivation of the lute song during the early seventeenth century was perhaps both an effect and, in its turn, a cause of greater skill in the art of solo singing in this country. This higher accomplishment must surely be behind the elaborate vocal scoring and the expert, flexible declamation of many of Gibbons' verse anthems. Byrd had been content to use no more than two soloists in his verse anthems, but Gibbons, whose verse anthems all belong to the first quarter of the seventeenth century, used a great variety of vocal scoring in his verses, which may freely employ anything from one to six soloists (one actually uses eight).

Likewise, many of Gibbons' verse sections are composed in a declamatory vocal style demanding expert soloists, while Byrd adhered to the older, more restrained manner. Byrd may have composed his verse anthems before this new vocal situation matured; in any case, as an older composer, he was likely to retain habits which he had long practised. His solo melodic manner was broad and measured, with variety provided by varying his usual duple metre with triple rhythm (as Weelkes does in Example 91). In the later verses of his verse anthems, there is sometimes a trend towards a greater rhythmic movement, and the final duet of *Christ is risen* is thoroughly declamatory, though without the plasticity which Gibbons achieved in his very best declamations—for instance, the solos of *Behold, Thou hast made my days* or *This is the record of John*. Some of the solos in Gibbon's other verse anthems do apply Byrd's rather heavy delivery, but in these two anthems he consistently uses a livelier pace approaching more closely that of real speech. Quavers abound in the lines and, since it is the sound of the words themselves that have done so much to make the vocal line what it is, the singer can make the words effective in a way impossible with Byrd's more spacious delivery. Often Gibbons' imagination will fasten upon a brief arresting phrase which he will then repeat sequentially so that the detail haunts the memory long after the anthem is done (Example 90). Indeed, if it is the quiet nobility of Byrd's best verse anthems that is their most memorable feature, it is details such as this which offer some of the most precious moments in Gibbons' verse anthems.

Ex. 90

GIBBONS: Behold, Thou hast made my days

O spare me a lit-tle, me a lit-tle, O spare me a lit-tle, that I may [recover my strength]

Weelkes' verse anthems belong chronologically to the period of Gibbons, yet it is notable that he uses elaborate solo scoring far less than Gibbons, and biases still to the older, more measured style of solo delivery characteristic of Byrd, though on occasions a more declamatory manner breaks through. As for the complement of soloists used in each anthem, most require three; only two are known to be for a single soloist,[1] while two of the eight complete or restorable anthems employ five,[2] and one momentarily uses six.[3] Thus the variety of scoring in the verses is wider than Byrd's but not as broad as Gibbons'. Not only does Gibbons use the multi-voice verse more than Weelkes, but he also shows greater variety in his handling of it. When using four or more soloists together, Weelkes treats them as component voices of a full texture—as a kind of semi-chorus. Gibbons did this sometimes, but he was more consistently aware of his soloists as *soloists*, maintaining their parity through a more open network in which the progress of the individual parts is clear and crucial. When linking soloists together as a single entity, he favoured the small group—duet or trio—which he could set off against other similar vocal groupings.

Ex. 91

All laud and praise with heart and voice, O Lord,— I give to Thee,

As noted earlier, the style Weelkes normally adopts for his soloists is not far removed from that of Byrd, and the older composer's most tangible influence is to be found in such passages as the openings of the first two verses of *All laud and praise*, and of all three verses of *Give ear, O Lord*, where the duple rhythm of the opening is straightway broadened into a triple rhythm continuation (Example 91). Like Byrd, Weelkes thought in terms of broadly spanned melody, even though he generally

[1] *In Thee, O Lord*, and perhaps the fragmentary *The Lord is my shepherd*.
[2] *Give ear, O Lord* and *Plead thou my cause*.
[3] *If King Manasses*.

inclined to a rather more mobile line than Byrd.[1] When Weelkes moved into a more animated manner he often retained the rhythmic stiffness typical of Byrd's more selfconsciously animated passages. Occasionally Weelkes did incline to a free declamatory manner like that of Gibbons, especially when writing for tenor or bass (as in *In Thee, O Lord* (see Example 100), or the tenor verse of *Plead Thou my cause* (Example 92)),

Ex. 92

and let the an-gel of the Lord per - se-cute them: For they have privi - ly laid a   net to de-stroy

me with-out a   cause: yea, ev'n with - out a cause have they made a   pit for my soul.

though rarely managing that absolute engagement between text and music which Gibbons could achieve so well. Weelkes concentrated less intensively on detail, though he would allow the text to prompt conventional musical symbolism (for instance, low note for 'pit' in Example 92); sometimes his representation of movement or exultation is perhaps over-enthusiastic, and leads to a little convulsion whose stiffness renders it curious rather than felicitous (Example 93).

Weelkes' conservative manner of word setting arose partly because he did not have Gibbons' easy response to the sound of words, and often because he was clearly composing for more limited musical forces. This raises the whole question of the purpose for which any of his verse anthems were written. The sources confirm that they were essentially liturgical works, for only one, *Give ear, O Lord*, exists at all in a secular source, Myrriell's collection of 1616 (and the organ part of this anthem survives only in a liturgical collection).[2] In any case, it seems unlikely that verse anthems would have been widely used for domestic performance, for there is no evidence to suggest that the chamber organ was a common household instrument in the early seventeenth century, and not one of Weelkes' verse anthems survives in an alternative viol-accompanied version. In addition, the undemocratic division of soloist(s) and chorus would hardly make verse anthems as satisfactory a form for domestic music-making as full anthems.

[1] Nevertheless, even in *Give the king Thy judgements*, the most impressive of all Weelkes' complete verse anthems, over four-fifths of the quaver pairs which occur in the solo voice parts are simply repeated quavers (i.e., crotchets broken in two).

[2] Paradoxically, this piece is one of the only three verse anthems by Weelkes which demands as many soloists as chorus parts. It cannot therefore be properly performed without a substantial group of singers in the chorus to contrast with the concerted soloists.

Ex. 93

Presumably most, if not all, were composed either for the Chapel Royal or for Chichester. The former had a large and expert choir, the latter a small and mediocre one, and it is tempting to assign the more complex anthems to the former and the less demanding to the latter. But the example of Byrd's verse anthems counsels caution. Is it not likely that his were composed for the Chapel Royal, for this was the centre of his activity for all but the earliest part of his creative life? All his manuscript verse anthems survive solely in liturgical sources,[1] and a Chapel Royal habitat seems especially likely in the case of the two which set texts praying for the sovereign. The texts of five of them are quoted in the Chapel Royal word book made by 1635,[2] together with the texts of four others of which the music has vanished. Yet their style is restrained, and there is little apparent ceremony in their mien. The answer to this may be that they were 'everyday' pieces to be sung when the full choir was not available, and a less lavish diet was required. Certainly it would be rash to assign Weelkes' individual verse anthems either to Chichester Cathedral or the Chapel Royal simply on the grounds of their plain or elaborate manner.

[1] With the exception of a single source for *Alack! When I look back.*
[2] Bodleian MS Rawl-poet 23.

There is, however, one factor which may have some very real bearing upon this question. The verse anthem could plainly be of great use when the choir was indifferent, since the main burden of the piece could be carried by one or two singers. One respect in which Weelkes does diverge from both Byrd and Gibbons is in the relative proportions he allots to the verse and chorus elements in his verse anthems. Byrd and Gibbons almost exclusively apportion more than one third of the whole to the chorus,[1] but there are a number by Weelkes in which the chorus has only a very small role. In eight, over a third of his surviving output, it has significantly less than one third of the total music, and in five of these eight it has less than one quarter.[2] Were these works composed specifically for the use of Chichester Cathedral? Indeed, did the suitability of this type of work to the limited capacity of the Chichester musical establishment explain why Weelkes has left us more verse anthems than full anthems? One of the eight works just mentioned is *If King Manasses*, the one composition by Weelkes which is evidently mentioned in the Chichester inventory of 1621.

But these are only guesses, and other explanations of the relative brevity of some of the choruses might be advanced. The likelihood is that, although Weelkes may have composed some verse anthems in actuality or ideally for the Chapel Royal (especially strong candidates are the two royal-texted anthems, *Give the king Thy judgements* and *O Lord, how joyful is the king*),[3] at the same time he had in mind the needs and limitations of the Chichester Cathedral choir, and tried to ensure that these verse anthems would not be completely beyond their abilities. The great majority of his verse anthems were probably works for Chichester, even though he sometimes stretched his soloists' resources to emulate some of the novel practices of the Chapel Royal.

Nor can we be any more precise about the dates at which any of them were composed. The earliest manuscript containing one of them is Myrriell's collection of 1616, which includes *Give ear, O Lord. If King Manasses* was evidently in the Chichester inventory of 1621, and *Behold,*

---

[1] The one by Byrd which does not is one of the royal-texted anthems, *Behold, O God.* But, being a prayer for the recovery of the sovereign, it was probably composed in an emergency, and the burden was deliberately thrown upon the soloists; it is perhaps significant that, of all Byrd's matured verse anthems, this is the one which makes the greatest use of repetition.

[2] These five are *All laud and praise, An earthly tree, Give ear, O Lord, O Lord, turn not away* and *Why art thou so sad?* The others are *Deal bountifully, If King Manasses* and *In Thee, O Lord.*

[3] Four of Weelkes' verse anthems were quoted in J. Clifford, *The Divine Services and anthems* (1663 and 1664). These are *All laud and praise, Give the king Thy judgements, Let us lift up* (no music extant), and *Plead Thou my cause.* None, however, are quoted in the Chapel Royal Word Book, compiled by 1635 (Bodleian MS Rawl-poet 23).

O Israel survives in an organ score of about 1620. This last anthem and
O Lord, how joyful is the king are labelled 'the fifth of November', and
must have been composed after 1605 to commemorate the deliverance of
the king and parliament from the treason of Guy Fawkes.

As for the words set, the most noteworthy divergence from Weelkes'
full anthems is in the use of metrical texts, for whereas three-quarters of
the full anthems use prose texts, five of the eight complete or restorable
verse anthems are composed upon metrical texts. Three of these are from
Sternhold and Hopkins' metrical psalter, and the other two are penitential
supplications by William Hunnis and Robert Southwell respectively. The
remaining three are prose extracts from psalms.

Returning to structural matters, we shall again find it profitable to
compare Weelkes' practices with those of Byrd and Gibbons. Besides the
three published in his 1589 volume, seven other complete verse anthems
by Byrd are extant, all preserved in much later sources. Two were printed
in his *Psalms, songs and sonnets* of 1611, and the remainder exist in
manuscripts of which the earliest dates from 1617. In general, Byrd's verse
anthems are considerably below the level of his best church music—
though an exception must be made of *Christ rising | Christ is risen*. In
manner they are restrained, but what is striking about them is their quiet
and broad exploration of the possibilities of solo-choral alternation, and
of repetition, especially expressive repetition within single verse-chorus
divisions. Two of the manuscript works, *Alack! When I look back* and
Behold, O God, show traces of the older tradition by repeating the music
of one series of verse-chorus alternations to different words. The latter
anthem also uses repetition to fashion a clear, carol-like structure, with
the music the same for all the choruses, and also identical for the latter
half of all the verses.[1] Nevertheless, though the words of the latter half of
each verse and the ensuing chorus are always the same, Byrd creates no
musical relationship between verse and chorus. The very opposite happens
in *O Lord, rebuke me not*, in which there is no textual relationship between
any of the verses or any of the choruses, but in which each chorus is
fashioned upon the music of the preceding verse, incorporating the solo
line either entirely or substantially into its treble part, but abbreviating
some of the rest groups and modifying the harmonic structure. In *Alack!
When I look back*, the first two choruses are simply two-bar echoes of the
ends of the preceding verses; the third chorus is more extended, but likewise draws its material from the end of the verse. Weelkes must surely
have known this verse anthem and have been haunted by the end of this

---

[1] The single surviving part of another verse anthem by Byrd, *Now Israel may say*,
indicates that the music, though not the words, of all the choruses is identical, and the equal
length of the verses hints that they may have employed the same music.

third verse and the following chorus ('Good Lord, with mercy do forgive the follies of my youth') when he came to set 'Mercy, good Lord, mercy' in his verse anthem, *Give ear, O Lord*. Byrd's *Thou God that guidest* uses the same music for the first two verses, and subsequently employs most effectively a close alternation of verse and chorus. A tight collaboration of verse and chorus is also used in *Hear my prayer, O Lord*.

If Gibbons had been the adventurous one in matters of vocal style, in the use of repetition his area of enterprise was much smaller than that of Byrd or, as we shall see, of Weelkes. Only one verse anthem, *Thou central orb*, uses the same choruses throughout, and these, with their sudden switch to triple time, seem as disassociated from the verses as the burdens of Byrd's 'carols'. Another verse anthem, *The secret sins*, is a two-strophe piece, made up of a single verse-chorus division. In only one really genuine verse anthem, *Grant, O Holy Trinity*, does he choose to set the music of one chorus to serve another.[1] Many choruses repeat the whole or part of the text of the preceding verse, and quite commonly there is also some musical repetition, though on many other occasions the old words are set to new music. Sometimes in such text-repeating choruses, Gibbons will juxtapose old musical ideas and new ones; the old music may be either literally repeated, or may provide material to fashion a new paragraph. Such repetitions may be used for some choruses of a verse anthem while other choruses of the same work ignore them completely. Hints of smaller, long-range repetitions, such as turn up in a number of Weelkes' verse anthems, are rare, and close antiphonal dialogue between verse and chorus is comparatively infrequent.

Like those of Gibbons, the majority of Weelkes' verse anthems are made up of three or four verse-chorus divisions, though he makes wider use of variations from this norm; two have six and one seven, all more than Gibbons ever used. As for his repetitive and variational procedures, only two of his verse anthems show no significant evidence of such relationships. The organ score of one of these, *If ye be risen again*, is enough to suggest that we have sustained some musical loss through the incompleteness of this anthem. The other, *O Lord, how joyful is the king*, has fortunately survived less imperfectly, and more will be said of this anthem later. Although none of Weelkes' verse anthems uses the device of repeating an entire verse in a chorus setting, as both Byrd and Gibbons had very occasionally done, a number do use material from a verse as the foundation of the ensuing chorus (occasionally *vice versa*). This is an expressive device, but on no occasion does Weelkes exploit its fullest possibilities, for the repetition is always softened by avoiding a literal

[1] In *See, see, the Word is incarnate*, the text prompts the final chorus to incorporate a few modified bars of the second chorus which had treated the same words.

reiteration of the material. He uses verse-chorus relationships on three occasions in *Christ rising / Christ is risen*,[1] but exploits it more systematically, if not very exactly, in *All laud and praise* and *What joy so true*, two anthems in which the chorus texts reiterate the last phrases of the preceding verses.

Ex. 94

It is important to note this freedom with which Weelkes varies what are obviously intentional echoes of something already heard, for it bears upon the significance of certain less regularly placed, varied cross-references which occur in some of his other verse anthems, and which may have arisen not through pre-meditation, but from the natural compositional instinct, already noted in the madrigals, to return to earlier thoughts. One of the most important ways this shows itself is in the 'headmotifs' which occur at the openings of some component sections of certain verse anthems. *Deal bountifully*, which survives only in an organ score, opens each of its last three sections with what sounds like a varied headmotif stemming from the opening bars of the piece (Example 94). There is a suggestion of a headmotif at the openings of verses one and three (and perhaps chorus

[1] In the last verse-chorus division of *Christ rising*, and the first and last divisions of *Christ is risen*.

three) of *Plead Thou my cause*, and three headmotifs may be recognised in *If King Manasses* (see below, Example 101). Headmotifs are used even more consciously, if not more systematically, in *In Thee, O Lord*, which has three verse-chorus divisions of which the first and last open with the same three bars; the beginning of the central verse is not unrelated to these (Example 95*a* and *c*). Likewise choruses one and three open similarly

Ex. 95

(Example 95*b*); chorus two lies outside the system, since it opts to echo the latter part of verse two.[1]

[1] A headmotif may be traced in three sections of the anthem pair *I love the Lord* / *The Lord preserveth* (the opening of the second verse of *I love the Lord* (Example 96*a*) is contra-

Ex. 96

Such multiple, widely spanned relationships between sections have a structural function, and by far the most positive and important of these are to be found between the chorus sections. Just on one half of the verse anthems bind their choruses together with some sort of very material relationship. In a few this is slight, and merely serves to confirm the stylistic consistency of the piece. In the verse anthem pair, *I love the Lord | The Lord preserveth*, the outer choruses of the whole double work are related through the use of the same thematic point (the 'mercy' point quoted as Example 102*a*), and material relationships may be traced between the second chorus of the first half, and the first chorus of the second half. But most inter-chorus relationships are much more precise and extensive. Literal repetition may occur. Despite its imperfect musical remains, it is clear that the three choruses of *Ye people all* are the same in words and music, although the verses are all different. Only a single voice part survives of the enigmatically named *Successive course* (chorus one opens with 'That mighty God that humble spirit raises') but from this we may gather that the second and last of the five choruses are identical musically though not verbally, and the opening two bars of the first chorus are the same as the beginnings of these two choruses. Rather curiously, this first chorus is also identical musically with chorus three in all respects *except* for the headmotif. The first and third choruses of *Give the king Thy judgements* are the same in words and music; the surviving organ score of *O Lord, turn not away Thy face* shows that the first two of its three choruses have the same music.[1] But it is quite as common for Weelkes to use some kind of variation, and the third chorus of this last anthem reworks and expands the elements that had gone into the first two identical choruses (Example 97). The same general outline is followed in *Behold, O Israel*; the second chorus is the same as the first in all but minor details, and the opening and closing moments of the third chorus are related to the earlier two. Likewise *Give ear, O Lord*, while employing the same text and melodic point for its three choruses, works the point differently on each occasion. In addition, it integrates verse and chorus by anticipating the material of the chorus at the end of each verse.

Byrd's use of repetitive procedures in his verse anthems revealed an interest primarily in their expressive potentialities; Weelkes was drawn to their structural possibilities. Those verse anthems by Byrd which

puntally applied to initiate the first verse and the second chorus of *The Lord preserveth* (Example 96*b* and *c*)); nor, it appears, are the two Amens unrelated. From the single voice part for the choruses, which is all that remains of *I lift my heart to Thee*, it appears that the first and last choruses of this anthem open with the same one and a half bars.

[1] Evidently the work is in fact cast in five verse-chorus divisions, for after the second chorus there is interpolated the instruction 'begin again'. Thus the first four choruses are identical.

Ex. 97

employ long-range repetition most intensively are either composed as thoroughly traditional carols, or as works which are still influenced by the form; his more matured verse anthems make much use of close, effective repetition between verse and chorus, but employ distant cross-references less, and we shall find confirmation of this in his Services, too. Weelkes knew the value of expressive repetition, though he never used it with the same intensity or insistency that is so striking in Byrd's *Hear my prayer, O Lord* or *Thou God, that guidest*. As for Gibbons, the use of repetition as an expressive device had only a limited appeal to him—certainly less than it had to Byrd—and he virtually ignored the structural possibilities of long-range repetition. This confirms Gibbons' conservatism, so clearly revealed in his *Madrigals and Motets* of 1612. Here Weelkes was the progressive; the various repetitions between the choruses of his genuine verse anthems have nothing of the formal 'burden' about them, but seem more like probes towards the ritornello structure of the concerto grosso. They are thoroughly consistent with the structural attitudes that he shows in his other works.

It now remains for us to look more closely at the five complete verse anthems and the three which can be reliably restored. Of these eight, *All laud and praise* is as likely as any to have been a Chichester anthem. Its four choruses are all short, all very simple, and are scored for only four voices. Although it officially needs four soloists, it can be perfectly well sung by only three. The solo scoring is progressively more complex to give successive verses more weight—a common feature of Weelkes' verse anthems. In the second and third verses there is a move towards a more vigorous declamation, and the former contains one of those sudden bursts of activity which sometimes seize Weelkes' vocal lines at the suggestion of the text (see Example 93). But the most beautiful verse is really the first, which unfolds its line in a thoroughly Byrd-like manner, but reveals the lurking madrigalist in the restrained but still quite ravishing setting of 'in all my pain and grief' (Example 98).

Ex. 98

Weelkes seems to have had a particular liking for the opening of this verse anthem, for the first five bars of *Give ear, O Lord* are essentially the same as this, and the opening of *What joy so true* is related to it.[1] Like *All laud and praise*, this latter anthem employs its three soloists more intensively in the successive verses. The sources bear the rubric 'Made for Dr Hunt', though no candidate has yet emerged who may credibly be identified with this person. It is a pleasant anthem which renders its

---

[1] It is also worth noting the odd way in which the Amen of *If King Manasses* is largely identical with the end of the final chorus *and* the Amen of *If ye be risen again* (Example 99). It is impossible to believe that this is just coincidence, though whether it was consciously

pictorial due to 'gliding', 'scattered', 'top', and 'pours down', but it is altogether less characterful than *All laud and praise*.

Plead Thou my cause requires five soloists, but unfortunately the music for one of these, a bass which should open verse two, has not survived; the other half of this verse is notable for employing the four soloists simultaneously. Perhaps the fierce imprecations of this vindictive psalm encouraged a more forceful utterance, and the tenor solo in the third verse delivers its uncharitable sentiments quite vividly (see Example 92). The solo writing of *In Thee, O Lord* is even more consistently forceful. This is the only one of these eight verse anthems which is for a single soloist. The singer who occasioned this work must have been quite first-rate, for it is the one really declamatory work among Weelkes' verse anthems, and has the most challenging, wide-ranging solo part of all (Example 100).

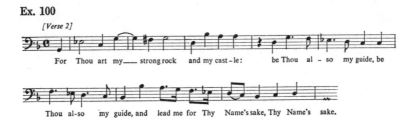

Ex. 100

[Verse 2]

For Thou art my___ strong rock and my cast-le: be Thou al - so my guide, be

Thou al-so my guide, and lead me for Thy Name's sake, Thy Name's sake.

The verses are the most commanding part of the work, and reveal that Weelkes was quite prepared to plunge his singer below the organ part so that he alone provides the bass; the choruses are short and appear to be for only four voices. The use of headmotifs has already been remarked.

done is uncertain. Small similarities of this sort are not uncommon between the verse anthems and offer further insight into the character and workings of Weelkes' mind.

Ex. 99

a If King Manasses *[organ only]*

[Amen]

b If ye be risen again *[organ part only survives]*

[Amen]

If King Manasses[1] is structurally the most unusual of these eight anthems. It has six verse-chorus alternations, though the grouping of these is unorthodox. The first three are normal, each verse introducing one of the three soloists, but beyond this point the regular subdivision of verse and chorus disappears; instead of three divisions it falls into two, of which the first is really a single three-voice verse incorporating a very short chorus, and the second an extended chorus embracing a very short six-voice verse. The scheme can be more easily grasped from a diagram, which also shows the system of headmotifs and other material relationships (Example 101). The simple word painting at the end of verse one on 'and lowly creep where flying threw it down' provokes another of Weelkes' convulsions; in this instance it is the organ part which becomes especially agitated.

The vocal manner used in the three verses of *Give ear, O Lord* is as committed to the older style as anything in Weelkes' work. There is nothing in the verses that Byrd might not have written, except perhaps the flurry on 'fly' in the final tenor verse. The words and melodic material of all three choruses are the same (Example 102), and the introduction of the final chorus by a semi-chorus of five soloists brings yet more variety and insistency to the plea: 'Mercy, good Lord, mercy'.[2] This is the one verse anthem by Weelkes which approaches that touchingly personal manner which Gibbons managed so marvellously in *Behold, Thou hast made my days*.

The remaining two verse anthems set prayers for the sovereign. One, *O Lord, how joyful is the king*, is the longest of all Weelkes' single anthems, not only in bars, but in the number of verse-chorus divisions (seven in all). The chorus stands on very equal terms with the soloists and the verses are rather short. Despite its size, this anthem is quite as memorable for some unobtrusive details—moments like the quaver-animated cadences which round off the first three verses (especially the second of these (Example 103), a melodic idea Gibbons might have conceived, though he would doubtless have extended it sequentially).

But it is the other royal anthem, *Give the king Thy judgements*, which is the finest of all these eight. The handling of the three soloists has a masterly breadth and dignity, and the choruses (all for six voices) are

[1] This exists in another version, entitled *In Thee, O Lord*. The sources of this are in Durham Cathedral Library. The voice parts are the same as those of *If King Manasses*, but the organ part is different. It seems that some Durham musician obtained the voice parts of *If King Manasses* (except for one treble book). These parts must have been textless. Knowing, perhaps, that Weelkes had composed an anthem entitled *In Thee, O Lord*, he reconstructed the text from Psalm 71, not knowing that Weelkes' setting of *In Thee, O Lord* was based on Psalm 31. He then devised his own organ part, which is quite unskilful.

[2] Weelkes evidently uses this same device of introducing a chorus section by a passage for soloists alone in his fragmentary verse anthem, *Christ rising / Christ is risen*.

Ex. 101

*These consecutive fifths are authentic

Ex. 102

a [Choruses 2 and 3]

Mer - cy, good Lord

b [Chorus 1]

Mer - cy, good Lord

sonorous and characterful. The whole piece has a powerful sense of unity. The first and last of the three choruses are identical in words and music, and the central one opens in a similar manner; this chorus is closely bound to the following verse, which continues the same line of musical thought. Since this verse sets the same text as the identical first and third choruses, it uses some material from these and then, it seems, founds its last part

upon the second chorus, which had just preceded it. The Amen takes over
the vigorous point of 'and look upon the face [of Thine annointed]' to
open the bass part, and a more unconscious identity between two phrases
of the first and second verses only serves to substantiate the notable consistency of manner between the different sections. This, of all Weelkes'
verse anthems, is the one that would have most worthily graced the Chapel
Royal services. It is labelled 'For the King's Day'—the anniversary of
either his birth or his accession.

Ex. 103

a crown of per-fect gold, a crown — of per-fect gold.

It is really impossible to by-pass one of the fragmentary verse anthem
pairs, though any comment can be little more than an epitaph. *Christ
rising / Christ is risen*, if it had survived intact, might well have proved the
peer of *Give the king Thy judgements*. It is influenced by Byrd's setting of
the same text for, although the surviving organ score of Weelkes' *Christ
rising* opens quite independently, the opening vocal phrase of Byrd's
setting can be made to fit very convincingly with it. *Christ is risen* draws
closer to Byrd, and the final point of both works is actually the same. But
Weelkes proceeds further, and adds an 'alleluia' to increase the festive
splendour of this anthem. His setting appears to use two soloists for most
of the verses, and a chorus of five voices for all except the final chorus
and Alleluia, which appear to be for six. The organ score is enough to
reveal the splendour and majesty of *Christ rising / Christ is risen*; the
missing parts are the most grievous loss from the Weelkes' anthem legacy.

XI. THE SERVICES

Though Weelkes' Services have never endured quite the neglect suffered by his verse anthems, their importance has rarely been properly recognised. Here credit must be returned to Fellowes, who may have done scant justice to the verse anthems by ignoring them completely, but who fully appreciated that Weelkes had, in his Services, made a most notable contribution to the repertoire. Indeed, he went so far as to assert that 'the position to which he advanced this branch of music was not reached again until the latter part of the nineteenth century'.[1] The compliment is a dubious one, but Fellowes was right in perceiving the creative vitality of these works. Weelkes was the most prolific purveyor of Services among all the major English composers of the time, and has left us ten as against Tomkins' seven, Byrd's four, and Gibbons' two. It will be useful to tabulate them here, partly to give a comprehensive list of sources, and also to fix a number to each for later reference. This is the more important since the older list of ten Services which Fellowes made needs revision. Fellowes did not realise that the fragments of three vocal parts of a Service 'in verse for a mean', which he listed as the Sixth Service, belong in fact to the First Service; in addition, he did not know of the fragments of *Jubilate* of an otherwise unknown Service which survive in the Bodleian Library, Oxford. The revised list[2] and numbering is as follows:

1. 'The First Service to the organs in Gamut'. *Te Deum, Jubilate, Offertory, Kyrie, Creed, Magnificat* and *Nunc dimittis* (Tenbury 791). In one set of sources for the incomplete vocal parts of *Te Deum, Offertory* and *Magnificat* (Wimborne Alto (*Te Deum* only), Tenor and Bass), this Service is described as 'in verse for a mean'. *Kyrie, Creed* and *Magnificat* are also preserved in Christ Church 88, and *Magnificat* and *Nunc dimittis* in Tenbury 1442, and Bodleian Mus. e23–25.

[1] E. H. Fellowes, *English cathedral music*, p. 95.

[2] In addition to these, there appeared in the periodical, *The Choir*, Nos. 47 and 48 (July and August, 1864), a piece described as 'The Responses to the Commandments, set to varied music by Thomas Weelkes A.D. 1620. From a MS in the possession of Edw. F. Rimbault . . . formerly belonging to Chichester Cathedral'. The source now seems to have disappeared. Weelkes had provided settings of these Responses for his First and Second Services, though in these the same music served the first nine Commandments, whereas in the set printed by Rimbault, each of the ten responses is set to different music. Nevertheless, each of these ten responses follows the practice of Weelkes' two authenticated settings by being planned as a chorus-verse-chorus scheme, and the last response uses a set of entries which was a particular favourite of Weelkes. However, Weelkes' authorship is less certainly proclaimed by some other features.

2. 'The Second Service to the organs in D-sol-re'. *Te Deum*, *Jubilate*, *Offertory*, *Kyrie*, *Creed*, *Magnificat* and *Nunc dimittis* (Tenbury 791).
3. Service 'to the organs in F-fa-ut'. *Magnificat* and *Nunc dimittis* (Tenbury 791).
4. Service 'for trebles'. *Te Deum* (Tenbury 791), *Magnificat* and *Nunc dimittis* (Tenbury 791, Durham A6, C1, C13, C18, E11A, Peterhouse 33, 34, 38, 39, and unnumbered treble and alto parts).
5. Service 'in medio chori'. *Magnificat* and *Nunc dimittis* (Tenbury 791).
6. Service 'in verse for two countertenors'. *Magnificat* and *Nunc dimittis* (Wimborne Alto, Tenor and Bass).
7. Short Service for four voices. *Venite*, *Te Deum*, and *Jubilate* (BM. Add. MS 29289, Royal Library 23.1.4), *Te Deum* and *Jubilate* (Durham A6, C13, C26, C31–3, E11A, Christ Church 437, St. John's (Oxford) organ book), *Magnificat* and *Nunc dimittis* (Durham A6, C13, C18, E11A, Peterhouse 36, 43, 45).
8. Service for five voices. *Te Deum*, *Jubilate*, *Magnificat* and *Nunc dimittis* (Tenbury 791).
9. Service for seven voices. *Magnificat* and *Nunc dimittis* (Durham C1, C18, Peterhouse 33, 34, 38, 39, and unnumbered treble and alto parts).
10. *Jubilate* (tenor and bass parts in Bodleian Mus. e24–25).

The first six are verse Services, and the remaining four are full Services. But the misfortune of these works is that only the morning canticles of the Short Service (No. 7) are intact. As with the verse anthems, not one was published during Weelkes' lifetime. Their fate was entrusted to manuscripts, and the surviving fragments of one Service (No. 10) are a mere two chorus parts, and of another (No. 6) are little more than three chorus parts; four others (Nos. 2, 3, 5 and 8) exist solely as organ scores. The remains of the First Service (an organ score and sections of three chorus parts) look more promising, and the choruses of *Te Deum*, *Magnificat* and *Nunc dimittis* (three extant vocal parts) can be reliably reconstructed; but all that has survived of the solos in the verses is four bass fragments. It is possible to reconstruct convincingly the remaining three Services – the evening canticles (but not *Te Deum*) of the Fourth Service, the whole of the Short Service, and the Ninth Service. To this list might be added the Eighth Service, of which the surviving organ score is unusually detailed; one can only guess at many details of the part-writing, but it is possible to re-create a five-voice texture which gives a very fair impression of Weelkes' intentions.[1]

[1] Fellowes attempted this with the evening canticles, publishing the result in TCM octavo series, No. 96. A revised edition was made in 1965 by David Wulstan. The organ score offers no authority at all for Fellowes' and Wulstan's *cantoris-decani* divisions, and Fellowes' realisation of some other parts of the score was unnecessarily free. The revised edition by David Wulstan is generally more faithful to the original.

The movements included within the separate Services are varied. Nine set the evening canticles, and four are simply Evensongs. Only two are comprehensive, affording not only settings of canticles, etc. for Morning Prayer, but also musical adornment for the Communion. The most interesting feature of these two is the Offertories which appear to be the only settings of this part of the Liturgy from the period. Offertory sentences had appeared in the Prayer Book of 1549 and were 'to be sung while the people do offer', but in the 1552 edition it was decreed that the celebrant should say the offertory, and this was still the official direction in Weelkes' time. One of the sentences set by Weelkes, 'Blessed be the man', was drawn from the Prayer Book selection, but the other, 'Blessed is he . . . Glory be to Thee, O Lord', had no place in this collection. It is known that experiments were sometimes made with the liturgy at this time, and it is worth noting that Lancelot Andrewes, Bishop of Chichester from 1605 to 1609, supplemented the Prayer Book selection of offertory sentences with some of his own.[1] 'Blessed is He . . . Glory be to Thee' is not in Andrewes' supplementary collection, but one wonders whether some other liturgical experiment of Andrewes is reflected by these two offertory settings of Weelkes, for, besides being sung instead of being said, they are exceptional in occupying a place before the Commandments instead of after the Creed, as was the official position.

Fellowes also wrote of the Services that in them is revealed 'the extent of Weelkes' inventive genius in exploring fresh methods and developing the design, especially with the object of adding interest and variety to this class of composition'.[2] This will seem a bold statement to those who see the musical Service as functional in the lowest sense, inferior to the anthem in which the composer could be so much freer. Granted that Service texts are mostly very lengthy, and the composer is therefore forced into a style that can be brief—granted that the need to set the same prescribed texts over and over again is likely to weaken the imaginative stimulus offered by these texts: the fact remains that the English composer of around 1600 found the Service an exciting form in which he could rise to achievements as notable in their own way as those of the anthem. Even the demand for economy was a challenge. As for the more circumscribed and uniform style imposed by the need to be business-like, a compensation for this was found in variety of scoring. It was no longer simply the mingling of full choir sections with stretches sung in alternation by the *cantoris* and *decani* sides of the choir, or the alternation of sections for soloist(s) and chorus; multi-voice verses might add variety to the choral palette of

[1] L. Andrewes, 'Notes on the Book of Common Prayer', included in *Two Answers to Cardinal Perron and other miscellaneous works*, pp. 153–4.

[2] E. H. Fellowes, *English cathedral music*, p. 95.

the full Service, and the resources of the verse Service might be augmented by the use of *cantoris-decani* alternations in the choruses. Verses might be long, or might alternate in close dialogue with the choruses; they might be for one or two soloists, or for a larger group—or even for both successively. The larger group might be deployed as an open contrapuntal network, or might be treated cohesively. The variations in the schemes of scoring were infinite, even in settings of the same text.

The truth is that the musical Service of Weelkes' time was in a particularly healthy state. It was a comparatively new form with no suggestion of degeneration or tiredness, where innovation and freshness had hardened into formula and convention, or where mannerism had replaced vital thought. But it was a form which created other problems besides the need for economy. In the first place, since the obligation to set repeatedly the same texts was bound to blunt their stimulus to the imagination, the composer was forced to employ a deliberately new musical approach in each setting if he wished to avoid a stale and sterile result. Secondly, the texts of the separate movements were mostly lengthy, and required a very considerable quantity of musical material; this encouraged the use of internal relationships to ensure that there was some focus to this material, and to tighten the structure of what could otherwise become a very sprawling movement. Thirdly, the fact that each Service was made up of at least two, and probably more, movements meant that some tangible musical relationship had to be created between them if their grouping was not to appear accidental.

In view of the concern he had already shown for musical integration, it would have been surprising if Weelkes had not responded vigorously to these challenges. As it is, one of the strongest first impressions gained from an examination of all the Services collectively is of the great variety between them, and the notable consistency within each of them. A good deal of this internal unity may be traced to already familiar techniques, for it is common to find thematic relationships as well as the repetition of segments within or between movements. But the Service had a special musical device which it had taken over from the Mass for establishing a relationship between its components. This was the head- or tailmotif—a musical fragment which appeared at the beginning or end of all or some movements of a particular Service. It could range from a true headmotif—that is, a thematic outline in the top voice (which might be varied from movement to movement until only a ghost of a resemblance remained) to a literal repetition of a section several bars long.

It is worth observing its use by other composers in order to place Weelkes' practices in perspective. Byrd had used the device freely, though his motifs were rarely elaborate. True, there is a very extended headmotif in his Second Service, an Evensong in verse form, but it is much more developed than anything in the other three Services; both canticles open with the same four bars and are closely related for a further four to five bars. The headmotif of the Third Service, another Evensong, is very much shorter—only a couple of bars. The Great Service employs two headmotifs, both of which are constantly varied. One relates *Venite* and *Benedictus* for some three bars, and a shorter one (little more than a tonic-subdominant progression) binds *Te Deum, Kyrie, Creed, Magnificat* and *Nunc dimittis*.[1] Only in the evening canticles is the latter headmotif extended into a fairly broad and varied common opening. There are three headmotifs in Byrd's Short Service, one of three to four bars, used with liberal variation to join *Venite* and *Te Deum*, another (more exact but shorter) to link *Benedictus* and *Creed*, and a third, likewise short, to relate *Magnificat* and *Nunc dimittis*.

Byrd had less use for tailmotifs. In the Great Service the last three bars of *Venite, Benedictus* and *Creed* share the same outlines, and the end of *Kyrie* is related to these, but *Te Deum, Magnificat* and *Nunc dimittis* are outside the system. The Short Service has only the most rudimentary traces of tailmotif in the similarities of certain of the final cadences (those of *Venite, Kyrie I* and *Nunc dimittis* on the one hand, and of *Te Deum, Creed* and *Magnificat* on the other). Such similarities are longer and stronger in the Second Service, but there are none at all in the Third Service.

Byrd's use of repetition in his Services is completely consistent with the practices already demonstrated in his verse anthems. In the Short Service, for instance, it is found that the morning canticles in particular are filled with immediate repetition of material between the *cantoris* and *decani* sides of the choir—and very effective it is, especially with phrases as memorable as many Byrd composed for this Service. Long-range, structural repetition had much less interest to him. This is shown not only by his easy-going use of headmotifs and tailmotifs, for other less systematic cross-references, such as are abundant in certain of Weelkes' Services, are also lacking. Gibbons used such cross-references on occasions in his First (Short) Service, though his use of headmotifs is very sketchy. Admittedly the opening of *Magnificat* reflects the whole of the second *Kyrie*, but the only other sign of a headmotif in the whole Service is the tendency of the treble to rise by step from an initial F. His Second Service has no headmotif at all, and the only tailmotif in either Service arises from the recurrence of Amen, a two-bar fragment serving this in both *Creed* and *Magnificat* in the First Service, and another linking the

[1] A distant connection between the two headmotifs is established through the uppermost voice parts at the beginnings of *Benedictus* and *Magnificat*.

Amens of *Jubilate*, *Magnificat* and *Nunc dimittis* in the Second Service. As for immediate repetition which plays such a part in Byrd's Short Service, Gibbons had little or no use for it—just as was the case in his verse anthems.

Of Weelkes' major contemporaries, Tomkins merits special attention not only as the most productive composer of Services (or, at least, of ones that have survived), but also because, like Weelkes, he used head- and tailmotifs not only at the extremities but also a little way inside the movement. Thus there could result a kind of double head- or tailmotif, though it was possible for the 'secondary headmotif' or the 'penultimate motif' to be used by itself. These measures thus took material relationships deeper into the individual movements, and created an even stronger bond between the components of a Service. Tomkins used a secondary head-motif in his Fifth Service. The regular headmotif of this Service is the most tenuous in all his Services, consisting solely of the structure under-lying the first two bars of the bass solo which opens all four canticles,[1] but in *Te Deum* and *Magnificat* the first choruses of both are the same for six to seven bars, and provide a powerful secondary headmotif. A penul-timate motif is also important in this Service, for though the last couple of bars of all four canticles are related, much more important is the penulti-mate motif which sets the entire first half of Gloria in both evening can-ticles (though in *Nunc dimittis* it is pitched a third higher than in *Magnifi-cat*). The evening canticles of the Fourth Service offer two penultimate motifs by themselves without the benefit of a regular tailmotif, for it is not Amen that is the same in both, but two brief passages in the preceding Gloria.[2]

Tomkins' use of orthodox head- and tailmotifs is little if at all stronger than Byrd's,[3] though there was nothing stereotyped in the way either he

---

[1] Since in each case this is preceded by an organ introduction, it has the placing of a secondary headmotif. In the following discussion the terms secondary headmotif and penultimate motif will be applied only to those which are used in association with another orthodox head- or tailmotif, or which occur by themselves in a section which is neither the very opening section nor the very last section of the piece.

[2] The same point is also used to set 'and to the Holy Ghost' in both canticles.

[3] It is perhaps worth recording Tomkins' further use of these devices. A varied headmotif of three to four bars links *Venite*, *Benedictus* and *Nunc dimittis* in the First Service, and the openings of *Te Deum* and *Magnificat* are not unrelated. A short firm phrase opens *Jubilate*, *Kyrie*, *Magnificat* and *Nunc dimittis* of the Second Service, and *Te Deum* is launched with two bars virtually identical with the variant of this headmotif offered by *Magnificat*, but the Third Service pays little attention to this device, only the evening canticles being at all related. The evening canticles of the Fourth Service match Byrd's Second Service not thematically, but in the way they are linked by an extensive headmotif presented as a solo supported by organ. Like Gibbons, Tomkins allowed textual repetition to be the foundation of a tailmotif, and the Gloria identities in the Fourth and Fifth Services have already been noted. In his First Service *Creed* and *Nunc dimittis* close with the same three-bar Amen, and

or Byrd applied them. But it was Weelkes who showed the greatest range when using them. In his madrigals his conservative contrapuntal tendencies in some had been opposed by his radical expressive adventures in others; in his Services the restraint with which head- and tailmotifs are used in some is balanced by the elaborate network of repetitions used in the First Service. Sometimes, like Byrd and Tomkins, Weelkes would ignore one or other of these devices completely, as in the very attractive Fourth Service which has no headmotif at all, or in the seven movements of the Second Service which contain only the barest hints of tailmotifs. The Ninth Service for seven voices, the most conservative but the finest of them all, confines its headmotif to an outline of four notes in the top voice (see Example 115*a*). Two other evening Services, the Third and the Fifth, each have a variable headmotif of three and a half bars (Example 104), but only three of the seven movements of the Second Service (*Te*

Deum, Jubilate and Offertory) are related through a similarly variable three-bar headmotif. Among the other Services which set both morning and evening canticles, the Short Service uses a very variable headmotif of three to five bars for four of its five movements, but the remaining one, *Jubilate*, is unrelated. Likewise, in the Eighth Service, one movement, *Nunc dimittis*, has a completely independent opening, though the other three are bound by a six-bar headmotif which is all the stronger for being invariable.

the last two bars of *Venite* are a close variant of this. In the Second Service the only trace of a tailmotif is the identical bass of the last three and a half bars of *Te Deum* and *Kyrie*, and the similarity of the last two bars of the treble in *Venite* and *Te Deum*. In the Third Service there is no tailmotif at all, except for some similarity of outline between the treble parts at the very end of *Magnificat* and *Nunc dimittis*.

This last headmotif is bold enough, but it was in the treatment of tail-motifs that Weelkes was most adventurous. Gibbons used the same musical Amen for two or more canticles, and Tomkins extended the identities to parts of the Gloria as well—but Weelkes applied the repetition to the whole Gloria and Amen in four or five of his Services. Thus what had been a kind of brief musical signature to a couple or more movements became a full-length final paragraph. There were clear precedents for this practice in Weelkes' earlier madrigals, for the two lyrics within each of the madrigal pairs, *Come clap your hands | Phyllis hath sworn* and *Thule | The Andalusian merchant*, had each ended with the same words, and Weelkes had matched the textual repetition with a musical one. He used the same Gloria-Amen for both canticles of the Sixth Service, and very likely did the same in the Fifth Service.[1] Yet he never made such a section common to more than two canticles; thus in the Short Service he pairs the morning canticles *Venite* and *Jubilate* in this way, but uses a different setting of Gloria-Amen to bind *Magnificat* and *Nunc dimittis*. The *Jubilate* and *Nunc dimittis* of the First Service have this section in common too, but in the Second Service it is only the latter half of Gloria (but not the concluding Amen) of *Jubilate* and *Nunc dimittis* that is the same.

Other tailmotifs are far briefer, less literal, yet firm. There is no mistaking the relationship between the last two to four bars of all four movements of the Eighth Service (Example 105), and the Ninth Service effectively achieves a tailmotif through the identical melodic foundation of the end of Gloria of *Magnificat* and of Amen of *Nunc dimittis*. In each of these Services it was characteristic of Weelkes to make the variations by changing the contrapuntal complex. Like Tomkins, Weelkes also used penultimate motifs. The link between the concluding areas of the evening canticles of the Fourth Service is made by taking two three-bar segments from the Gloria of *Magnificat*, interpolating two extra beats into the first, re-ordering the rhythmic structure of the second, and then knitting the two segments together to launch the Gloria of *Nunc dimittis* (Example 106). Even if it should prove that the *Magnificat* and *Nunc dimittis* comprising the Fifth Service do not in fact share the same Gloria, they certainly have in common the last two and a half bars of the treble in each canticle. As for the Short Service, the listener is prepared for the identical Glorias of *Venite* and *Jubilate* by the similarities between passages immediately preceding the Gloria in each. So, too, *Te Deum* and *Magnificat* of the Eighth Service share four bars shortly before their respective conclusions.

It remains to look at these features in Weelkes' First Service. This is by far the most highly unified of the ten, and the system of cross-references

[1] The sole extant source provides no Gloria for *Nunc dimittis*.

Ex. 105

a Te Deum

b Jubilate

c Magnificat

d Nunc dimittis

is so highly complex that a diagram can convey only a very imperfect impression of these relationships (Example 107). Not only are the relationships very numerous and exact, and often involve very substantial sections, but they recur freely between the head- and tailmotifs, and also appear in the inner areas of movements. One significant fact is that the Offertory, *Blessed is he*, does not tie into the system, which strongly suggests that it was not originally conceived as part of the Service. Nevertheless, Weelkes left no more consciously integrated work, nor one that proves more conclusively his concern for such matters.

A feature of considerable interest is the appearance in certain of Weelkes' Services of material also used in his anthems. Sometimes the relationship is only for a brief section and may be coincidental, but on other occasions a whole section is transferred bodily from one work to another. It is difficult to believe that such appropriations were the result of sterility; it seems much more probable that certain anthems were

Ex. 106

designed to be associated with particular Services. An instruction in one bass part of the First Service states that the anthem to be sung with this work was *Thou art my portion, O Lord,*[1] though unfortunately there appears to be no trace anywhere of music for this.

We are more fortunate in the case of the Sixth Service, for the anthem specified for this, *Why art thou so sad,* has survived in fragmentary form; the slender remains of both anthem and Service reveal no identity of material between the two works. On the other hand, it is only material identities that lead to the assumption that certain other Services and anthems are intended to be paired, though the apparent liturgical relationship of these various pairings is the more probable since all the major instances of such identities occur between works composed for the same

[1] The full rubric after *Magnificat* (the *Nunc dimittis* is lacking) reads: 'anthem is the first verse of the eighth part, the first verse of the tenth part, the last verse of the ninth part, the last two verses of the thirteenth part, and the fourth verse of the second part of the hundred and nineteenth psalm'.

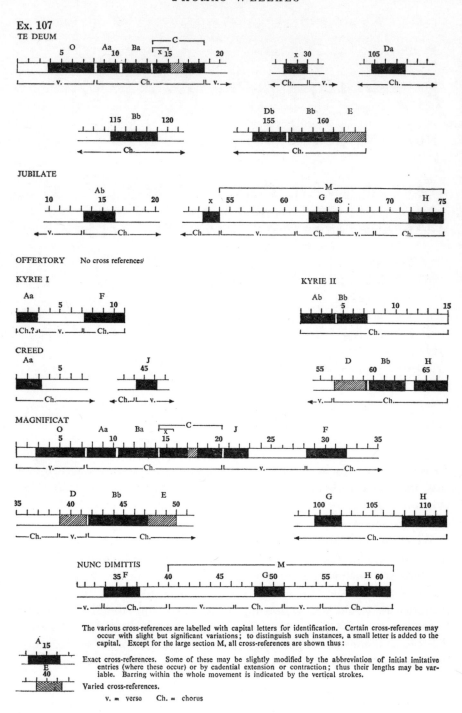

Ex. 107

TE DEUM

JUBILATE

OFFERTORY   No cross references

KYRIE I

KYRIE II

CREED

MAGNIFICAT

NUNC DIMITTIS

The various cross-references are labelled with capital letters for identification. Certain cross-references may occur with slight but significant variations; to distinguish such instances, a small letter is added to the capital. Except for the large section M, all cross-references are shown thus:

Exact cross-references. Some of these may be slightly modified by the abbreviation of initial imitative entries (where these occur) or by cadential extension or contraction; thus their lengths may be variable. Barring within the whole movement is indicated by the vertical strokes.

Varied cross-references.

v. = verse   Ch. = chorus

complement of performers. The Ninth Service for seven voices shares two substantial passages with the seven-voice *O Lord, grant the king a long life*; one is a ten-bar section which appears in *Magnificat*,[1] and the other occurs in the Amen of *Nunc dimittis*, which is largely the same as the Amen of the anthem. A similar Amen relationship is present in the Eighth Service, for *Magnificat* shares its last seven bars with the five-voice anthem, *O how amiable*, and the headmotif opens with the same two and a half bars as the Amen of *All people, clap your hands*. The largest single Service-anthem identity is located in the Fourth Service, in which a dozen bars, comprising the latter half of the Gloria of *Nunc dimittis*, are identical with the setting of the Latin acclamation in *Alleluia! I heard a voice*. We may also note some briefer and less conclusive relationships between the Second Service and the verse anthem, *O Lord, turn not away Thy face*, while the Short Service comes very close for seven bars of its *Te Deum* to a passage from *O Lord God Almighty*. The validity of this last parallel is undermined by the differing forces required to perform Service and anthem.

The musical language of the Services is in general the most restrained in all Weelkes' work. There is no chromaticism except of the very mildest sort, and even that is rarely applied. There is a certain amount of moderate musical symbolism. All five settings of *Te Deum* accord their proper relative altitude to 'Heaven and earth', and the 'sharpness of death' always occasions the chromatic raising of some notes. In two Services, the Fourth and Eighth, this textual suggestion is broadened to shift the whole musical passage into another key. In three Services (the First, Fourth and Eighth) a sudden change from verse to chorus is made for the words 'to all believers', emphasising how comprehensive will be the celestial posting of the faithful. But Weelkes is far from obsessed by musical symbolism, and 'lift them up' only occasions a very mild rising response in most cases. Three of the five settings of *Jubilate* set 'serve the Lord with gladness' to running quavers, and an interesting feature of Weelkes' two *Creed* settings is that both appear to treat 'and was crucified also for us' to exactly the same musical phrase. Likewise, in *Te Deum* four of the five settings use essentially the same music to set 'Holy, Holy', an identity which is all the more surprising since the musical phrase is quite unremarkable (Example 108). In almost all Weelkes' settings of *Magnificat* the proud are scattered in a vigorous rhythmic figure (♩.♫♩), and 'he hath put down' is set to a descending phrase in all except the Fifth Service; in the Eighth Service the downward leap of a seventh (especially when it is a major seventh) is quite startling (Example 109), both to listener and singer. The Second Service, it seems, chooses a descending sequence to illustrate their de-

---

[1] *Magnificat:* 'and the rich he hath sent empty away', and *O Lord, grant the king:* 'so shall we always sing and praise Thy Name'.

Ex. 108

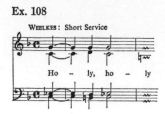

WEELKES: Short Service

Ho — ly, ho — ly

Ex. 109

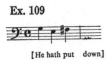

[He hath put down]

Ex. 110

clension (Example 110). The exaltation of the humble and meek is achieved via the expected rising phrase.

Any comments on the more detailed characteristics and the quality of Weelkes' Services are obviously restricted by the drastic incompleteness of most of them. Nevertheless it seems worth attempting some sort of closer scrutiny and assessment of each. There is little point in dwelling further on the integrating features of these works, partly because their incompleteness is likely to prevent most of them ever becoming an active experience to the reader, and partly because these phenomena merely reinforce what has already been exhaustively demonstrated in the examination both of the madrigals and the anthems. It may, however, be useful to footnote in due course some of the more important cross-references in those Services which have been published. One point is worth noting. While, in some Services, cross-references in addition to the head- and tailmotifs are made through small particles of a bar or two, which may be literally repeated, but are more often at least a little varied, in the more contrapuntally inclined Services (notably the Fifth and Ninth) the unfolding manner is less favourable to such block transferences. Instead thematic relationships are prevalent in these works, and nearly all the points in each Service may be placed in one of a number of thematic families. However, in the Eighth Service, which is also thoroughly contrapuntal, there are likewise a good many instances of block repetitions.

Although the First Service is described in some vocal sources as being 'in verse for a mean', it is quite clear that a number of soloists are involved, and the rubric must refer to the solo scoring of the initial verse. The only fragments surviving of any of the solos are four short passages for a bass, which confirm that Weelkes was quite prepared to take his singer below the organ part. Some verses are fairly roomy, suggesting only one or two soloists, but others are barely long enough to accommodate the text assigned to them, and must surely be for a group of several soloists treated as a semi-chorus. This is especially true of the *Creed*, both in this and the Second Service. From its remains we may gather that the First Service was at least a very admirable specimen of the simple verse Service. The verse-chorus planning is varied, some sections being quite extensive, while in *Te Deum* verse and chorus are used in very close alternation on two occasions. Weelkes was not especially interested in striking details in this Service—which must not be taken as a defect, but rather as a reflection upon the efficiency with which the whole text is presented.

The Second Service is quite different yet equally consistent in character. Even from the organ score alone it conveys an air of distinguished simplicity. *Te Deum* makes much use of *cantoris-decani* alternations in its chorus sections, and this, coupled to the evident variety of vocal forces employed in the verses, makes it the most varied in scoring of all Weelkes' works. Nevertheless, very little use is made of expressive repetitions between the two sides of the choir, and the other movements all appear to use the chorus as a single unit, never divided. A momentary madrigalism emerges in the sequence evidently designed for 'Thou didst not abhor the Virgin's womb' in *Te Deum*, and provides the most arresting moment in the movement (Example 111), but it is in *Magnificat* that some of the most striking music is to be found. The dissonance in the passage which sets (apparently) 'all generations shall call Me blessed' is expressive, even though basically conventional (Example 112), and 'throughout all generations' occasions a switch to triple time, a rhythmic change repeated at the opening of Gloria. *Nunc dimittis*, too, must have been impressive in its gentle way.

The Third Service has a very definite relationship with the First Service, for the first verse and first chorus of *Magnificat* open with virtually the same music in both Services, and there is a further corresponding passage towards the end of this canticle in each Service. In his Third Service

Ex. 111

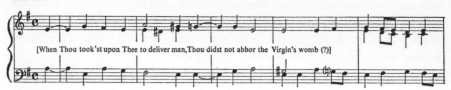

[When Thou took'st upon Thee to deliver man, Thou didst not abhor the Virgin's womb (?)]

Ex. 112

[all generations shall call me blessed (?)]

Weelkes sets *Magnificat* in a notably expansive manner, and the verses of the whole Service probably only require one or two soloists.[1] Like the First Service it makes liberal use of B flat inflections of what is a prevailing C major. Some of the opening portions of *Magnificat* are very routine, but the Service improves to present some pleasant music.

Nevertheless, this music is far less appealing than that of the Fourth Service, which employs the high 'treble' voice as the top line in the choruses, instead of the lower and more normal 'mean'. Only an organ score survives of *Te Deum*, but there are also sufficient vocal parts extant of the evening canticles to permit a convincing reconstruction of these.[2] *Te Deum*

[1] Unfortunately the organ score gives no indication of the verse-chorus scoring of *Nunc dimittis* beyond the first verse which starts in bar 8.

[2] This has been done by Peter le Huray (London, 1962), whose edition supplants that of Fellowes (London, 1931). Dr. le Huray has discussed the problems of reconstructing this Service in the Preface to his edition. The following are the literal or only slightly modified cross-references to be found in this Service (including those in *Te Deum*). The tailmotif of *Magnificat* and *Nunc dimittis* was noted earlier.

Magnificat: 'for, behold, from henceforth' and 'Glory be to the Father'; *Nunc:* 'of Thy people Israel' (2 bars).

Te Deum: 'Make them to be numbered with Thy Saints'; *Magnificat:* 'he hath filled the hungry' (3–4 bars).

contains the most unusual final cadence, both in its structure and 'dominant' inconclusiveness, in all Weelkes' work; it is also used as the main central cadence to divide the movement in two (Example 113). The verses seem to have been quite beautiful, especially the tightly contrapuntal setting of 'Thou art the everlasting Son of the Father', and there are some light touches of what may be pseudo-antiphony in the last two verses. As in the First Service, Weelkes sets 'we believe that Thou shalt come to be our judge' to a close alternation of verse and chorus, and the same technique is used in the Glorias of both *Magnificat* and *Nunc dimittis*. A

Ex. 113

[in G minor]

good part of the choruses of the evening canticles are homophonic and straightforward in manner, and the most precious parts of the whole Service lie in the verses. In *Magnificat* Weelkes freely indulges his liking for quasi-antiphonal effects in the delivery by two pairs of soloists of 'For He that is mighty hath magnified me, and Holy is His Name'. The twenty-bar canon for two trebles (and, except for the modification of one interval, it is a real canon) which sets 'He remembering His mercy hath holpen His servant Israel' is very touching, and its habit of doubling back upon itself is very reminiscent of the pseudo-antiphony of Weelkes' madrigals. The duet which opens *Nunc dimittis* is chastely charming, and the madrigalian connotations of this style are made more specific still by the adaptation of a passage from *What have the gods?* (six-voice madrigals of 1600) to set 'according to Thy Word'. For sheer attractiveness, this is unsurpassed among Weelkes' Services.

In Weelkes' Fifth Service, 'in medio chori', it is clear that the three-voice sections labelled 'medio' are for a group of singers quite distinct from those participating in the normal verses and choruses (apparently for five voices) that comprise the rest of the music. The term 'in medio chori' is still used

Te Deum: 'Thou art the King of Glory, O Christ' (conclusion (see Example 113)); *Nunc:* 'For mine eyes have seen' (1½–2 bars).
  Te Deum: 'to deliver man'; *Nunc:* 'before the face of all people' (first half; 2½ bars).
  Te Deum: 'in glory everlasting'; *Nunc:* 'before the face of all people' (second half; 3 bars).
  Te Deum: 'All the earth doth worship Thee'; *Nunc:* 'Glory be to the Father' (2 bars).
  The textual reconstruction of *Te Deum* is conjectural. All these identities are between Chorus sections.

in the rites of the Roman Catholic Church, and simply means 'between the choir stalls' (assuming that the choir is placed in the normal rows of stalls facing inwards). This had been the normal place for the precentor and the rulers of the choir to stand during Mass on major festivals, and it is apparent that Weelkes intended an additional group of singers to be sited thus for a performance of this Service. It is doubtful whether he envisaged soloists for the group 'in medio chori', for these passages and the full chorus sections clearly employ the Elizabethan high 'treble' voice which Weelkes uses in his Fourth Service only in the chorus sections, never in the verses. In the Fifth Service the verses appear to be allocated almost entirely to two countertenors, apart from the second verse of *Magnificat*, which a rubric in the source specifically allots to two basses. In style the Fifth Service is thoroughly contrapuntal, and turns out to be one of the most expansive of Weelkes' settings, with a *Magnificat* whose length is matched only by its counterpart in the Ninth Service (the deficiency of Gloria makes the length of *Nunc dimittis* uncertain). As in the First Service it is the consistency rather than the highlights of this setting that is more impressive, and the variety between verse, 'medio' and chorus, together with the sonorous texture and spacious dimensions, must have made a splendid effect.

Little can be said of the last of Weelkes' verse Services, the Sixth. From the meagre remains of three chorus parts and a few fragments of verse solos, it would appear to be one of the more unremarkable of his works. The same may be said of the Tenth Service; the two surviving parts of *Jubilate* indicate that it was a full Service, simple in manner, and using *cantoris-decani* alternations.

When Byrd came to compose his Short Service, he adopted a homophonic manner relieved by gentle counterpoint, but he never permitted a single set of imitative entries, even of the simple kind such as Gibbons was to use in his Short Service (No. 1). Weelkes' Seventh Service, *his* Short Service, lies stylistically between these two, for its homophony is frequently relieved by the familiar device of allowing one of the four voices to anticipate the others by two beats, though in all five movements there are only two sets of the briefest and most simple entries. As in *Te Deum* of the Second Service, the constant *cantoris-decani* alternation occasions very little repetition of phrases between the two sides.[1] The three morning

---

[1] The momentary identities between the separate canticles are less precise in this Service than in some of the others. The version of the headmotif in *Venite* opens a major division of *Te Deum* ('Thou art the everlasting Son of the Father'), and recurs yet again later in the same movement ('O Lord, let Thy mercy lighten upon us'); the openings of the common Gloria of *Venite* and *Jubilate* is clearly related to this too. 'Today if ye will hear his voice' in *Jubilate* is slightly modified to set 'We therefore pray Thee . . . with Thy precious blood' in *Te Deum*.

canticles (this is the only Service by Weelkes to set *Venite* as well as *Te Deum* and *Jubilate*) are of fine quality–plastic and resourceful within the limitations of their simple style, with admirable breadth of phrase. But the evening canticles are rather disappointing, melodically and harmonically constricted, with less variety in their harmonic progress and in their cadential course.

Despite the fact that the Eighth Service is essentially a full Service, each movement is planned as a broad scheme of choruses interlarded with briefer verses.[1] *Te Deum* has four such verses, but the remaining three canticles have only one each at their respective centres. Some, probably all, of the verses are for four singers,[2] and normally employ clearly defined groups of either high or low voices. A number of these verses employ pseudo-antiphony, or a closely related technique, and the verse in *Nunc dimittis* is actually labelled ' "4 pts: Gimell" ' in acknowledgement of its quasi-canonic 'twinning' of the two upper and two lower voices. The constant use of these tiny, haunting repetitions in the slender-textured verses makes an intimate contrast with the more constantly changing counterpoint of the full sections.[3] Fellowes observed that this Service 'shows marked individuality of style among the Tudor settings of the Canticles',[4] and it seems intended to occupy a place between the economy of the Short Service and the elaboration of the Great Service, offering counterpoint which is concise without being constricted. The most impressive movement is *Te Deum*, which contrasts a noble grandeur in praising God with a supplication for mercy which reaches its most intimate on the words: 'O Lord, save Thy people'. Weelkes' Eighth Service is a splendid composition, achieving an excellent balance between the contrapuntal need to expand and liturgical pressures for conciseness.

[1] In view of the definite verse-chorus organisation of the morning canticles, it seems that the centre of each evening canticle must also be a verse, for the section beginning 'he hath shewed strength' in *Magnificat* is labelled '4 pts: for men', and that beginning 'to be a light' in *Nunc dimittis* is also marked '4 pts'.

[2] Three verses in *Te Deum* are not actually marked for four voices, though it seems clear that these were the forces Weelkes used for them.

[3] There are very numerous identities between the four canticles:

Te Deum: 'continually do cry' and 'whom Thou hast redeemed'; *Jubilate*: 'World without end'; *Magnificat*: 'Amen' (2 bars).

Te Deum: 'Thine honourable, true' and 'and we worship' (2 bars).

Te Deum: 'Thou didst not abhor'; *Jubilate*: 'it is He that hath made us' (2 bars).

Te Deum: 'As our trust is in Thee'; *Magnificat*: 'and His mercy' (1½ bars).

Jubilate: 'that the Lord, He is God'; *Magnificat*: 'Glory be to the Father' (2½ bars).

Jubilate: 'and not we ourselves. We are His people'; *Magnificat*: 'magnified me, and Holy is His Name' (4 bars); also related to 'the Father of an infinite majesty' in *Te Deum*.

Jubilate: 'and to the Holy Ghost'; *Nunc*: 'before the face of all people' (3 bars).

Magnificat: 'all generations' and 'Abraham and his seed' (2½–3 bars of identical entries).

Te Deum: 'and lift them up'; *Magnificat*: 'as He promised' (3½ bars).

[4] Footnote to Fellowes' TCM octavo edition of the evening canticles.

The most splendid of all Weelkes' Services is the last of these works, the Ninth Service. Weelkes was clearly determined to make this the grandest work of which he was capable, with spacious, even gigantic paragraphs, and imposing sonorities. It employs the largest complement of voices ever used by him; though no more than seven voices are used simultaneously (except, it seems, to launch Gloria of *Nunc dimittis*), it contains some sections, apparently verses, requiring as many as four altos. Only a large and expert choir could hope to do it justice and, of all Weelkes' Services, this must surely have been designed for the Chapel Royal. It is the one Service from the period which really rivals the achievement of the evening canticles in Byrd's Great Service as much in style and technique as in scale and elaboration, and it is as close as Weelkes ever came to composing a Service that is thoroughly and fully polyphonic. True, his typically virile, close-knit counterpoint fills many passages, but we need only compare the settings of 'He remembering His mercy' in both Services to see how close Weelkes has drawn to Byrd in places (Example 114). No work emphasises more pointedly Weelkes' liking for

Ex. 114

strongly dissonant false relations, for Byrd's Great Service, the work of a master in whose work such asperities could figure largely, is harmonically far less astringent than some passages in Weelkes' Service.

If *Magnificat* is notable for its strong and vigorous counterpoint, its unity blended with variety, its splendidly strong yet restrained harmonic language, and its bold use of dissonance,[1] *Nunc dimittis* is even more impressive. It is less easy to appreciate its thematic singlemindedness from

[1] Perhaps the similarities of the Amen of Weelkes' *Magnificat* and that of the *Nunc dimittis* of Byrd's Great Service are not entirely coincidental.

the score than from a performance, although if we tabulate the first half dozen main points as they appear in either or both of the treble parts (Example 115), we may note their tendency to shape themselves round the four notes of *a* in Example 115*b*. This Service has been criticised for the

Ex. 115

a

Lord, now let — test Thou thy ser[vant]

b

a

ac - cord - ing to Thy—— Word

c

For mine eyes have seen

d

which Thou hast pre - par - ed

e

be-fore the face of [all people]

f

[transposed]

To be a light

restricted range of the individual voice parts, but the effect of this work comes far more from the contrapuntal interaction of the lines than from the expressive qualities of individual parts. Weelkes' melodic invention is controlled by great singleness of expressive purpose. Couple this to the breadth of the whole conception and the masterly strength of the counter-point, and the result is perhaps the most lastingly impressive experience in the whole range of his music.

XII. WEELKES: AN ASSESSMENT

The Englishman of today finds himself in a situation peculiarly favourable for an understanding of Weelkes and his contemporaries. Since the Second World War we have seen much of the insularity of English music disappear, and the doors of our musical life open to receive the influence of continental practices. Schoenberg and Webern are now a regular part of our musical diet, and English composition has been revitalised by an infusion of what to English musicians are the novel practices of mid-European serialism. Britten was an established master before ever these new influences were fully felt, but even he has not been unaffected by them, while a group of younger composers has emerged from this situation whose works have enthusiastically embraced these new manners, and whose talents have been warmly recognised by the open-minded listener. But if we retreat just over three and a half centuries, substitute Italian madrigal for mid-European serialism, if we think of men like Weelkes, Wilbye and Morley as the 'younger composers' instead of Maxwell Davies, Goehr and Bennett, if we put Ferrabosco and Marenzio in place of Schoenberg and Webern, replace Britten by Byrd—even, perhaps, read 'Spanish Armada' instead of 'Second World War', we have a not unfair appraisal of the musical situation in England in the years around 1600. Even the marked tendency of some English composers of the later 1960s to retreat from their former advanced positions is matched by the tendency, shared by Morley, Weelkes and Wilbye, to employ a greater contrapuntalism in their later madrigals. The important difference between the two situations is that the madrigal was music for middle class amateur performance, while most serial music is very much the preserve of the highly professional executant.

The Italian madrigal had revitalised English composition, and opened up fresh, stimulating possibilities. A situation of this sort is particularly favourable to minor talents who in another context might have passed almost unnoticed. The excitement of exploring these new territories of sound draws from such talents the fullest response of which they are capable, and they may rise to achievements of real note and merit. In such a situation creativity does not have to come from an evolving inner vision striving to catch a new view of an established musical language, for a whole new world of sound is there for the taking, and the composer has only to enter and explore in order to discover new musical vistas. However when familiarity has lessened the power of these new aural stimuli, only the composer's inner growth can open new possibilities from which may come really creative works. This inner growth is the thing which distinguishes the great (or potentially great) from the merely talented composer; because of this, for instance, Vaughan Williams became a more important composer than Walton, though he was a less talented musician. Byrd and Britten have this spiritual growth in abundance, but the majority of the madrigalists did not—and one suspects that this will prove true of many of the talented young English composers of today. Most of the madrigalists were simply mildly gifted men who produced one or two volumes, and then fell silent simply because to have said more would have been to repeat gestures.

When Weelkes' whole creative work is reviewed, he emerges as both a beneficiary and a victim of the musical situation into which he was born. As a young composer, he accepted the new musical stimuli whole-heartedly, rapidly composing three volumes of madrigals which were to be one of the most important products of this confluence of English and Italian styles. It has already been shown how his imagination responded to the new possibilities, and how the apprentice became the master while composing these works. But as Weelkes' mastery grew, so the paradox emerged that this most progressive of English composers was, in fact, just as much a conservative. It is usually forgotten that the startling musical phenomena of *O care / Hence, care* or *Thule / The Andalusian merchant* are quite exceptional even for Weelkes. Most of their companion works pursue a much less sensational course, with the ready imaginative response tempered by pressures for purely musical quality and coherence. At heart Weelkes was a contrapuntist who turned away from the madrigal partly because his more brilliant and imaginative works were almost certainly too advanced for all but very limited circles, partly because of the circumstances connected with his move to Chichester and his Chapel Royal aspirations, but also because the trends which had been developing in his work were hardly suited to a further pursuit of the madrigal. The sphere in which they could find a full and fitting expression was church music, and when Weelkes moved to Chichester, he plainly took the decision to pour everything into this type of composition.

Because of his contrapuntal proclivities and his disposition to full, sonorous textures, the lute song would not have appealed to Weelkes as an alternative form in which his more radical impulses might have found an outlet. In addition—and this is of fundamental importance—it would have been unsuited to him because melodic invention was the most uneven of his gifts. He could evolve efficiently a broad, restrained solo line in Byrd's measured manner, but he had nothing like the same ability for inventing memorable melodic details. Admittedly he did devise some excellently apt melodic points for works of a forthright, festive character (anthems like *Alleluia! I heard a voice* and *Hosanna to the Son of David*, or madrigals like *As Vesta was descending* and *Like two proud armies*), but he showed far less aptitude in melodic invention of a more reflective, more tender and more intimate nature. Weelkes' best works are always splendidly extrovert (even the mystical *Laboravi* is a work with a sense of occasion), for he was never a composer of really personal works in the way that Byrd or Gibbons could be. *O care / Hence, care*, for all the lamentation of the lyric, conveys nothing of that personal poignancy so touchingly expressed in Gibbons' *Behold, thou hast made my days*.

The trouble was that Weelkes was not particularly responsive to words themselves. We may recall that in the dedication of his five-voice madrigals of 1600 he professed no aptitude for anything but music, and one suspects that he was not a man of broad cultural interests. For him the sound and the sense of the words was not to be savoured together, and then felicitously matched with an apt musical phrase. It was the meaning of the words and any suggestions they offered for musical imagery that alone mattered. His treatment of such suggestions is always imaginative in a calculated and self-conscious way; certainly it seems that his creative processes included nothing of the experience of Byrd, who could write that 'there is such a mysterious and hidden power in the words themselves, that in some fashion (I know not how) the most fitting notes occur spontaneously to the man who ponders and seriously meditates upon them'.[1]

As a result of this, the melodic point itself in a work by Weelkes is not usually a particularly compelling part of the musical experience. Thus there was no reason why the same point might not serve for many contexts, and this is substantiated by the very frequent recurrence of certain points from one work of Weelkes to another. The point of Example 116a turns up over and over again in different works though, signifi-

Ex. 116

cantly, the resourceful contrapuntist always produces a different paragraph from it. Example 116b is used even more often, and as the little one-bar

[1] Preface to *Gradualia* (1605).

cell of 116c it becomes a distinctive fingerprint in one third of the verse anthems. Even the 'mercy' theme (Example 116d), which likewise occurs in a number of different works, is a closely related idea. But the fact that a rather functional musical entity could be the basis of a splendidly devised paragraph is a confirmation that the strength of Weelkes' work, as in that of any contrapuntist, lay not in the basic idea, but in the structure which he erected from it. In one way at least this lack of fertility in the creation of a basic idea was an advantage; it enabled Weelkes to establish thematic relationships more easily, since he was less troubled by the temptation such melodic facility would have created to make every point absolutely apt for each phrase of text.[1]

In contrapuntal works—madrigals or full anthems—Weelkes' melodic limitations were not any very great drawback. Composers often used stock formulae or borrowed their material from elsewhere, and one might hesitate to pronounce Weelkes weak in this dimension on the evidence of such works alone. It is in the solos of the verse anthems that his melodic limitations become most apparent. He may have favoured the archaic melodic style partly to accommodate the restricted skills and tastes of Chichester, but it seems just as likely that it was because the older neutral manner did not demand an intense response to the individual phrases of the text. Certainly the best verses in the verse anthems impress less by their details than by their growth and breadth. This is very apparent in the verse-chorus divisions of *Give the king Thy judgements*, for instance, where the calculated growth of the verse and its fulfilment in the chorus reveals Weelkes' masterly grasp of *broad* musical thinking. It is significant that the texts which he did choose to set in a more modern declamatory manner are those which favour the firm and forthright melody which he invented most readily.

As for Weelkes' limited potentialities as a composer of lute ayres, we have only to compare some of the more melodic of his *Ayres* of 1608 with the best of Campion's to see just how inferior Weelkes was in this particular field to the lesser composer. It is not only that the individual phrases of Weelkes' ayres are mostly less distinctive, for they have none of the ability of Campion's to unfold from phrase to phrase in fresh, easy invention, accumulating into a broad, *purely melodic* entity. Weelkes' tunes are made

---

[1] One other point is worth noting. It has been observed that a number of Weelkes' verse anthems virtually share the same opening; just as the devising of a point for each phrase of text in a fully contrapuntal work was a cold process after which creation could follow, so in these instances also it appears that invention did not readily flow until the first calculated step had been taken. Therefore it may not have been only that Weelkes was not particularly responsive to the words themselves; it seems also probable that he was a composer whose imagination did not always start to function freely until it had been given a point of departure.

to grow largely through sequences which can all too easily become mechanical. Here, too, Weelkes was happiest when inventing virile melody, as in the hearty (though still very sequential) ayre, *Come, sirrah Jacko*.

Thus Weelkes centred his creative attentions upon church music, and in doing so he abandoned the more startling eruptions which had occasionally appeared in his madrigals. This has commonly been considered a regression—a regrettable if unavoidable capitulation to the pressures for a more staid expression in music for worship. This view is quite wrong. Weelkes' music really lost nothing essential through foregoing its more purple moments. It has already been noted that most of the madrigals eschew sensational incidents or passages; when they do occur, they are calculated effects, flirtations with some of the new procedures of contemporary music. Sometimes he had applied these effects with brilliant musicality to create some of his best madrigals, and not the least remarkable feature of *O care | Hence, care* is the mastery with which these startling expressive devices are compounded into a thoroughly satisfying musical experience. But such devices were still effects peripheral to his style, not an essential part of the style itself. Thus he was able to abandon them with only a marginal loss, and in the whole of his church music there is only one really arresting chromaticism,[1] and one really striking piece of calculated musical symbolism.[2] *His mature style, established in the madrigals and confirmed in the best of his church music, was a synthesis of the older counterpoint of the Renaissance with the splendid extrovert expression of the Baroque.* This is seen most clearly in the point-saturated textures at the conclusions of *When Thoralis delights to walk* or *As Vesta was descending*, the turbulent yet monolithic paragraphs of *Like two proud armies*, or in the combination in some of his anthems of a traditional, contrapuntally-minded texture with a broad harmonic progress of great strength. The balance between old and new might be shifted to produce works as different as *Laboravi* and *Thule | The Andalusian merchant*, but the engagement is always there in his best works.

No feature of Weelkes' work is more transitional than his use of recomposition. This, surely, is a sign of an instinct to create a balanced and integrated structure within a technique which had no ready precedents for such integration, and whose essence had been the constant unfolding of new ideas. Weelkes accepted polyphony not from external compulsion, nor because there was no ready alternative, but because it was the most congenial, natural way for him to think. He handled it with resourcefulness and individuality, with a most virile approach to dissonance, and a masterly control which is scarcely flawed by occasional consecutive fifths

---

[1] The setting of 'to tune' in *Gloria in excelsis Deo.*
[2] The opening portion of *Alleluia! I heard a voice.*

and octaves. In his contrapuntalism he was conservative; in his instinct to build a new contrapuntal paragraph around the framework of an earlier passage from the same work he was progressive. However, there was no future for this type of recomposition. It was a polyphonist's instinctive solution to the problem of repetition, and its effectiveness in practice was very limited; with the passing of polyphony and the firm establishment of other repetitive practices for the erection of an integrated structure, the technique became redundant. In the verse anthems, whose sectional structures especially suggested the use of repetitive procedures, the move towards a more systematic and exact use of repetition is pronounced, though even here it would be overbold to claim that Weelkes more than approached the threshold of the *concerto grosso* principle. Indeed, the amount of attention that has been given in this study to various repetitive devices must not cause the significance of individual applications to be overestimated. Many instances of their use are comparatively unimportant; what is significant is their consistent reflection of Weelkes' instinct to achieve a purely musical integration within a work.

We have no way of knowing what drove Weelkes to become an alcoholic, nor whether his alcoholic excesses were the cause or the effect of his later failures. The greatest single misfortune that we can isolate in his career was his lack of success in securing for himself a place in the Chapel Royal. This was not simply a failure to achieve a personal ambition, for the best of his church music demands a large and expert choir to do it justice, and it seems reasonable to expect that membership of this establishment would have given him ample incentives to exploit further that splendid ceremonial manner in which he was unsurpassed. In the end we have to recognise that he was a disappointment—a composer with the makings of greatness, but who failed lamentably to fulfil the boundless expectations aroused by his great musical endowments and early achievements. He seems to have been in several ways a misfit in the England of his time—a progressive madrigalist whose conservative tendencies debarred him from more than a limited exploitation of that line, a rather limited melodist who was ill-equipped to follow the fashions of the lute song or to achieve any really broad success with the verse anthem, and whose immense gifts as a composer of full anthems were frustrated by failure to find circumstances in which they could be fully exploited. But when we turn to his finest achievements—madrigals like *O care | Hence, care, Thule | The Andalusian merchant* or *Hark, all ye lovely saints above,* to name only three: when we meet the finest of the anthems—*Alleluia! I heard a voice, Hosanna to the Son of David, O Lord, arise, Laboravi in gemitu meo* or *Give the king Thy judgements,* for instance: or experience the spacious paragraphs of the Service for seven voices, we can have no doubt that here is a major creative mind at work. Whether such works thrust spectacular imagery at us, or retreat into a more sober polyphony, there is no question that the former is mere avant-garde gimmickry, or the latter worn anachronism. Brilliant response is always set within a splendidly firm musical framework, and solemn counterpoint is always stirring. Weelkes was in every way a transitional figure, standing with one foot in the Renaissance and the other in the Baroque, applying the contrapuntal legacy of the former to the incipient demands of the latter, and producing, through the fertilising power of one upon the other, some of the most splendid compositions of this most splendid period of English music.

MODERN EDITIONS OF WEELKES' WORKS

This catalogue does not include the numerous editions of separate works which are included in the larger collections listed below.

SECULAR VOCAL MUSIC

A complete edition of Weelkes' madrigals is published as *The English Madrigal School* (edited by E. H. Fellowes), vols. 9–13. London, 1916. This series is in process of revision as *The English Madrigalists* (edited by Thurston Dart).

OTHER REPRINTS OF SEPARATE VOLUMES AND PIECES:

The First set of madrigals (1597). Published as *Musical Antiquarian Society*, vol. 8 (edited by E. J. Hopkins). London, [1843].

Ballets and madrigals (1598). Published as *The Old English Edition*, vols. 13–15 (edited by G. E. P. Arkwright). London, 1895.

Airs or fantastic spirits (1608). Published as *The Old English Edition*, vols. 16–17 (edited by G. E. P. Arkwright). London, 1895–96.

Grace my lovely one. Edited by W. B. Squire. London, [1888]. New edition by David Brown. London, 1969.

The Cryes of London. Edited by F. Bridge. London, [1919].

INSTRUMENTAL WORKS

In nomine for five viols, and *Pavan* [No. 2] for five viols. Printed in *Jacobean consort music*, published as *Musica Britannica*, vol. 9 (edited by Thurston Dart and William Coates). London, 1955.

Lachrimae and three pavans. Edited and arranged [for recorders] by Denis Arnold. London, 1960. (Pavane III is by R. Micho).

[Fantasia] for two basses. Printed in G. Reese, *Music in the Renaissance*. London, 1954.

Pieces for keyed instruments. Transcribed and edited by Margaret Glyn. London, 1924.

CHURCH MUSIC

Collected anthems. Published as *Musica Britannica*, vol. 23 (edited by David Brown, Walter Collins and Peter le Huray). London, 1966.

Magnificat and *Nunc dimittis* (Service No. 1). Reconstructed and edited by David Brown. London, 1969.

Evening Service for two trebles (Service No. 4). Edited by E. H. Fellowes and P. C. Buck. London, 1931. This is superseded by: *Evening Service 'for trebles'*. Newly edited by Peter le Huray. London, 1962.

Short Morning and Evening Service for four voices (Service No. 7). Edited by E. H. Fellowes. London, 1931. New edition of the morning canticles (including *Venite*) by David Brown. London, 1969. Revised edition of the evening canticles by David Brown. London, 1968.

Evening Service for five voices (Service No. 8). Edited by E. H. Fellowes. London, 1937. Revised edition by David Wulstan. London, 1965.

SELECTED BIBLIOGRAPHY

The Acts of the Dean and Chapter of the Cathedral Church of Chichester,
1545–1642. Edited by W. D. Peckham. Published as *Sussex Record*
Society, vol. 58 (1959).

H. K. Andrewes, *The Technique of Byrd's vocal polyphony.* London, 1966.

D. Arnold, 'Thomas Weelkes and the madrigal' (*Music & Letters,* vol. 31
(1950), pp. 1 ff.).

J. Barnard, *Selected church music.* London, 1641.

M. C. Boyd, *Elizabethan music and musical criticism.* Philadelphia, 1940.

Sir F. Bridge, *Twelve good musicians.* London, 1920.

D. Brown, 'The Anthems of Thomas Weelkes' (*Proceedings of the Royal*
Musical Association, vol. 91 (1964–65), pp. 61 ff.).

D. Brown, 'Thomas Weelkes' (*Recorder and Music Magazine,* vol. 2
(1967), pp. 137 f.).

J. S. Bumpus, *A History of English cathedral music.* London, [1908].

H. C[hitty], 'Winchester College: the organist and the quiristers' master'
(a reprint (with some alterations) from an article in *The Wykehamist,*
No. 523 (1913), pp. 84 ff.).

J. Clifford, *The Divine Services and anthems usually sung in the cathedrals*
and collegiate choirs in the Church of England. London, 1663. A second
edition is titled *The Divine Services and anthems usually sung in His*
Majesty's Chapel and in all cathedrals and collegiate choirs in England
and Ireland. London, 1664.

W. S. Collins, *The Anthems of Thomas Weelkes* [unpublished Ph.D.
dissertation. University of Michigan, 1960].

W. S. Collins, 'Recent discoveries concerning the biography of Thomas
Weelkes' (*Music & Letters,* vol. 44 (1963), pp. 123 ff.).

A. E. F. Dickinson, 'Thomas Weelkes'. Published in *The Music masters,*
edited by A. L. Bacharach. London, 1948–54.

J. S. Drew, *Compton near Winchester.* Winchester, 1939.

E. H. Fellowes, *English cathedral music.* London, 1941.

E. H. Fellowes, *The English madrigal composers,* 2nd edition. London,
1948.

E. H. Fellowes, 'Thomas Weelkes' (*Proceedings of the Royal Musical*
Association, vol. 42 (1915–16), pp. 117 ff.).

W. K. Ford, 'Chichester Cathedral and Thomas Weelkes' (*Sussex*
Archaeological Collections, vol. 100 (1961), pp. 156 ff.).

M. B. Foster, *Anthems and anthem composers.* London, 1901.

G. Holst, 'My favourite Tudor composer' (*Midland Musician*, vol. 1, (1926), pp. 4–5).

G. Holst, 'The Tercentenary of Byrd and Weelkes' (*Proceedings of the Royal Musical Association*, vol. 49 (1922–23), pp. 29 ff.).

J. Kerman, *The Elizabethan madrigal: a comparative study*. New York and London, 1962.

P. le Huray, 'Towards a definitive study of pre-Restoration Anglican Service music' (*Musica Disciplina*, vol. 14 (1960), pp. 29 ff.).

P. le Huray, *Music and the Reformation in England, 1549–1660*. London, 1967.

Sir W. Leighton, *The Tears or lamentations of a sorrowful soul*. London, 1614.

W. Mellers, *Harmonious meeting: a study of the relationship between English music, poetry and theatre, c. 1600–1900*. London, 1965.

D. Morse, *Word-painting and symbolism in the secular choral works of Thomas Weelkes* [unpublished Ph.D. dissertation. University of New York, 1961].

W. D. Peckham, 'The vicars choral of Chichester Cathedral' (*Sussex Archaeological Collections*, vol. 78 (1937), pp. 126 ff.).

G. Reese, *Music in the Renaissance*. London, 1954.

Statutes and constitutions of the Cathedral Church of Chichester. Edited by F. G. Bennet, R. H. Codrington, and C. Deedes. Chichester, 1904.

D. Stevens, *Thomas Tomkins*. London, 1957.

D. Stevens, *Tudor church music*. London, 1961.

D. Tovey, *Essays in musical analysis*, vol. 5 (*Vocal Music*). London, 1937.

Tudor Church Music. Edited by P. C. Buck, E. H. Fellowes, G. Ramsbotham and S. Townsend Warner. 10 vols. London, 1922–29.

C. A. Welch, 'Two cathedral organists, Thomas Weelkes and Thomas Kelway', published as *The Chichester Papers*, No. 8 (1957).

W. Woodfill, *Musicians in English society*. Princeton, 1953.

INDEX OF MUSIC

I. COMPOSITIONS BY WEELKES

A. SECULAR VOCAL MUSIC:

A country pair (1597), 64, 65, 67
A sparrow-hawk proud (1600), 115, 134
Alas, O tarry but one half hour (1608), 123
All at once well met, fair ladies (1598), 81, 82
As deadly serpents lurking (1608), 120, 123
As Vesta was from Latmos Hill descending (*The Triumphs of Oriana*), 109, 110, 134, 202, 204
As wanton birds (1600), 105, 106, 107, 134
Ay me, alas, hey ho! (1608), 124, 125
Ay me, my wonted joys forsake me (1597), 53, 67, 68, 75, 93, 131

Cease now delight (1598), 88, 115, 116
Cease sorrows now (1597), 57, 64, 65, 66, 96
Clear wells spring not (1597) [see *My flocks feed not*]
Cold winter's ice is fled (1600), 97
Come clap your hands/Phyllis hath sworn (1598), 93, 187
Come, let's begin to revel't out (1608), 104, 122
Come, sirrah Jacko (1608), 122, 204

Death hath deprived me of my dearest friend (1608), 115, 116, 117, 121
Donna, il vostro bel viso (1608), 73, 121, 123

Fa la. Now weep, now sing (1608), 121
Farewell, my joy (1598), 84, 88, 115
Four arms, two necks, one wreathing (1608), 102, 121

Give me my heart (1598), 85
Grace my lovely one (MS), 17, 136

Ha! ha! This world doth pass (1608), 104, 120, 121
Hark, all ye lovely saints above (1598), 84, 205

211

2. COMPOSITIONS BY OTHER COMPOSERS

A. COLLECTIONS OF MUSIC:

INDEX OF NAMES